CW01024908

Ghostly Apparitions

Ghostly Apparitions

German Idealism, the Gothic Novel, and Optical Media

Stefan Andriopoulos

ZONE BOOKS · NEW YORK

2013

© 2013 Stefan Andriopoulos

ZONE BOOKS
1226 Prospect Avenue
Brooklyn, NY 11218

Printed in the United States of America.

Distributed by The MIT Press,
Cambridge, Massachusetts, and London, England.

Library of Congress Cataloging-in-Publication Data

Andriopoulos, Stefan.
     Ghostly apparitions: German idealism, the gothic
novel, and optical media / Stefan Andriopoulos—
First edition
          pages   cm
     Includes bibliographical references and index.
     ISBN 978-1-935408-35-2
               1. Idealism, German. 2. Kant, Immanuel,
1724–1804. 3. Gothic fiction (Literary genre)—History
and criticism. 4. Paranormal fiction—History and criticism.
5. Ghosts—Miscellanea. I. Title.

     B2745.A53 2013
     133.1–dc23
                              2013013067

Contents

To Shiaolan

Figure 1. "Fantasmagorie de Robertson dans la Cour des Capucines," frontispiece of Etienne-Gaspard Robertson, *Mémoires récréatifs, scientifiques et anecdotiques* (Paris, 1834). The darkness of the theater, the black ground of the magic lantern slides, and the back projection onto hidden screens and smoke allowed for the special effect of magnifications that were perceived as a terrifying approach of the projected figure.

Introduction

In the fall semester of 1805–1806 Georg Friedrich Wilhelm Hegel gave a lecture course, The Philosophy of Nature and Spirit, at the University of Jena. It was at the same time that he wrote his *Phenomenology of Spirit* (1807), which described a succession of different "spiritual shapes"[1] in the progress toward absolute knowledge—from subjective through objective to absolute spirit. A teleological sequence of spirits was also at the center of Hegel's Jena lectures, in which he explicitly referred to the optical technologies involved in the visual medium of the phantasmagoria. These spectral performances, first staged in postrevolutionary Paris by Paul Philidor and Etienne-Gaspard Robertson, perfected the use of the magic lantern for the purpose of simulating spirit apparitions. In the dark subterranean vault of a former Capuchin monastery, Robertson achieved stunning effects by suddenly magnifying ghostly projections that seemed to loom out at terrified audiences (Figure 1).

In Hegel's lectures on the philosophy of nature and spirit, one early passage describes a stage of interiority that has to be overcome in the subject's teleological progress toward knowing. In representing pure selfhood, Hegel invokes the darkness and terror that were at the center of Robertson's phantasmagoria: "This is the night, the inner of nature that exists here—pure self. In phantasmagorical presentations it is night on all sides; here a bloody head suddenly surges forward, there another white form abruptly appears, before vanishing again. One catches sight of this night when looking into the eye of man—into a night that turns dreadful; it is the night of the world that presents itself here."[2]

9

Even though Hegel's representation of the "night of the world" has been analyzed in several readings, it has not been linked to the visual medium whose name introduced the word "phantasmago- ria" into French, German, and English in the 1790s.[3] Tracing the interaction between the cultural use of media technologies and new philosophical theories, the following explorations juxtapose ideal- ist philosophy with phantasmagorical projections and a scientific debate about the possibility of spiritual apparitions. For it is not only Hegel's notion of spirit and his invocation of "phantasmagorical pre- sentations" that link the emergence of German idealism to optical media and theories of the occult that gained widespread currency in the late eighteenth century. Immanuel Kant's critical epistemology also draws on spiritualist notions when conceiving of *Erscheinung* as an "appearance" or "apparition" that is constituted by our forms of intuition, but nonetheless related to a supersensory thing in itself. At the same time, Kant's doctrine of transcendental illusion described the "mirage" (*Blendwerk*) of speculative metaphysics by invoking the phantasmagorical images of the magic lantern, which are real, even if no material bodies correspond to them. This recourse to contem- poraneous media technology becomes even more pronounced in the writings of Arthur Schopenhauer, who described our perception of the empirical world as a "cerebral phantasmagoria."[4]

This book explores the intersection of the ghostly with various media and discursive fields between 1750 and 1930. The opening chapters reveal the central role of the magic lantern and of spiritual- ist notions in the work of Kant, Hegel, and Schopenhauer. Shifting to contemporaneous print culture, the book then examines ghost narratives, the Gothic novel, and Romantic representations of clair- voyance. Contextualizing a more recent visual medium from the early twentieth century, the final chapter centers on the dynamic relationship between occultism and the emergence of television. By merging media archaeology with a historicist reading of philosophi- cal discourse, my analysis of German idealism highlights previously ignored preconditions that made thinking Kant's, Hegel's, and Scho- penhauer's philosophical arguments possible.[5] However, I do not contend that their theories were solely or primarily determined by optical media and spiritualism. Each of these authors draws on the same set of ghostly and medial figures, but they do so in various ways, surreptitious or overt, and for different argumentative purposes.

Kant emphasizes the structural affinity of philosophical metaphysics and spiritualism in an early, precritical treatise entitled *Dreams of a Spirit Seer, Elucidated by Dreams of Metaphysics* (1766). There, he develops the surprising "metaphysical hypothesis" of genuine apparitions that arise from a "real, internal spiritual impression."[6] In certain persons of unusual sensitivity, these internal impressions could be transposed to the external world, Kant suggests, thereby creating "the outer appearance of objects corresponding to them."[7] Yet immediately after establishing how genuine appearances might be conceptualized, Kant develops a second, diametrically opposed explanation. In order to expose spiritual visions as a sensory delusion, Kant compares the "brain phantoms" (*Hirngespenster*) of an inflamed, enthusiastic imagination to an optical "spectre" (*Spectrum*) created by means of a concave mirror.[8] This skeptical account of ghostly apparitions anticipates Kant's doctrine of transcendental illusion, for in his critical writings, he repeatedly draws on contemporaneous optical media in order to describe the fallacies of speculative reason. Kant characterizes speculative metaphysics as a "magic lantern of brain phantoms."[9] In doing so, he transforms the optical instrument into an epistemic figure for the limits of philosophical knowledge.

The ghostly apparitions from this period also intersect with an emerging popular print culture that gave rise to the Gothic novel and immersive reading practices, an interrelation analyzed in Chapters 3 and 4. In *Dreams of a Spirit Seer*, Kant deplored the "haunting circulation" of ostensibly authentic ghost narratives.[10] In a criticism similar to current indictments of the Internet, he responds to an exploding print market and the concomitant proliferation of nonscholarly writings by warning against "rumor" and "hearsay" as undermining critical reasoning and scientific judgment. At the same time, the new literary genre of the Gothic novel adapted spiritual apparitions as a serial narrative device of shock and terror. The immersive appeal of these popular tales even raised concerns about "reading addiction" (*Lesesucht*) as leading to a pathological loss of reality.

Literary, scientific, and philosophical representations of animal magnetism and clairvoyance also blurred the boundary between the factual and the fictional in the first half of the nineteenth century. Adapting an allegedly factual German case history about a somnambulist clairvoyant who was for seven years arrested between life and death, Edgar Allan Poe published a fictional tale about a mesmerist experiment that was reprinted as an authentic news item in various newspapers and popular-science journals. Finally, in the concluding chapter, I will explore a reciprocal interaction between occultism and engineering in the early twentieth century. At that time, spiritualist research into the psychic "television" of somnambulist clairvoyants enabled the gradual invention and implementation of electrical television.

While not the central focus of individual chapters in this book, other media that emerged in the nineteenth and twentieth centuries, such as photography, telegraphy, cinema, and radio, were also closely connected with the occult. This striking proximity between different waves of spiritualism and the rise of various new technologies has been noted by several scholars.[11] Among the first to highlight the double sense of the term "medium" was the influential media theorist Friedrich Kittler, who at one point went so far as to suggest that there is "no difference between occult and technical media."[12] Jacques Derrida's *Specters of Marx* (1993), by contrast, adopts an exclusive focus on language as a source of spectrality. In his reading of Marx, Derrida disregards the cultural use of the magic lantern in phantasmagorical projections, and he subscribes to a common, but incorrect etymology of "phantasmagoria" as describing a public speech act.[13] The following explorations, however, do not privilege either language or technology as a sole, determining cause; instead, they seek to preserve the historical specificity of these various conjunctures of media and the occult by analyzing the complex and reciprocal interaction between technological innovation and cultural change.

Kittler's work has shaped the field of German media studies in the 1980s and 1990s by providing important insights into the history of new information technologies and their cultural impact. Yet ultimately, Kittler considers "hardware" to be more important than the discourses and imaginations that allow for its emergence and shape its contingent realization and appropriation. This focus on a technological a priori led Kittler to reintroduce the distinction between spiritualism and technology by making the one-sided claim that "from the very beginning occult media have necessarily presupposed technical ones."[14] According to Kittler, it was the invention of the Morse alphabet that "was promptly followed by the tapping specters" of American spiritualism, and he dismisses "literatures or fantasies" as "irrelevant" for the conception and implementation of television.[15] In short, Kittler asserts a general primacy of technology over culture. Technological innovation may generate spiritualism, but not vice versa.

This book adopts a more nuanced, post-Kittlerian approach that does not claim to reconstruct a comprehensive a priori—be it cultural or technological. Its chapters examine several, but not all, of the various cultural and technical materialities that allowed for the philosophical, literary, and medial invocations of ghosts around 1800 and for the emergence of television around 1900. In this vein, I establish late nineteenth-century spiritualist research into the psychic television of somnambulist clairvoyants as crucial for the construction and implementation of the technical medium. Spanning from the 1890s into the first decades of the twentieth century, television's gradual emergence in no sense relied exclusively on "factors immanent to technology."[16] The slow accumulation of technical and physical knowledge that led to the first experimental television broadcasts in the late 1920s cannot be separated from its contingent cultural contexts. Psychical research on telepathy and "television" (*Fernsehen*), carried out in the same period by spiritualists who emulated the rules and procedures of science, played a constitutive role for the technological inventions and developments of the medium. The archaeology of television reveals not a one-sided primacy of hardware or culture, but a reciprocal interaction between the newly

13

emerging technology and spiritualist research. Electrical and psychic television mutually presuppose each other.

Technological innovation and its cultural and epistemic conditions feature less prominently in my analysis of ghostly apparitions from the eighteenth and nineteenth centuries. Yet in exploring optical and print media from that period, I also avoid a simple determinism that would reduce culture to a mere epiphenomenon. In juxtaposing Kant's critical epistemology with the cultural use of the magic lantern in phantasmagorical projections, I conceive of the magic lantern as both a material object in an arrangement of cultural practices and a discursive figure within philosophical texts. This approach builds on Jonathan Crary's account of the camera obscura's mixed status as optical instrument and epistemological figure in his *Techniques of the Observer* (1990). At the same time, I propose a revision of Crary's description of the magic lantern as preserving and adhering to the epistemological model of the camera obscura, a model predicated on a paradigm of disembodied and purely receptive perception.[17] *Techniques of the Observer* describes an epistemic shift that occurred in the early nineteenth century and that was linked to the emergence of optical instruments such as the stereoscope and the phenakistoscope. My interpolation of Kant and the magic lantern, by contrast, has its focus on the second half of the eighteenth century. At that time, the magic lantern's open display in scientific demonstrations was gradually supplanted by its use for the back projection of phantasmagorical images.[18] Concomitantly, the medium's deceptive power became an important discursive figure in epistemological discussions about the unreliability of sensory perception and the limits of philosophical knowledge. Kant's critical epistemology describes a subject that projects its forms of intuition onto the external world and that is inclined to mistake subjective ideas for objectively given substances.[19]

But in appropriating contemporaneous optical media and spiritualist notions, Kant was following two opposite impulses. His doctrine of transcendental illusion adapts his early account of false optical specters and transforms the visual instrument of the magic lantern into an epistemic figure for the limits of philosophical knowledge. Kant thus describes an empirical appearance as constituted by our forms of intuition. Nonetheless, Kant still insists that an appearance can be conceived as linked to an unknowable thing in itself. In doing so, he adapts his early metaphysical hypothesis of genuine apparitions and defines *Erscheinung* as "an indication of a supersensory substrate."[20] In addition to tracing this tension between skeptical and metaphysical arguments in Kant's philosophical writings, the opening chapters contrast Schopenhauer's and Hegel's response to Kant's critical epistemology.

Schopenhauer's "Essay on Spirit Seeing" (1851) explicitly compares a spirit apparition to an appearance in the normal, empirical world. In *The World as Will and Representation*, he furthermore introduces optical categories into his summary of Kant's critical epistemology, praising Kant for "disassembling...the whole machinery of our cognitive faculties that brings about the phantasmagoria of the objective world."[21] Schopenhauer thereby foregrounds medial concepts in an altogether aggressive manner. Similar to Schopenhauer, Hegel concedes a "kinship" of speculative philosophy and magnetic clairvoyance in the third volume of his *Encyclopedia of the Philosophical Sciences* (1817/1830). But whereas Schopenhauer openly cites spiritualist notions and media technologies, Hegel seeks to conceal the material conditions of his ostensibly universal theories of absolute knowledge. Striving to suppress his reliance on occultist terms, Hegel also avoids acknowledging his appropriation of contemporaneous phantasmagorical projections.

The differentiation between the various surreptitious or overt adaptations of the ghostly and the magic lantern in the work of Kant, Hegel, and Schopenhauer reveals the crucial role of spiritualism and optical media for the emergence of German idealism. But the specific philosophical theories of these authors alter and transform the medial and spiritualist notions they draw upon, adapting them in different ways. Schopenhauer highlights his reliance on physiology and media technologies by describing our intellectual faculties as a material apparatus of cognition. Hegel's *Phenomenology of Spirit*, by contrast, emulates the phantasmagoric projection of spiritual shapes in the textual realm of speculative philosophy without naming the visual medium. Its final chapter describes "absolute spirit" apprehending itself in a "gallery of images" that presents a "slow motion and sequence of spirits."[22]

By tracing the divergent modes in which Kant, Hegel, and Schopenhauer appropriate spiritualism and optical media the following chapters contribute to and extend the kind of historical epistemology exemplified by *Techniques of the Observer* and Lorraine Daston and Peter Galison's *Objectivity*.[23] Michel Foucault's *Archaeology of Knowledge* (1969) formulated the notion of a "historical a priori" whose rules govern all discursive utterances at a given historical moment—a concept transposed from the discursive to the technological by Kittler's media history. Rather than replicating the assumption of an ostensibly unified general a priori, this book reveals specific cultural and technological preconditions that rendered possible the emergence of new philosophical arguments. The juxtaposition of idealist philosophy, popular print culture, phantasmagorical projections, and spiritualism does not assign primacy to any of these cultural spheres. But it allows for a merging of nuanced, close readings of philosophical texts with a historical exploration of cultural and medial practices that shaped these philosophical theories without determining them.

It is this interest in seemingly marginal cultural and technical materialities that distinguishes this account of ghostly apparitions from a conventional history of ideas. Traditional intellectual historians rarely stray beyond the realm of academic discourse, thereby disregarding the constitutive exchange across the permeable boundaries between philosophical thought and contemporaneous media and culture. In doing so, they inadvertently replicate Kant's wish for an impermeable boundary between philosophy and other cultural practices. Even a recent well-researched and comprehensive historiography of German spiritualism upholds this segregation by claiming that the spirits of occultism had "nothing to do . . . with the absolute spirit of Hegel's philosophy."[24] It is of course true that German idealism and spiritualism constituted distinct cultural spheres.

But in drawing on a shared set of ghostly and phantasmagorical notions, they responded to and molded the cultural use of optical technologies and print.

By interpolating canonical philosophical texts with visual media and popular print culture, this book also differs from most of contemporary academic philosophy. The aim of my reading of Kant, Hegel, and Schopenhauer is not to resolve contradictions or ambiguities in their thought. Rather than reformulating these authors in a way that would make their arguments "rigorous" or consistent, my goal is to historicize their texts in a manner that takes note of the strangeness of their theories and terminology, thereby transforming our understanding of the philosophical canon. The juxtaposition of spiritualism, phantasmagorical projections, and Kant, Hegel, and Schopenhauer may seem frivolous or crude to a specialist in German idealism. It is, however, suggested by a reading of these texts. Kant himself decided to give his treatise *Dreams of a Spirit Seer* the subtitle *Elucidated by Dreams of Metaphysics*, and in 1767, Moses Mendelssohn reviewed the book as leaving "the reader somewhat unsure as to whether Mr. Kant would rather render metaphysics risible or ghost seeing plausible."[25]

Derrida's *Specters of Marx* was crucial for establishing the rhetoric of ghostliness as a subject worthy of serious critical study by highlighting the constitutive role of ghostly and phantasmagorical figures in Marx's writings.[26] Yet the historicist approach adopted in the following chapters differs not only from Kittler's notion of a technological a priori, but also from Derrida's poststructuralist mode of reading. In analyzing "The Communist Manifesto" (1848), "The Eighteenth Brumaire" (1852), and *The German Ideology* (1845), Derrida reveals the role of Max Stirner's philosophy in the proliferation of the spectral in Marx's early writings. In a footnote, Derrida also mentions Schopenhauer's "Essay on Spirit Seeing."[27] He does not, however, engage in a reading of any contemporaneous spiritualist texts, and his preoccupation with language as the only source of spectrality leads him to disregard the cultural and medial conditions of Marx's invocation of ghosts. In his reading of Marx's chapter on the commodity's "phantasmagorical form," Derrida thus ignores the modes in which *Capital* (1867) appropriates optical media and Kant's doctrine of transcendental illusion—an adaptation I will shortly outline here.

In *The German Ideology*, Marx represents the "camera obscura" of idealism as producing a cognitive error that is false, but that can be turned into a faithful representation of reality by a simple inversion: "In all ideologies, human beings and their circumstances [appear] upside-down as in a camera obscura."[28] But in *Capital*, Marx sets out to expose a much more intricate and persistent illusion that he describes in analogy to the magic lantern and its use in the visual medium of the phantasmagoria. Kant had explained traditional metaphysical problems as based on "hypostatizing" or reifying a "mirage" that is mistaken to be a real object, and he characterized this process as if referring to the projections of a phantasmagoria that a credulous observer falsely considers to be a real physical object.[29] In his chapter on "commodity fetishism," Marx adapts Kant's warning that we mistake "that which exists merely in thought" for a "real object outside of the thinking subject," and he transforms Kant's doctrine of transcendental illusion into a critique of our tendency to reify social relations.[30] By invoking the modes in which capitalism gives a "thinglike semblance" to "the social determination of labor" Marx accounts for the commodity's "phantasmagorical form" and its "spectral objectivity."[31]

Derrida and others have ignored this appropriation of Kant's doctrine of transcendental illusion in *Capital* and in later Marxist theories of "reification." The following explorations lay the groundwork for correcting that omission, but they do not engage in a detailed, diachronic history of the notion of phantasmagoria in the work of Marx, Georg Lukács, Walter Benjamin, or Theodor W. Adorno.[32] Instead, the main focus of my analysis is on interrelations between cultural fields and medial practices that are contemporaneous with each other.

Rather than following a strictly chronological order, the sequence of chapters in this book proceeds from the magic lantern to print culture to television. Chapter 1 juxtaposes Kant's *Dreams of a Spirit Seer* to late eighteenth-century spiritualism and the cultural use of the magic lantern in phantasmagorical projections. Tracing Kant's transformation of the optical instrument into an epistemic figure also allows for a new, provocative reading of his critical philosophy. Chapter 2 contrasts Schopenhauer's and Hegel's response to Kant's critical epistemology and examines their diverging modes of adapting medial and spiritualist notions. Shifting from the interrelation of canonical philosophy and optical media to the realm of print culture and literary history, Chapters 3 and 4 analyze ghost narratives, the Gothic novel, and Romanticism in the late eighteenth and early nineteenth centuries. That period witnessed not only the emergence of new projection technologies, but also a profound change in print culture in which reading was no longer restricted to religious and scholarly purposes. The rise in popular literacy, the concurrent rise of the lending library, and the proliferation of Gothic fiction and occultism were all part of a newly emerging popular print culture, a decisive cultural transformation that has been characterized as a "reading revolution."[33] Accordingly, this book juxtaposes late eighteenth-century anxieties about "reading addiction" with the dissemination of nonscholarly writings and with the allure of new serial genres.[34]

Chapter 3 analyzes ghost narratives, the Gothic novel—especially Friedrich Schiller's *The Ghost Seer*—and new immersive reading practices. In *Dreams of a Spirit Seer*, Kant had repudiated the proliferation of ostensibly genuine ghost stories in an exploding print market, even though his own treatise contributed to their "haunting circulation." Within the realm of literary fiction, Horace Walpole's *The Castle of Otranto: A Gothic Story* (1764) simultaneously became the founding text of a new genre whose enormous success was based on the literary appropriation of supernatural apparitions as a narrative device of shock. Similar to the sequence of sudden optical magnifications that assault the phantasmagoria's viewer, Friedrich Schiller's sensational novel *The Ghost Seer* (1787–89) administered a series of shocks to its protagonist and to its readers. In its wake, numerous sequels and spin-offs by other authors sought to emulate the commercial success of Schiller's novel as one of the most widely read literary texts of the eighteenth century.

But the immersive appeal of these popular tales also caused considerable alarm. One extreme episode of "reading addiction" (*Lesesucht*), analyzed in more detail in Chapter 3, was Ludwig Tieck's recitation of a popular Gothic novel that Tieck and two of his friends read aloud to each other, taking turns for the duration of ten hours. When Tieck had finished reading the novel's second volume at two in the morning (his friends were asleep by then), he suffered a nervous breakdown marked by intense and frightening hallucinations in which he almost killed his companions. Warning against the harmful effects of "reading addiction" and "reading rage" (*Lesewut*), conservative critics drew on similar anecdotes to invoke a pathological loss of reality as the inevitable consequence of reading too many Gothic novels. According to these conservative indictments of new media in the late eighteenth century, print's dissemination of nonscholarly writings and the Gothic novel's appeal to the imagination of addicted readers paralleled the mirage of contemporaneous optical technologies.

Chapter 4 extends the analysis of literary representations of the marvelous to the first half of the nineteenth century, when Romantic texts about animal magnetism and clairvoyance also blurred the boundary between fact and fiction. E. T. A. Hoffmann's "The Magnetizer" (1814) transforms its representation of the magnetic rapport between mesmerist and somnambulist into a poetological model for an immersed reader who is mentally and physically affected by Hoffmann's novella. Justinus Kerner, by contrast, presents his treatise *The Seeress of Prevorst* (1829) as a purely factual account of the somnambulist Friederike Hauffe, who remained for the duration of seven years in a state of magnetic clairvoyance. Yet by giving a peculiar explanation of Hauffe's ability to see into the beyond, Kerner's case history lent itself to a sensational literary adaptation. According to Kerner, the seeress perceived the material as well as the spiritual realms because she was—for the whole extended period—"arrested by some fixation in the moment of dying between life and death."[35] Edgar Allan Poe's "The Facts in the Case of M. Valdemar" (1845) appropriates and transforms this account of the clairvoyant somnambulist in a ghastly and shocking manner. In describing an ostensibly real scientific experiment, Poe's tale replicates and undermines Kerner's claims to factuality within the realm of literary fiction. Yet even though Poe's text was a literary one, its fictional mode of producing reality effects was so compelling that the novella was reprinted as an authentic case history in various newspapers and popular-science journals—similar to the haunting circulation of ghost narratives in eighteenth-century print culture.

The final chapter reveals a reciprocal interaction between spiritualist research and the gradual emergence of electrical television in the late nineteenth and early twentieth centuries. At that time, the German spiritualist Carl du Prel appropriated Kant's critical philosophy in a curious manner that allowed him to define psychic "television in time and space" as a function of the "transcendental subject."[36] In addition to presenting occultism as the "very philosophy of technology," du Prel introduced Ernst Kapp's theory of technology as "organ projection" into his spiritualist account of new media.[37] Du Prel even imagined an engineer "well versed in occultism" who would draw on this expertise to construct an apparatus for the wireless transmission of moving images.[38] The closest real-life equivalent to this fantasy may have been the British physicist, chemist, and spiritualist William Crookes, who undertook research on thought transference and who also invented the cathode ray tube. But Crookes was not an isolated figure; under the auspices of the Society for Psychical Research, other renowned scientists, such as Oliver Lodge and William James, also conducted experiments in thought transference and telepathy.

The various conjunctures between the ghostly and new media technologies in the twentieth and twenty-first centuries would have allowed for extending this book's historical range. In the Cold War period, Günther Anders conceptualized the mass medium of television under the title "The World as Phantom and Matrix," and the recent history of digital technologies could have served as the subject of another chapter that examines a link between the spectral and the medial. This book, however, ends with the first experimental television broadcasts in the late 1920s, when "wireless television" was described, somewhat hyperbolically, as "perhaps not only the most magical, but also the most consequential . . . of all inventions of our time."[39]

CHAPTER ONE

The Magic Lantern of Philosophy:

Specters of Kant

Otherwise there would follow the absurd proposition that there is an appearance without anything that appears.

—Kant, *Critique of Pure Reason*

Illusion is the kind of mirage that persists even though one knows that the ostensible object is not real.

—Kant, *Anthropology from a Pragmatic Point of View*

The first edition of *Dreams of a Spirit Seer, Elucidated by Dreams of Metaphysics* was published anonymously in 1766.[1] Two years earlier, *The Castle of Otranto: A Gothic Story* initially came forth as the alleged translation of a medieval Italian manuscript. In the second edition of each book, Immanuel Kant and Horace Walpole acknowledged their authorship and chose the same dictum from Horace as an epigraph.[2] In *Ars poetica*, the Roman author had criticized the pictorial representation of monstrous bodies. But also, in the realm of literature, Horace rejected a text "whose fantastic forms are fashioned like the dreams of a sick man so that neither head nor foot merge to a whole."[3] Anticipating Kant's denunciation of Swedenborg as a deluded maniac, the title page of *Dreams of a Spirit Seer* quotes Horace almost accurately: "Empty semblances are fashioned like the dreams of a sick man."[4] Walpole, however, altered Horace's sentence in a manner that subverted its original meaning: "Empty shapes are fashioned so that head and foot nonetheless merge to a whole."[5]

By inverting Horace's classical aesthetic, Walpole's "Gothic story" affirmed a poetics of monstrous architectural and textual

23

bodies. Simultaneously, its narrative interest centered on the gradual manifestation of an enormous specter that materializes, literally, piece by piece. The text opens with a giant helmet suddenly falling from the sky and killing Conrad, the son of the novel's principal villain, Manfred. Later in the novel, more outsized body parts—an enormous hand, an enormous foot—appear in the castle that has been usurped by Manfred. The book ends with the apparition of Alfonso, the founder of Otranto. His "form . . . dilated to an immense magnitude" finally becomes visible as a whole, reinstalling the rightful heir, Theodore, before ascending to heaven.[6] In the "translator's" preface to the first edition, Walpole apologized that the medieval tale centered on "miracles, visions, necromancy, dreams and other preternatural events, which are exploded [sic] now even from romances."[7] But the enormous success of Otranto led Walpole to acknowledge his authorship, and it served to legitimize the literary representation of spirit apparitions.

In the preamble that introduces his theoretical treatise, Kant, by contrast, criticized the popularity of supposedly authentic ghost stories, which were intruding upon philosophical theory: "But why is it that the popular tales, which find such widespread acceptance . . . circulate with such futility and impunity, insinuating themselves even into scholarly theories?"[8] Three years earlier, in 1763, Kant had been favorably impressed by various reports about Swedenborg's ghostly visions, and he even characterized one incident as "remov[ing] any conceivable doubt" about the veracity of these narratives.[9] But in Dreams, Kant casts doubt on these stories, and he postpones their discussion to the second, "historical part" of the text, which I will analyze in Chapter 3. The first, "dogmatic part" gives a detailed theoretical account of how spirit apparitions might be conceived of—an issue that Kant deliberates in conjunction with classical metaphysical questions such as the relationship between mind and body.

The "Practical Conclusion Drawn from the Treatise as a Whole" attempts to put an end to "zealously overeager speculation," and in passing, Kant here formulates a new definition of metaphysics as the "science of the limits of human reason."[10] This delimitation of philosophical speculation has often been read as anticipating the *Critique of Pure Reason*, and it may seem Kant's final and dismissive word on the issue of spiritual apparitions.[11] But a closer reading reveals a fundamental ambiguity of Kant's treatise, whose subtitle announces the "elucidation" of the "dreams of a spirit seer" by the "dreams of metaphysics."[12] Toward the end of the book, Kant himself declares that he brought the reader "to precisely the same point of ignorance from which he set out in the first place."[13] This "indecision" vis-à-vis possibly authentic ghost stories has produced strikingly divergent interpretations of Kant's book, which has been cited by skeptics as well as by spiritualists.[14] Even in the first, "dogmatic part" of the text, Kant developed two diametrically opposed theories of spirit apparitions without clearly marking his own position. Like Moses Mendelssohn, Jacob Friedrich Abel consequently criticized Kant's treatise as "ultimately leaving everything open to question."[15]

In Chapter 3, I will interpolate Kant's critique of ghost narratives with a newly emerging popular print culture and the literary genre of the Gothic novel. In this chapter, however, I am going to juxtapose *Dreams of a Spirit Seer* to the cultural use of the magic lantern in phantasmagorical projections. Viewed in this context, we can trace the conflicting metaphysical and skeptical impulses inherent to *Dreams* and how they persist in Kant's critical philosophy. While defining *Erscheinung* as an indexical apparition of a supersensory thing in itself, Kant simultaneously warns against the mirage of speculative reason, which he describes as a "magic lantern of brain phantoms."

Dreams of a Spirit Seer: "The Dogmatic Part" and Optical Media

Kant opens his theoretical analysis of how to conceive of spirit apparitions by defining spirits as simple, immaterial beings that are endowed with reason, but lack spatial extension.[16] But this reiteration of the Cartesian opposition of *res cogitans* and *res extensa* gives rise to the question as to how to conceptualize the unity of the human body and spirit: "How mysterious is the community [*Gemeinschaft*] which exists between a spirit and a body?"[17] Kant seeks to resolve this mind-body problem, which also preoccupied the young Friedrich Schiller in his medical dissertations, by describing the soul as partaking in both the bodily and the spiritual worlds: "The human soul, already in this present life, would therefore have to be regarded as being simultaneously linked to two worlds."[18] However, the soul's spiritual dimension eludes our bodily perception. A "clear intuition" or "view" of the spirit world (*das klare Anschauen*), which mesmerist theories would later term "clairvoyance," can be achieved only in the afterlife.[19]

Consequently, Kant formulates the assumption that "the human soul, even in this life, stands in an indissoluble community with all the immaterial natures of the spirit world—that standing in a mutual interaction with these natures, it both has an effect upon them and receives impressions from them. But the soul as a human being is not conscious of them, provided that everything is in good order."[20] For the purpose of further elucidating and supporting this hypothesis, he introduces a "real and generally accepted observation" in a digression on social phenomena.[21]

Vaguely relying on Jean-Jacques Rousseau, Kant describes the reconciliation of "private" and "common interest" as the consonance of the individual soul in a ghostly harmony that comprehends the aggregate unity of all "spiritual natures."[22] Kant's surprisingly detailed foray into moral philosophy postulates an "immediate community of spirits."[23] It is a "spiritual republic" that arises as "a consequence of the natural and general mutual interaction" between private and general will.[24] Kant emphasizes that "the forces which move the human heart...find the focal point of their union outside ourselves," and he links this disregard for our own interests to an imperceptible influence of the general will.[25] As Kant puts it: "When we relate external things to our need, we cannot do so without at the same time feeling ourselves bound and limited by a certain sensation; this sensation draws our attention to the fact that a foreign will, as it were, is operative within ourselves, and that our own inclination needs external assent as its condition. A secret power compels us to direct our will towards the welfare of others or to regulate it in accordance with the will of another, although this often happens contrary to our own will."²⁶

The description of being controlled by a "secret power" resembles the economic and Gothic invocations of an "invisible hand" whose ghostly intervention compels us to promote the public interest.²⁷ But Kant is more interested in deducing this phenomenon from a general moral law and concludes: "As a result, we recognize that, in our most secret motives, we are dependent on the rule of the general will. It is this rule [*Regel*] which confers on the world of spiritual beings a moral unity and systematic constitution according to purely spiritual laws."²⁸ The "rule" of the general will—a phrase that oscillates between external coercion and adherence to a universally valid formula—can thus be interpreted as our being controlled by a foreign will and as anticipating the formal principle of practical reason and its ethical legislation.²⁹ Kant goes on to equate our "moral feeling" with "this sensed dependency of the private will on the general will."³⁰ Introducing a further speculative explanation of this phenomenon, he relates the mutual attraction of kindred spirits to "pneumatic laws" that may function similar to Newton's laws of gravitation.³¹ Kant does not clearly subscribe to a belief in this analogy of physics and pneumatology as a science of spiritual forces. Nonetheless, he maintains that the compelling influence exerted by the general will constitutes a "real and generally accepted observation." The aggregate specter of the "spiritual community" is therefore a "common and ordinary thing."³²

The rarity of ghostly visions seems strangely at odds with the constant interaction between our soul and the spiritual republic. Yet Kant explains this apparent discrepancy by distinguishing between the soul's "immaterial intuition" (*immaterielles Anschauen*) and the sensory intuition and perception of material objects, which are "altogether different" from each other.³³ The unity of this difference within one single subject can therefore be maintained only in a precarious manner—by introducing the unexpected and initially enigmatic distinction between subject and person. In Kant's words: "While it is true that there is one single subject, which is simultaneously a member of the visible and the invisible world, it is nonetheless not one and the same person."[34] Describing the mysterious community of body and spirit, Kant invokes the splitting of one subject into two distinct "persons" that know nothing about each other. What we perceive "as a human being" retreats from our intuition "as spirit," while spiritual "ideas" are inaccessible to our sensory perception.[35] As an empirical analogy to this strange theory of the subject, Kant even refers to the "dual personality of sleepwalkers, who on occasion in this state display greater than usual understanding, even though they remember nothing about it when they wake."[36] The unity of body and mind in one subject corresponds to the identity of a split personality.

Yet according to Kant, the division between the spiritual and the material worlds can be overcome at certain points, "even in this present life," when "spiritual impressions...arouse kindred fantasies in our imagination."[37] This can take place "in persons with organs of unusual sensitivity."[38] Such "strange persons," Kant suggests, amplify the images of their fantasy to such a degree that they are "assailed by the appearance of certain objects as being external to them." The true cause of these apparitions, however, is an internal "genuine spiritual influence." This spiritual influence "cannot be perceived immediately, but it reveals itself to consciousness by means of kindred images of our fantasy that assume the semblance of sensory perception." While presenting mere "shadow images of material objects," ghostly visions are "founded upon a real spiritual impression."[39] But the actual qualities of the manifesting spirit remain unknown, since the ghost seer's perception of such an appearance does not allow for immediate conclusions about its underlying spiritual substrate.

Summarizing this "metaphysical hypothesis," Kant again explains genuine spiritual apparitions as hallucinations that are based on sensory deception and that nonetheless have an objective cause.[40] He writes: "Departed souls and pure spirits can never, it is true, be present to our outer senses, nor can they in any fashion whatever stand in community with matter, but they may indeed act upon the spirit of man, who belongs, with them, to one great republic. And they can exercise this influence in such a way that the representations, which they awaken in him, clothe themselves, according to the law of his fantasy, in images which are akin to them, and create the outer appearance of objects corresponding to them."[41]

Kant thus asserts the possibility of genuine apparitions that are based upon our constant partaking in a "republic" of spirits. After the book's publication, Kant received a no longer extant letter from Moses Mendelssohn, who later, in a review of *Dreams*, would convey his surprise about Kant's ambivalent stance on ghost seeing and metaphysics. In his response to Mendelssohn's letter, Kant claimed that his attempt at an "analogy between a real moral influence by spiritual beings and the force of common gravitation" was "actually not a serious proposition," but "merely intended as an example of how far one can go in philosophical fabrications, completely unhindered, when there are no data."[42] This statement has been taken as indicating that the whole first chapter of *Dreams* does not have to be taken seriously. But Kant's uneasy renunciation pertains only to the parallel between Newton's laws of gravitation and the explanation of our moral actions by "pneumatic laws."[43] He never questions the "real and generally accepted observation"[44] of our moral feeling being directed by a secret power. In addition, Kant elaborates the surprising "metaphysical hypothesis"[45] of genuine spirit apparitions in great detail, and he even feels the need to emphasize that despite apparent similarities, he conceived his theory of ghost seeing independently from Swedenborg's *Arcana coelestia*.[46]

Yet immediately after establishing how genuine spirit appearances could be conceptualized, Kant's treatise formulates a diametrically opposed, equally "dogmatic" model that dismisses ghost seeing as the perception of delusive phantoms. Kant's metaphysical theory of genuine apparitions puts particular emphasis on the parallel between spiritual visions and the moral influence of the general will. But in explaining the false and deceptive images created by a fanatic and inflamed imagination, Kant's treatise foregrounds a medial analogy: the optical production of a ghostly illusion or "mirage" (*Blendwerk*) that a credulous observer mistakenly assumes to be real.[47] This "phantasmagoria," as it was soon to be termed by Paul Philidor, perfected the use of the magic lantern for the purpose of simulating spirit apparitions by projecting images on smoke. Within *Dreams of a Spirit Seer*, Kant makes explicit the parallel between ghostly visions and the perception of optical illusions in a passage that denounces the seeing of apparitions as the delusion of an enthusiastic imagination.[48] He does not explicitly introduce the term the term "projection," which in German became common around 1850 in referring to mental and optical processes.[49] But he describes how pathological spirit seers locate the figments of their own imagination "outside of themselves," mistaking these chimeras for the actual presence of a specter.[50] In 1791, Jakob Friedrich Abel wrote in nearly identical terms: "We see, outside of ourselves, what merely haunts our own head."[51] In an etymologically grounded pun, Kant therefore refers to these *Hirngespinste*, these "figments of the imagination" as "brain phantoms"—*Hirngespenster*; and he explains their emergence by invoking the "optical deception" of visual media.[52] According to this second, skeptical model of how to explain spiritual apparitions, the deranged spirit seer refers the "mirage of his imagination" to the exterior world, thereby assigning a false, imaginary "focal point" to the perceived object—"as also happens for example when, by means of a concave mirror, the spectre [*Spectrum*] of a body is seen in mid air."[53]

The creation of such optical specters by means of concave mirrors was described in numerous contemporaneous texts on natural magic, such as Bonaventure Abat's *Philosophical Amusements on Various Parts of the Sciences* (1763) or the third volume of Edme Gilles Guyot's *New Physical and Mathematical Amusements* (1769).[54] Guyot's text gave a detailed description of the special effects produced with concave mirrors that allowed for "presenting the image of an object in such a way that even if one imagined holding it in one's hand, one could clutch only the semblance of it."[55] Providing his readers with extensive instructions for building the necessary apparatus (Figure 2), Guyot explained how "by means of this mirror, all kinds

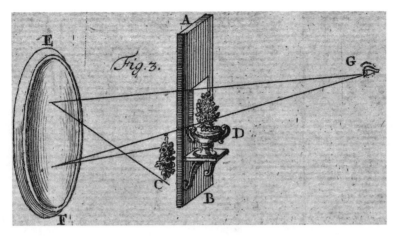

Figure 2. Creation of an optical "specter" by means of a concave mirror: a plant hidden from sight behind the wall A–B and located at point C is reflected by the concave mirror E–F and perceived by the observer G as located at point D. From Edme Gilles Guyot, *Neue Physikalische und mathematische Belustigungen* (Augsburg, 1772).

of objects, painted or in demirelief, could be shown, for instance, an absent person of whom one has only a portrait, or figures of ghosts . . . and many other things."[56]

In addition to this description of optical tricks rendered possible by the use of concave mirrors, Guyot also presented various modes of employing hidden magic lanterns, such as the simulation of spirit apparitions by projecting images onto clouds of smoke. This use of the optical instrument became very popular in the late eighteenth century, since it lent the ghostly apparitions the semblance of corporeality (Figure 3). As Guyot put it: "The observers [will] not know to whom they should ascribe the sudden apparition of this ghost whose head seems to emerge from out of the smoke."[57]

Technical innovations such as Ami Argand's development of an oil burner that, after 1783, replaced simple candles as the light source of magic lanterns allowed for the optical conjuring of spirits before larger audiences. Especially popular were Etienne-Gaspard Robertson's "phantasmagorias," which took place in the dark subterranean vaults of a former Capuchin monastery in Paris, accompanied by the unearthly sounds of Benjamin Franklin's glass harmonica. In

Figure 3. Phantasmagorical projection of ghostly images onto smoke. From Johann Georg Krünitz, *Oeconomisch-technologische Encyklopädie* vol. 65 (Berlin, 1794).

staging his elaborate performances, Robertson relied on the phantascope, a magic lantern that was equipped with movable glass slides
and mounted on wheels (Figure 4). The moving back projection of
the images allowed for powerful special effects that were created by
increasing the distance between projector and image. In the darkness of the vault, astounded audiences perceived the resulting mag-
nification as a terrifying approach of the projected figure. As Hegel
puts it in his description of the night of the world, "here a bloody
head suddenly surges forward, there another white form abruptly
appears, before vanishing again." Highlights of Robertson's phantasmagoria included the apparition of the "Bleeding Nun" (Figure 5), a
figure from Matthew Lewis's Gothic novel *The Monk* (1796). Equally
popular was the summoning of Louis XVI, who had been executed
in January of 1793.[58]

Robertson's spirit shows aimed for the production of dread by
staging an illusion that could be recognized as produced by smoke
and mirrors, but that nonetheless exerted a powerful bodily effect
on its observers. By contrast, Gothic novels such as Friedrich Schiller's *The Ghost Seer: From the Memoirs of Count O* (1787–89), Cajetan
Tschink's *The Victim of Magical Delusion* (1790–93) and Carl August
Grosse's *Horrid Mysteries* (1791–95) described credulous observers
who mistook the ghostly projections of a hidden magic lantern for
genuine spirit apparitions.[59] Simultaneously, within the realm of
instructional literature, theoretical essays attempted to "enlighten"
their readers, warning against the deception and manipulation of
gullible victims by impostors such as Johann Georg Schröpfer and
Cagliostro, who were among the most notorious necromancers in
the German-speaking countries of the late eighteenth century.[60]
A contemporaneous Prussian law even prescribed incarceration
between six months and two years as the adequate punishment for
"fraud by means of ostensible or false magic."[61]

In the wake of Guyot's *New Physical and Mathematical Amusements*,
numerous texts on natural magic appeared that put forward skeptical and esoteric accounts of spirit apparitions. These books included
a treatise by Karl von Eckartshausen that was published in three

Figure 4. The phantascope, a magic lantern on wheels, and its use in a phantasmagoria. From Adolphe Ganot, *Cours de physique purement expérimentale à l'usage des gens du monde* (Paris, 7th edition, 1859).

Figure 5. "Le nonne sanglante," phantasmagoria glass slide, Thomas Weynants Early Visual Media Collection. In addition to the dagger in her right, the "bleeding nun" also held a lantern in her left hand, missing in this slide, but indicated by her lifted arm and her extended index finger and thumb. A second slide was projected with a different magic lantern onto the same screen, showing an arched walkway through which the figure advanced toward the audience. See Etienne-Gaspard Robertson, *Mémoires récréatifs, scientifiques et anecdotiques*, 2 vols. (Paris: Robertson, 1834), vol. 1, pp. 342–44).

volumes under the title *Revelations on Magic from Verified Experiences in Occult Philosophical Sciences and Rare Secrets of Nature* (Figure 6).[62] Eckartshausen even gave directions for building a "pocket magic lantern" with a built-in cooling system to prevent the supposed necromancer's clothes from going up in flames. By such means, Eckartshausen asserted, an unsuspecting companion on an evening stroll could be terrified through "optical spirit apparitions."[63]

But apart from this practical demonstration of optical deceptions, Eckartshausen, a former member of the Illuminati who had turned to theosophy, also gave a psychological and a metaphysical explanation of apparitions. Kant's *Dreams of a Spirit Seer* presented its two theories of ghostly visions as mutually exclusive, even though it remained unclear whether Kant himself adhered to the metaphysical hypothesis of genuine apparitions or whether he embraced the skeptical denunciation of brain phantoms. Eckartshausen, who did not explicitly refer to Kant, instead asserted the simultaneous existence of "three kinds of spirit apparitions," defined in the following manner: "The first one is purely artificial, consisting of an optical deception. The second kind is produced through the images of the imagination, that is, by the imagination creating a [false] external image outside of the body. And the third is the true spirit apparition, visible only to the inner sense, and transformed by this very inner sense into an image for the outer senses, which is in fact the true apparition."[64]

Eckartshausen's typology puts the various explanations of ghostly apparitions inherent in Kant's *Dreams* side by side. Yet what is surprising about Eckartshausen's psychological and metaphysical account of spiritual appearances is an underlying similarity to the "purely artificial" optical specter. According to Eckartshausen, the second, "false" apparition emerges as a purely subjective figment of the imagination, whereas the "true" apparition is based on an objective, spiritual influence. But both models are marked by a structural affinity with the simulation of a specter by means of a magic lantern, since they presuppose the projection of an inner mental picture onto the exterior world. An alternately overt and surreptitious recourse

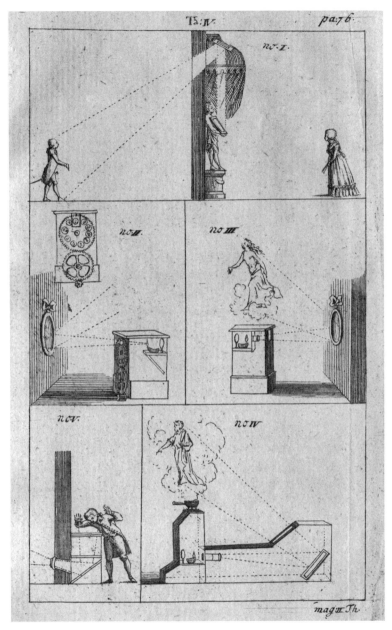

Figure 6. A series of optical deceptions that are achieved by concave mirrors. From Karl von Eckartshausen, *Aufschlüsse zur Magie* (Munich, 1790). Especially interesting is Eckartshausen's inclusion of the viewer's bodily reaction of terror or surprise within the technical drawing. (See lower left, drawing no. v.)

to contemporaneous visual media can also be seen in Kant's *Dreams of a Spirit Seer*. There, the explicit reference to creating the "spectre of a body" by means of a concave mirror serves to discredit the belief in imaginary brain phantoms—by explaining how a fanatic enthusiast refers the figments of his or her imagination to the external world.[65] Yet Kant's theory of genuine spirit appearances implicitly adopts the same mode of explanation, for Kant characterizes authentic visions as arising from spiritual impressions that are transposed to the external world as "shadow images of material objects."[66] Even Kant's digression on the moral forces that govern our practical actions draws on an optical model of projection in asserting that these forces "find the focal point of their union outside ourselves."[67]

In Kant's *Dreams*, the explicit invocation of visual instruments serves a skeptical, antimetaphysical function. But Kant's description of real spiritual impressions, which are received internally and then projected toward the external world, is also predicated on the cultural use of concave mirrors and magic lanterns in phantasmagorical projections. Eckartshausen, who seeks to prove the reality of spirit apparitions, even goes so far as to refer to the working of an optical instrument in his account of genuine spiritual appearances. Explaining how "the inner sense influences the outer senses," he writes about the "true apparition" that "it is as with a concave mirror: the object, which is invisible to the eye, is reflected in the concave mirror. The mirror concentrates the simple imprint of the image in its hollow, thereby forming an external body visible to our organic system. This is also the way it works with the inner sense—it receives an image that is invisible to us, concentrates its reflected imprints on our outer senses, and thereby we see."[68]

Eckartshausen's typology of three different kinds of spiritual apparitions highlights the constitutive role of optical technologies for late eighteenth-century accounts of false and of genuine apparitions. Yet in addition to explaining various kinds of ghostly manifestations, Eckartshausen employed the concept of *Erscheinung* in its meaning of "empirical appearance." Assigning the same degree of reality to spiritual apparitions and empirical appearances, Eckartshausen

affirmed that even the "normal kind of appearances" do not correspond to the "reality of things."[69] Nine years after the first edition of
Kant's *Critique of Pure Reason*, Eckartshausen's treatise thus suggests
a spiritualist interpretation of Kant's critical notion of *Erscheinung*.

Empirical Appearance and Supersensory Thing in Itself

In *Dreams of a Spirit Seer*, Kant had defined metaphysics as the "science of the limits of human reason."[70] He sought to give a new scientific foundation to this philosophical discipline in his *Critique of
Pure Reason*. Turning against the "dogmatic slumber" of scholastic
philosophy,[71] Kant's famous Copernican turn undertook a chiastic
inversion of the traditional assumption that human knowledge is
shaped by the cognized object: "Up to now it has been assumed
that all our cognition must conform to the objects; but all attempts
to find out something about them a priori through concepts that
would extend our cognition have, on this presupposition, come to
nothing. Hence let us once try whether we do not get further with
the problems of metaphysics by assuming that the objects must
conform to our cognition."[72] Concurrent with this reversal of the
relation between subject and object, Kant distinguishes between
Erscheinung—"appearance" or "apparition"—and the thing in itself.
Our cognition "reaches appearances only, leaving the thing in itself
as something real for itself but uncognized by us."[73]

Kant's "transcendental" analysis of perception therefore sets out
to grasp the conditions of possibility of our experience, explaining how an "appearance" conforms a priori to the subject's forms
of intuition. Yet even though the objects cognized by us are "mere
appearances" (*bloße Erscheinungen*),[74] Kant nonetheless maintains
that there is a relation between this appearance and the thing in
itself—a relation, however, of which we cannot gain any knowledge
and that seems to contradict the assumption that appearances are
in fact constituted by the knowing subject.[75] Objects are given to
human knowledge only as appearances. But as Kant continues: "The
reservation must also be well noted, that even if we cannot cognize
these same objects as things in themselves, we at least must be able

to think them as things in themselves. For otherwise there would follow the absurd proposition that there is an appearance without anything that appears [*Denn sonst würde der ungereimte Satz daraus folgen, daß Erscheinung ohne etwas wäre, was da erscheint*]."[76]

Even though Kant elsewhere warns against "moving into the realm of chimeras . . . by cloaking unfounded claims through popular language," he relies here on the very same mode of argumentation.[77] He introduces the concept of *Erscheinung*, which is defined in relational terms in the contemporaneous discussion on spirit apparitions, and thereby lends a "cloak" of plausibility to his own speculative claim of a relation between appearance and thing in itself. Elucidating the distinction between perceivable phenomena and conceivable noumena, Kant conflates the distinct meanings of appearance as distortion of reality and appearance as indexical manifestation by asserting: "It . . . follows naturally from the concept of appearance [*Erscheinung*] in general that something must correspond to it which is not in itself an appearance, for appearance can be nothing for itself and outside our mode of presentation; thus, if there is not to be a constant circle, the word appearance must already indicate a relation to something."[78]

But while this "something" is conceivable, it cannot be proven to exist in reality. The precarious relationship between the "something" and its apparition thus takes on the same epistemological status as Kant's "metaphysical hypothesis" of spirits that affect us in real spiritual impressions and then become perceptible in sensory appearances transposed to the external world by our imagination. Kant's critical epistemology presumes that our senses are "affected" (*affiziert*) by a principally unknowable thing in itself.[79] Yet this assumption cannot be upheld without logical inconsistencies and seems strikingly reminiscent of Kant's previous theory of a genuine spiritual influence that is transformed by the spirit seer into a sensory impression. It is the *Critique of Judgment* (1790) that defines *Erscheinung* as "an indication of a supersensory substrate,"[80] but the very same phrase could also have been taken from Kant's *Dreams of a Spirit Seer*.

Introducing a metaphysical hypothesis that postulates the existence of a thinkable entity was exactly what Kant himself had
strongly criticized in an earlier letter to Mendelssohn. There, he
compared such a mode of argumentation to the "dreams" of spirit
seeing: "Conceivability (whose semblance derives from the fact that
impossibility cannot be proven either) is pure mirage; I would myself
dare to defend Schwedenberg's dreamings if someone should attack
their possibility."[81] Kant highlights the structural parallel between
the metaphysical postulation of possible entities and Swedenborg's
speculative account of the spiritual realm. In his Copernican turn,
Kant sought to substitute scientific statements for these spiritualist
"dreamings." Nonetheless, his critical epistemology corresponds in
its terminology and its logical structure to his earlier representation
of immaterial beings whose sensory appearance is "founded upon a
real spiritual impression."[82] In *Dreams of a Spirit Seer*, these apparitions are described as a kind of objective hallucination that does not
correspond to any material object in the outside world, but that can
nonetheless be traced back to a "genuine spiritual influence."[83] Yet
at the same time, *Erscheinung* as it is defined in the *Critique of Pure
Reason* is also an objective hallucination, as it were, constituted by
the cognizing subject and nonetheless vaguely related to an unde-
fined and ungraspable thing in itself.

According to Kant, in both cases, the sensory appearance does not
allow for any conclusions about its underlying substrate. Therefore
the most important difference between these phenomena derives
from the fact that spirit apparitions become visible only to "persons
with organs of unusual sensitivity."[84] The apparition through which
the thing in itself "affects" our senses, by contrast, is perceptible
to everybody. Yet even in his critical writings, Kant insists that
the word *Erscheinung*, in its double meaning of "appearance" and
"apparition," necessarily implies "a relation to something," thereby
placing the epistemology of transcendental idealism in precarious
proximity to the contemporaneous debate about spirit apparitions.[85]
Kant's Copernican turn may have been intended as a transformation
of philosophical metaphysics into a "pure," enlightened discipline,

but late eighteenth-century occultist assumptions about a link between sensory and supersensory realms retain a crucial role for his critical distinction between appearance and thing in itself.

In *Dreams of a Spirit Seer*, Kant first introduced metaphysical assumptions in his description of an "immediate community of spirits" before transferring the notion of a real spiritual impression to his theory of genuine spirit apparitions. In Kant's critical philosophy, the concept of *Erscheinung* fulfills a comparable argumentative function, since it is meant to ground the speculative claim of an indexical relation between an appearance and a supersensory thing in itself. But the explicit invocation of optical media that underlies Kant's skeptical turn against imaginary brain phantoms also finds a continuation in the *Critique of Pure Reason*. In formulating his doctrine of "transcendental semblance" or "illusion" (*transzendentaler Schein*), Kant conceives of the dialectic of speculative reason by comparing its mirage (*Blendwerk*) to the seemingly paradoxical status of phantasmagorical projections.

Transcendental Illusion and Optical Media

According to Kant, the transcendental illusion seduces us into employing the concepts of our understanding in an enthusiastic, transcendent, rather than transcendental manner that oversteps the limits of sensory experience. It is the inner dialectic of pure speculative reason that gives rise to this transcendental illusion. Therefore Kant insists on a strict differentiation between transcendental and empirical semblance: "Our concern here is not to treat of empirical (e.g. optical) semblance . . . rather, we have to do only with transcendental semblance [*Schein*], which . . . contrary to all the warnings of criticism, carries us beyond the empirical use of the categories, and holds out to us the mirage [*Blendwerk*] of extending the pure understanding."[86] Yet despite this distinction between optical and transcendental semblance, Kant again and again invokes contemporaneous optical instruments in his description of speculative reason. In doing so, his critical philosophy transforms the material apparatus of the magic lantern and its use in the visual medium of the phantasmagoria into an epistemic figure that highlights the limits and unreliability of philosophical knowledge.

For Kant, the dialectic of pure speculative reason corresponds to a "logic of semblance."[87] It emerges from the inner nature of reason, which, based on a knowledge of finite conditions, seeks to draw conclusions about the unconditioned or absolute. The mirage of transcendental illusion may therefore be seen through, but it cannot be abolished—in Kant's terms: "Hence there is a natural and unavoidable dialectic of pure reason . . . [that] even after we have exposed its mirage . . . will still not cease to mislead our reason with imaginary objects, continually propelling it into momentary deceptions that always need to be corrected again."[88] Kant explains this persistence of "transcendental illusion" by invoking the persistence of optical illusions that deceive our sensory apparatus despite our better knowledge.[89] As Kant writes, even an astronomer, who knows better, perceives the moon to be larger at the horizon than high in the sky.[90] Or to quote a statement from Kant's *Anthropology from a Pragmatic Point of View* that is key for understanding his doctrine of dialectical semblance, since it goes beyond this traditional example of perceptive distortion: "Illusion is the kind of mirage that persists even though one knows that the ostensible object is not real" (Illusion ist dasjenige Blendwerk, welches bleibt, ob man gleich weiß, daß der vermeinte Gegenstand nicht wirklich ist).[91]

Kant thus defines illusion as different from a mere distortion of reality. Describing a conflict between knowledge and perception, his notion of *Blendwerk* (mirage or delusion) is modeled on the use of concave mirrors and magic lanterns for simulating an "ostensible object" that does not really exist. In refuting the paralogisms and false conclusions of pure reason, Kant repeatedly invokes optical terms, warning against the transcendental illusion that "deceives" us with the "mirror image" of the soul as a material entity.[92] Yet as Kant affirms, the single proposition of rational psychology—"I think"—does not presuppose any kind of substance. Traditional metaphysical problems, such as the seemingly impossible "community of the soul with an organic body," are therefore based on

43

"hypostatizing" or reifying a "mirage" that is mistaken to be a real object.[93] Kant describes this process as if referring to the images of a phantasmagoria that a credulous observer falsely considers to be a real physical object: "Now I assert that all the difficulties which one believes to find in these questions...rest on a mere mirage, according to which one hypostatizes that which exists merely in thought and thus assumes it to be a real object outside of the thinking subject."[94] The transcendental illusion emerges from mistaking a subjective idea for an objectively given substance, and it is worth noting that Marx's account of the "thinglike semblance of the social determination of labor" in the chapter on "commodity fetishism" in *Capital* remains surprisingly faithful to Kant's critique of the dialectic of reason that leads us to reify the subjective conditions of appearances.

In announcing that Hegel's philosophy "stands on its head, but that one can discover its 'rational kernel'" by "overturning it,"[95] Marx's preface to the second edition of *Capital* reiterates the argument made in *The German Ideology* (1845) that "in all ideologies, human beings and their circumstances [appear] upside-down as in a camera obscura."[96] Yet in his chapter on "commodity fetishism," Marx sets out to expose a much more intricate and persistent illusion that he describes in analogy to the magic lantern and its use in the visual medium of the phantasmagoria. Idealist philosophy gives a distorted picture of reality, but as with a camera obscura, its falsification can be corrected by a simple inversion. Economic structures of capitalist exchange, by contrast, produce the mirage of a physical object, a simulacrum that has no referent in the material world. Marx thus adapts Kant's warning that we mistake "that which exists merely in thought" for "a real object outside of the thinking subject,"[97] and he transforms Kant's doctrine of transcendental illusion into a critique of our tendency to reify social relations. Explaining the "thinglike semblance of the social determination of labor," Marx describes the commodity's "spectral objectivity" (*gespenstige Gegenständlichkeit*) as emerging from the social formation of capitalism: "It is only the specific social relation of human beings that here

44

assumes...the phantasmagorical form of a relation of objects."[98]

But whereas Marx locates the source of this mirage in capitalist exchange, Kant describes the four antinomies of traditional metaphysics as emerging from the inner dialectic of pure speculative reason. While anticipating Marx's turn against conflating the social with the objective realm, Kant characterizes these antinomies as arising from our tendency to take "subjective conditions of our thinking for objective conditions of things themselves and to consider a hypothesis that is necessary for the satisfaction of our reason for a dogma."[99] The "skeptical method" employed by Kant in his famous staging of the conflict between thesis and antithesis therefore does not refute their content, but rather corrects the epistemological status of both propositions. Kant presents this strategy as "the method of watching or even occasioning a contest between assertions, not in order to decide it to the advantage of one party or the other, but to investigate whether the object of the dispute is not perhaps a mere mirage [*Blendwerk*] at which each would clutch in vain."[100]

Confusing an idea with an object or a hypothesis with a dogma is here once more described in terms that seem to cite Kant's own account of an optical "spectre" created by means of a concave mirror[101]—or a text such as Guyot's *New Philosophical Amusements*, with its instructions on how to "present the image of an object in such a way that even if one imagined holding it in one's hand one could clutch only the semblance of it."[102] Kant's August 1789 letter to Friedrich Heinrich Jacobi also deploys notions that come quite close to this critical account of speculative reason and its dialectical semblance. Turning against Johann Gottfried Herder's philosophical "syncretism," Kant characterizes his philosophical opponent as "very adept at producing a mirage that, like a magic lantern, makes wonderful things for a moment real before they vanish forever; meanwhile uninformed observers marvel that something extraordinary would have to be behind this, which they strive in vain to clutch."[103]

Transforming the optical instrument of the magic lantern into an epistemological figure, Kant's critical philosophy asserts that the antinomies of traditional metaphysics do not emerge from incorrect deductions; the specific content of any particular thesis or antithesis is not necessarily false. The problem is instead that we mistakenly conceive a necessary hypothesis as a theoretical dogma. Kant's emphasis on the persistence of this speculative illusion could also relate to the inescapable deception of our eyesight by the *trompe l'oeil*, a sensory delusion that Kant refers to in his *Anthropology*.[104] But his critical explanation of how we "hypostatize that which exists merely in thought and thus assume it to be a real object outside of the thinking subject" is clearly modeled on the projections of the magic lantern that lead us to assign a false imaginary focal point to an optical specter.[105] Kant assumed this dialectic to be operative even within theology, a discipline that he regarded as the apex of philosophical metaphysics. In his *Critique of Practical Reason* (1788) Kant thus reaffirms the "speculative restriction" undertaken by the *Critique of Pure Reason*,[106] and in an explicit invocation of contemporaneous media technology and its spectral projections, he emphasizes that only the critical limitation of speculative reason could prevent philosophical enthusiasm from producing "theories of the supersensory, to which we can see no end...thereby transforming theology into a magic lantern of brain phantoms."[107]

Within Kant's critical writings, this passage constitutes one of the few overt references to the magic lantern and its cultural use in phantasmagorical ghost projections. But it is important to note that his whole doctrine of transcendental illusion is predicated on a notion of "mirage" (*Blendwerk*) that is fundamentally and inextricably linked to late eighteenth-century visual media. The reference to the use of concave mirrors and magic lanterns in phantasmagorical projections has therefore a constitutive, rather than illustrative function for Kant's theory of transcendental illusion. One could even go so far as to say that the reader of Kant's *Critique of Pure Reason* who has followed the skeptical solution of the antinomies parallels the enlightened observer of a phantasmagoria. That viewer knows about the imaginary status of the magic lantern's ghostly projections and is nonetheless—to use terms from Kant's description of transcendental semblance—thrown into "momentary deceptions" by the reality of the phantasmagoric images and the "power of their illusion."[108] As Kant asserts in regard to the transcendental illusion: "There is a natural and unavoidable dialectic of pure reason...[that] even after we have exposed its mirage...will still not cease to mislead our reason with imaginary objects, continually propelling it into momentary deceptions that always need to be corrected again."[109] The images of a phantasmagoria truly exist, and the conflict between sensory deception and skeptical knowledge does not disappear once we recognize the lantern's projections to be a simulation, rather than a ghost: "Illusion is the kind of mirage that persists even though one knows that the ostensible object is not real."[110]

In the same manner, the mirage of dialectical semblance does not disappear, even after we have worked through the critique of pure speculative reason. Instead, our constant oscillation between skeptical knowledge and "momentary deceptions" (*augenblickliche Verirrungen*) leads us repeatedly to cross the limits of pure speculative reason. In doing so, we "hypostatize" a subjective idea as an objectively given substance and thereby transform philosophical metaphysics into a "magic lantern of brain phantoms."[111] Similarly, on the level of optical projection, we are led again and again, "for an instant" or, literally, "for the blink of an eye" (*augenblicklich*) to mistake visual semblance for reality and to ascribe a material body to the magic lantern's phantasmagorical projections. Kant distinguishes between optical and transcendental semblance. Yet he describes our tendency to mistake a subjective idea for a material object by drawing on contemporaneous optical projections. On the one hand, the *Critique of Pure Reason* adapts and appropriates its notion of *Erscheinung* as apparition and appearance from a contemporaneous debate about ghostly visions. Yet at the same time, Kant's doctrine of transcendental illusion transforms the material apparatus of the magic lantern and its use in the visual medium of the phantasmagoria into an epistemological figure. Spiritualist notions and the analogy between pure speculative reason and the visual instrument of the magic lantern are thus inherent to and constitutive of Kant's critical philosophy.

47

In the next chapter, I will contrast Schopenhauer's and Hegel's response to Kant's critical epistemology and trace their diverging modes of adapting medial and spiritualist notions. Schopenhauer praises Kant's distinction between thing in itself and appearance, and he aggressively foregrounds medial and spiritualist notions in his appropriation and transformation of Kant's critical philosophy. Hegel, by contrast, seeks to suppress his reliance on ghostly and phantasmagoric notions, while his philosophical system of absolute knowledge is meant to undo Kant's insistence on the limits of our cognition.

CHAPTER TWO

Ghosts and Phantasmagoria in
Hegel and Schopenhauer

The inner eye projects these forms as far as possible to where the outer
eye sees nothing, into dark recesses, behind curtains that suddenly
become transparent, and generally into the darkness of night.
—Schopenhauer, *Essay on Spirit Seeing*

Arthur Schopenhauer opens his *Essay on Spirit Seeing and Everything Connected Therewith* (1851) by asserting that a genuine spirit
apparition does not presuppose the physical "presence of a body."[1]
According to Schopenhauer, the very "notion of a spirit" implies
that it becomes known to us in a manner "altogether different"
from how we perceive a material object. Seeing a spirit is based on
the "presence of an image in an intuiting intellect" (Anwesenheit
eines Bildes in einem anschauenden Intellekt). While this image is
"perfectly indistinguishable from one caused ... by a body through
the medium of light, it nonetheless arises without the actual presence of such a body."[2]

In contrast to a purely subjective phantasm, a genuine apparition does refer to something outside the perceiving subject. But
the real "qualities of such a remote, external cause" are obscured
by the difference between the spirit and its appearance. Explicitly
invoking Kant's critical epistemology, with its distinction between
appearance and thing in itself, Schopenhauer writes: "Just as in the
corporeal world, we would here arrive at the question concerning the relation between appearance and thing-in-itself. But this is
the transcendental perspective which might reveal that the ideality

attached to the spirit apparition [*Geistererscheinung*] equals the ideality attached to the bodily appearance [*Körpererscheinung*]; the latter
is, as we know, inevitably subject to idealism and can therefore be
traced to the thing-in-itself, i.e. the truly real, only indirectly."[3]

Ascribing the same degree of reality to corporeal and to spiritual appearances, Schopenhauer thus formulates a theory of ghostly
manifestations that appropriates Kant's critical epistemology, as
well as Kant's metaphysical hypothesis of genuine apparitions from
Dreams of a Spirit Seer.[4] But Schopenhauer's adaptation of Kant's
terminology cannot conceal fundamental differences that emerge
from Schopenhauer's metaphysical notion of the will and his equation of will and thing in itself. As Schopenhauer states: "But just as
the thing-in-itself which manifests itself in the appearance of the
external world is *toto genere* different therefrom, so by analogy may
it be with that which manifests itself in the spirit apparition; in fact,
what reveals itself in both may perhaps be ultimately the same thing,
namely the will."[5] In contrast to Kant, Schopenhauer identifies
the thing in itself with the will and holds it to be accessible to our
experience. He borrows a concept of "communication" from empirical, physiological representations of the human nervous system to
describe metaphysical phenomena and thereby blurs the boundary
between empirical observations and metaphysical statements. Kant
emphasized the impossibility of any cognition that would go beyond
the realm of empirical appearances. But according to Schopenhauer,
spiritual visions and clairvoyance allow for a glimpse of the supersensory realm.

Media Technologies, Physiology, and Spiritualism in Schopenhauer
In distinguishing between a genuine spirit apparition and a purely
subjective phantasm, Schopenhauer emphasizes that a true spirit
vision does not refer to a material body, but is nonetheless caused by
"something truly external that is wholly independent of the subject."
For this something to be "cognized" by the ghost seer, it must "enter
into some communication with the interior of his organism."[6] The
"dream organ," which becomes active when our normal sensory

perception is shut off, then translates the data of this communication into an internal image, thereby serving as the "medium of intuitive seeing" (*Medium der Anschauung*).[7]

Schopenhauer explains the "arising of the dream organ,"[8] as well as the relation between waking and the dream in general, by referring to the projections of a magic lantern that become visible in darkness: "only when [the normal activity of the brain and the senses] is at rest can the dream occur, just as the pictures of a magic lantern can appear only after the lights of the room have been extinguished."[9] In addition, Schopenhauer explicitly introduces the term "projection," which had not been deployed in Kant's philosophical writings, in order to describe the transposition of these internal, spiritual images onto the external world. According to Schopenhauer, a clear spirit vision is based on a separation of external and internal images; therefore, "the inner eye projects these forms as far as possible to where the outer eye sees nothing, into dark recesses, behind curtains that suddenly become transparent, and generally into the darkness of night."[10]

Schopenhauer describes the seeing of inner spiritual images in analogy to the use of the magic lantern in the visual medium of the phantasmagoria, and he repeatedly draws on various optical instruments to account for the constitution of empirical appearances by the subject's cognitive apparatus. Reiterating Kant's conception of time and space as a priori forms of our empirical intuition, Schopenhauer characterizes our perception of the external world as always filtered "through our optical lens of time."[11] In doing so, Schopenhauer ascribes a bodily substrate to Kant's pure cognitive faculties, representing a material apparatus of cognition that functions like an optical instrument. Merging philosophy and contemporaneous physiology, he identifies Kant's disembodied faculty of "understanding" or "intellect" (*Verstand*) with our brain.[12]

The second volume of Schopenhauer's *World as Will and Presentation* (1819/1844) defines our cognition of the empirical world as "a very complicated physiological process in an animal's brain whose result is the consciousness of an image at that very spot."[13] Kant's

disembodied concept of *Vorstellung* (presentation) is thereby refor-
mulated in a manner that highlights the brain as the material site
of our intellectual functions. In his *Parerga*, Schopenhauer similarly
blends medial and physiological categories and characterizes our
intellect as a material mechanism that produces our perception of
the external world. Alluding to the optical box of the magic lantern,
he coins the unusual phrase of "a presentation machine in the human
brain box" in order to describe the material base of our cognition of
the empirical world.[14] According to Schopenhauer, the dream organ
transforms the data of an internal spiritual communication into
an image, which is transposed toward the external world. But the
normal activity of our intellect also consists of "projecting images
in space and time."[15] Both Schopenhauer's account of genuine spiritual apparitions and his explanation of the subject's constitution of
empirical appearances in our forms of intuition are modeled on the
projection of images by means of a magic lantern—a recourse to
contemporaneous media technology that does not just illustrate, but
that shapes his philosophical arguments.

Equivalent statements are to be found in an appendix on Kant in
the first volume of *The World as Will and Presentation*. There, Schopenhauer casts the fundamental "distinction between appearance
and thing-in-itself" in spiritualist and medial terms that threaten
to undo Kant's differentiation between semblance and appearance:
"What Kant refers to as the appearance (*Erscheinung*) in contrast to
the thing-in-itself... [is] a magical effect conjured into being, an
unstable and inconstant semblance [*Schein*] without substance, comparable to the optical illusion and the dream.... This clear cognition
and calm, deliberate representation of the dreamlike quality of the
whole world is indeed the foundation of the whole Kantian philosophy... and its greatest merit."[16] In the second edition of his main
treatise from 1844, Schopenhauer expands upon this argument by
stating that Kant "achieved all this by disassembling and presenting
piece by piece the whole machinery of our cognitive faculties that
brings about the phantasmagoria of the objective world."[17]

In his *Parerga*, Schopenhauer employs similar physiological and medial terms to describe Kant's transcendental enterprise of investigating the conditions of possibility of our cognition. He refers to Kant's critical epistemology as "a philosophy that makes us conscious of the fact that the first and essential laws of the world as it is perceived by us...are rooted in our brain and are therefore known a priori. It is called transcendental, because it goes beyond the whole given phantasmagoria to its origin."[18] This description of a "cerebral phantasmagoria" offers a stark contrast to Kant's invocation of contemporaneous optical technologies.[19] In *Dreams of a Spirit Seer*, Kant introduced the creation of an optical specter by means of a concave mirror in order to denounce the mirage of imaginary brain phantoms, and Kant's critical philosophy described speculative metaphysics as a "magic lantern of brain phantoms" to warn against the deceptive power of transcendental illusion.[20] In Kant's "metaphysical hypothesis" of genuine spirit apparitions, however, optical tropes were relegated to a surreptitious role, and Kant's definition of appearance as an indexical manifestation of a supersensory thing in itself refrained from an overt invocation of spiritualist notions. Schopenhauer, by contrast, ascribes the same degree of reality to spiritual apparitions and empirical appearances, and he explicitly describes both modes of phenomenal manifestation in spiritualist and medial terms. As a result, he compares our perception of empirical phenomena to the "dream," the "optical illusion" and the "phantasmagoria," nearly obliterating Kant's distinction between *Schein* (semblance) and *Erscheinung* (appearance, apparition).[21]

The altogether aggressive invocation of media technologies, physiology, and spiritualism in Schopenhauer's epistemology may be related to the fact that unlike Kant, Schopenhauer believed it possible to reveal the reality behind the "veil" of appearance.[22] Kant had represented the mirage of transcendental semblance as "an inevitable but not insoluble illusion."[23] But at the same time, Kant considered any attempt to cognize the thing in itself by going beyond empirical appearances as doomed to failure. Schopenhauer's metaphysics of the will, by contrast, oversteps this limitation by postulating an unmediated communication that occurs in the supersensory realm of the thing in itself and that may emanate toward the world of empirical appearances. According to Schopenhauer, it is the will as thing in itself that underlies both empirical appearances and spiritual apparitions. Yet in contrast to an empirical appearance, a genuine apparition is marked by a dissolution of the spirit seer's forms of intuition: "For the perplexity attaching itself to the seeing of visions and spirit apparitions really arises from the fact that, with these perceptions, the boundary between subject and object, which is the first condition of all knowledge, becomes doubtful, indistinct and indeed quite blurred."[24]

Even though Schopenhauer states at one point that in spirit visions, something "wholly independent of the subject...is cognized," his account of ghostly manifestations shifts from a theory of empirical cognition to a metaphysics of communication.[25] In a spirit vision, the boundary between subject and object, which constitutes "the first condition of all knowledge," gives way to a communication that undoes "the dividing walls of individuation and separation."[26] Yet in order to formulate this metaphysical theory of an allegedly immediate or unmediated communication, Schopenhauer surreptitiously draws on concepts of empirical, mediated communication. In explaining the genuine ghost apparition, Schopenhauer emphasizes that the appearing spirit must enter into "some kind of communication" with the dream organ of the spirit seer.[27] But at the same time, he asserts that this communication "cannot ever be demonstrated empirically" and is "empirically, i.e. physically, not even conceivable." For Schopenhauer, this can "be understood" only "metaphysically," as "something independent of all phenomenal laws...and occurring in the thing-in-itself...which we understand by the name of a magical action."[28] Schopenhauer therefore describes ghostly manifestations as arising from an "unmediated communication, which is grounded in the essence-in-itself of things."[29]

Schopenhauer affirms that this communication cannot be demonstrated or conceptualized empirically, but he nonetheless employs empirical and medial terms to represent this ostensibly unmediated communication. Indeed, even his notion of "communication" itself is borrowed from contemporaneous scientific descriptions of the human nervous system. While the optical instrument of the magic lantern serves as the model for Schopenhauer's account of how we constitute and perceive the world of phenomenal appearances, it may be the telegraph that underlies this notion of metaphysical communication. Schopenhauer invokes the new technology only obliquely, by quoting from the North American occultist journal *The Spiritual Telegraph*.[30] The first explicit reference to "communication" in Schopenhauer's *Essay on Spirit Seeing* occurs instead in a paragraph that summarizes Johann Christian Reil's theory of the human nervous system—in particular the distinction between the "cerebral" and the "ganglionic system" introduced by Reil around 1800 in order to explain the phenomena of somnambulism.[31] In the *Essay on Spirit Seeing*, the concept of "communication" is thus initially deployed to describe the "difficult, feeble, and *mediated* communication" that connects the brain and the ganglionic system "only indirectly."[32] Reil even referred to this intermittent connection between cerebral and ganglionic system as a "semiconductor."[33] Schopenhauer adapts the term from Reil's physiology of the human nervous systems, and he transfers it to the representation of a metaphysical communication that is allegedly prior to all empirical phenomena and "unmediated."

A comparable conflation of empirical and transcendental arguments can also be observed in Schopenhauer's attempt to present the phenomena of animal magnetism as factual evidence for Kant's distinction between appearance and thing in itself. Kant's critical epistemology had asserted that appearances conform a priori to our subjective forms of intuition and are therefore available to us only in time and space. From this, Kant drew the conclusion that in contrast to the appearance, the thing in itself must lie outside of time and space (a proposition that may be true or not, since, according to Kant, we do not know anything about things in themselves). Kant therefore proclaimed the "empirical reality" and "transcendental ideality" of time and space as fundamental assumptions of his epistemology.[34] In 1813, Joseph Philippe François Deleuze adapted this epistemological doctrine in his *Critical History of Animal Magnetism*. Introducing Kant's conception of time and space as forms of our empirical intuition, Deleuze explained that "pure spirits" could cognize things in themselves independently of these forms and therefore apprehend the past, present, and future.[35] Deleuze thus invoked Kant's epistemology in order to lend philosophical legitimacy to the assumption that magnetic clairvoyance could extend to the past and the future. Thirty years later, Schopenhauer conceived of the facts of animal magnetism and clairvoyance as beyond any doubt, introducing them as positive proof for Kant's distinction between appearance and the thing in itself. In his *Essay on Spirit Seeing*, Schopenhauer presents the surpassing of time and space in somnambulist clairvoyance or "television"[36] as giving a "factual confirmation, as it were ... for the Kantian doctrine of the ideality of time and space."[37] The initial caution of Schopenhauer's "as it were" disappears only three pages later, when he one more time refers to the overcoming of time and space in actions at a distance—as "a confirmation, as unexpected as it is certain and factual, of Kant's fundamental doctrine of the distinction between the appearance and the thing-in-itself."[38]

Yet Schopenhauer not only attempts to prove transcendental arguments about the conditions of possibility of our perception by referring to empirical observations. Even within his metaphysical theories, which are, in Kantian terms, simply transcendent, Schopenhauer relies on scientific data. Quoting from ostensibly authentic narratives about spirit visions and magnetic clairvoyance, which we will analyze in more detail in Chapter 4, he refers to "the facts of animal magnetism" as corroborating his metaphysical assumptions.[39] In Schopenhauer's philosophy, these "facts" assume the strange status of being physical and metaphysical at the same time—a paradox that cannot be disentangled in a coherent manner. On the one hand, Schopenhauer asserts that the "unmediated communication" that gives rise to ghostly visions cannot be verified or conceptualized empirically. On the other hand, the "experimental metaphysics" of animal magnetism with its factual accounts of "sympathetic cures, magic ... spirit-seeing, and visions of all kinds" provides us with "a certain and irrefutable indication of a nexus of entities that rests on an order of things entirely different from nature."[40] The "intrusion of the spirit world upon our own"—to quote the terms that Justinus Kerner chose for the subtitle of his book on *The Seeress of Prevost* (1829)—is hence "factual, as it were," but not empirical.[41] Alluding to Marx's later analysis of the commodity form, one could also say that the phenomenon of seeing ghosts is a "sensory supersensory thing."[42] This logical dilemma extends to Schopenhauer's representation of the will as an entity that precedes any empirical appearance and that can nonetheless be described only in recourse to empirical concepts. Schopenhauer not only treats the "facts of animal magnetism" as an "indication" (*Anzeige*) of the will's unity that is prior to any individuation,[43] he also introduces these physical metaphysical phenomena when describing the will itself, or to be more precise, "the unmediated communication that is grounded in the essence in itself of things" and that is therefore "independent of all phenomenal laws."[44]

In the second volume of *World as Will and Presentation*, as he himself admits, Schopenhauer relies upon a "language of mystical images" in order to speak of this "transcendent theme."[45] Schopenhauer here describes an unmediated communication in the human species—Kant's "spiritual republic,"[46] as it were—by invoking a monstrous bodily analogy: "Thus even this simile may pass, that the human species can be figuratively represented as an animal compositum, a life form of which many polyps present instantiations.... Just as in the case of these, the head portion isolates each individual animal...so the brain with its consciousness isolates human individuals; the unconscious part, on the other hand, the vegetative life with its ganglionic system, into which cerebral consciousness submerges in sleep...is a common life of all. By means of it they can even communicate in exceptional cases, as occurs, for example, when dreams are transmitted without any mediation, when the thoughts of the magnetizer pass over into the somnambulist, and finally also in the magnetic or generally magical actions which arise from intentional willing."[47]

The "immediate community of spirits,"[48] which in Kant's *Dreams of a Spirit Seer* constitutes a unity prior to all social differentiation, thereby ensuring the ghostly influence of the general will on our moral actions, is here likened to the bodily aggregate of a polyp.[49] But the renewed reference to Reil's theory of the ganglionic nervous system simultaneously testifies to the paradox that Schopenhauer can describe the ostensibly unmediated communication of ghostly visions only by borrowing from physiological representations of nerve pathways, which function as material media of communication.[50] In Kant's critical epistemology, the optical instrument of the magic lantern is transformed into an epistemological figure that plays a central role for his doctrine of transcendental illusion. Schopenhauer, by contrast, explicitly ascribes the same degree of reality to bodily and spiritual appearances, and he represents both modes of phenomenal manifestation in categories of optical projection that undermine Kant's distinction between illusion or semblance (*Schein*) and appearance (*Erscheinung*). In addition to this transformation of Kant's critical epistemology, Schopenhauer's philosophical work also puts forward a metaphysics of communication. Yet in order to describe the ostensibly unmediated transmission in the thing in itself, Schopenhauer draws on physiological theories that conceive of the ganglionic nervous system as a material medium of communication.

Despite his conflation of empirical science, transcendental philosophy, and metaphysics, Schopenhauer does acknowledge a "language of mystical images" as his sole means of formulating statements on this "transcendent theme." This epistemological restraint marks a significant difference between Schopenhauer's metaphysical statements and the speculative systems of F. W. J. Schelling, Johann Gottlieb Fichte, and Hegel. Schopenhauer distinguishes between his critical epistemology, which theorizes the "world as presentation," and his metaphysical theory, which centers on the "world as will." This demarcation of epistemology and metaphysics disappears in the philosophical systems of speculative idealism, which reject Kant's insistence on the limits of our cognition. But a careful comparison of Schopenhauer's *Essay on Spirit Seeing* with Fichte's theory of intellectual intuition (*intellektuelle Anschauung*) reveals surprising points of convergence between Schopenhauer's philosophy and that of his speculative antagonists, whom he attacks with stunning derision and aggression.

In his *Introductory Lectures to the Doctrine of Science* (1813), Fichte explicitly declared it impossible to understand his philosophy without a spiritual, inner seeing. In Fichte's words: "This doctrine presupposes an entirely new inner sensory tool, which gives us a new world, quite unavailable to the ordinary person. This is not to be understood as an exaggeration, or as some kind of oratorical phrase made for its own sake ... but rather as meaning literally what it says. Thus I say it again: This doctrine is completely incomprehensible for people as they usually are; for the objects it refers to are simply not there for them, as they have not the sense by and for which these objects exist."[51] Fichte's description of those who can comprehend his philosophy comes close to Kant's definition of ghost seers as "strange persons" with "organs of unusual sensitivity."[52] But according to Fichte, the "new sense" that is indispensable for perceiving the objects referred to by his philosophy exists in a "rudimentary form" in all human beings.[53] The "spiritual seeing" required to grasp Fichte's doctrine merely presupposes "that the eye open itself up to the curious aspect of this intuitive vision [*Anschauung*], which stands opposed to ordinary being."[54]

Fichte's invocation of a "spiritual seeing" (*Sehen des Geistes*) makes spirit the subject, rather than the object of this intuitive vision. Yet the opening of this inner eye seems nonetheless quite similar to the "arising of the dream organ" as theorized in Schopenhauer's *Essay on Spirit Seeing*. It may be precisely this proximity between Fichte's account of a spiritual seeing and his own description of inner spiritual visions that generates Schopenhauer's scathing critique of the "windbaggery of intellectual intuition."[55] At one point however, Schopenhauer notes in more sober terms a methodological difference between his and Fichte's philosophy. Addressing the validity of various modes of substantiating metaphysical claims, Schopenhauer asserts: "Even less guarantee is given by the systems that start from an intellectual intuition, i.e., from a kind of ecstasy or clairvoyance. All cognition so gained must be rejected as subjective, individual, and consequently problematic."[56] Schopenhauer here criticizes cognitive claims that are based on a speculative intuition or vision that, "even if actually given," could still not be "communicated by concepts and words."[57] He refutes nonconceptual intellectual intuition as a philosophical method, whereas Fichte presupposes such a "performative action" (*Thathandlung*) on the part of his readers as necessary for understanding his philosophy.[58]

Spiritual Forms and Phantasmagorical Presentations in Hegel

Prematurely abandoning the "strenuous effort of the concept" is also criticized in the preface to Hegel's *Phenomenology of Spirit* (1807), where Hegel attacks the "shrine of inner, divine, intuitive seeing."[59] Hegel here turns against Schelling and Fichte, simultaneously revising his own definition of speculation, which he had given, closely aligning himself with Schelling, in his early text *The Difference between Fichte's and Schelling's Systems of Philosophy* (1801). There, Hegel had described speculation as an internal vision that goes beyond the limitations of external empirical perception. According to the young Hegel, seen from the perspective of understanding (*Verstand*), the absolute identity of the subjective and the objective can appear only in the form of antinomies and contradictions. Reason (*Vernunft*) as the faculty of speculation, by contrast, is able to resolve these antinomies by means of an intuition that is not empirical, but intellectual or transcendental: "By our intuition [*Anschauung*] becoming transcendental, the identity of the subjective and the objective, which are split from each other in empirical intuition, enters our consciousness.... Speculation is producing the consciousness of this unity, and because in speculation ideality and reality are one, it is an intuitive seeing [*Anschauung*]."[60]

In his early writings, Hegel thus defined the concept of speculation in proximity to its literal meaning as an intuitive vision or seeing that, in contrast to empirical perception, gives us access to the absolute as the "identity of identity and nonidentity."[61] In his *Phenomenology of Spirit*, however, Hegel turns against the "nonmethod of presentiment and enthusiasm" as a way of thinking the unity of difference.[62] Hegel here rejects esoteric intuition as a means of overcoming Kant's delimitation of metaphysics, propagating instead an approach that rests on the "labor of the concept."[63] Yet without naming Kant, Hegel still refutes Kant's critical insistence on the limits of cognition. Hegel criticizes the assumption "that...securing for consciousness through cognition what exists in itself is a contradiction in terms, because there is a boundary between cognition and the Absolute that utterly separates them."[64] In lieu of such an epistemological restraint, Hegel postulates an "absolute knowledge" as the final stage of a teleological progression of consciousness.

Schopenhauer adapted Kant's critical philosophy by identifying our cognitive faculties with our brain functions, comparing this material apparatus of cognition to optical instruments. Hegel, by contrast, asserts that cognition does not function like an "instrument," which would "form and alter" the observed object, or a "medium," which would make us receive the truth not "as it is in itself, but only as it is through and in this medium."[65] Describing an absolute knowledge that is ostensibly independent of any media or material preconditions, Hegel seeks to refute the supposition that "the absolute stands on one side and cognition on the other, independent and separated from it."[66] He emphasizes that such a skepticism can claim certainty of its own knowledge only by means of a performative contradiction. He calls for a "mistrust [of] this very mistrust,"[67] since—as he later puts it in the *Encyclopedia of the Philosophical Sciences* (1817/1830)—the assumption that we could recognize boundaries of our knowledge undermines itself: "The very fact that we know of a limit is evidence that we are beyond it," because "only the unknown would be a limitation of knowledge; the known limit, by contrast, is not a limitation of knowledge; therefore to know of one's limitation means to know of one's unlimitedness."[68]

According to Kant, it is an "abysmal gulf" that separates the supersensory realm from the world of sensory appearances. But what Kant describes as an "impassable boundary" that would forever limit philosophical knowledge constitutes for Hegel merely a distinction that will be overcome in the progress of knowledge toward a higher unity.[69] The dialectic of speculative reason and its "logic of semblance,"[70] which Kant had characterized in his doctrine of transcendental illusion by invoking the visual medium of the phantasmagoria, constitute for Hegel the dialectical movement of the concept toward absolute knowledge. As we have seen in Chapter 1, Kant explains the mirage of "dialectical semblance" (*dialektischer Schein*) as emerging from the inner nature of speculative reason, which, based on a knowledge of finite conditions, seeks to draw conclusions about the unconditioned or absolute.[71] Characterizing the excess of speculative reason as a "magic lantern of brain phantoms," his critical philosophy warns against cognitive claims that go beyond the realm of empirical appearances. Hegel's *Phenomenology of Spirit*, by contrast, functions as a textual invocation of a sequence of "spiritual forms," and it presents their succession not as "dialectical semblance," but as a teleological progression toward knowledge. What Kant described in his solution to the antinomies as a series of optical specters constitutes for Hegel the "whole sequence of the shapes of consciousness in their necessity"—moving from subjective through objective to absolute spirit.[72]

This reversal of Kant's critical turn against the mirage of dialectical illusion is already indicated by the title of Hegel's philosophical treatise. In 1764, Kant's intellectual ally and correspondent Johann Heinrich Lambert had published a new methodological organon under the title *Phenomenology, or, the Doctrine of Semblance*. In addition to relating the "ghost stories" of "so-called visionaries" to the deceptive power of an enthusiastic imagination, Lambert developed a typology of different forms of illusion and semblance.[73] In diametrical contrast, Hegel's *Phenomenology* is intended as a doctrine of indexical apparitions. His treatise does not provide a theory of illusion or semblance; instead, it functions as a textual representation—and invocation—of "appearing knowledge" (*das erscheinende Wissen*) as it manifests itself on the path toward absolute knowledge.[74]

Kant insisted on the fundamental difference between appearance and thing in itself, emphasizing that our perception of "mere appearances" does not give us knowledge of things in themselves.[75] But Hegel asserts that it is the "essence" of the supersensory that manifests itself in the appearance: "The inner world, or supersensory beyond...arises from the appearance and the appearance is its mediation; in other words, the appearance is its essence and, in fact, its fulfillment."[76] For Hegel, the supersensory is "the sensory and the perceived...as it is in truth."[77] Akin to a spiritual apparition in which spirit and manifestation are one and the same, the ideal can be perceived by our senses in an ordinary appearance. Conversely, the "truth of the sensory...is to be *appearance*"; it serves as an indexical epiphany that refers us to the supersensory.[78] Ideality and reality are interwoven in a reciprocity that is also emphasized in Hegel's description of the mutual "solicitation" of the sensory and supersensory worlds: "We have seen, however, that this play of primary forces is so constituted that the force which is solicited by another force is equally the soliciting force for that other, which is only thereby solicited."[79]

The concepts of "appearance" and "solicitation," which Hegel employs here and in his *Science of Logic*, may be taken from late eighteenth-century texts about the "citation" of spirits.[80] But an explicit reference to spectral apparitions is to be found only in the *Lectures on Aesthetics*, where Hegel characterizes the "appearance of the ghost in *Hamlet*" as an "objective form of Hamlet's inner presentiment."[81] Here, too, Hegel postulates a reciprocal confirmation of solicited appearance and soliciting presentiment: "In the dark feeling that something monstrous must have happened, we see Hamlet enter the stage; now his father's ghost appears to him and reveals to him all the heinous crimes."

In passing, Hegel also refers to the ghost of Hamlet's father in his *Lectures on the History of Philosophy* in a passage that describes the self-recognition of absolute spirit in its previous shapes.[82] But before undertaking a more detailed analysis of how Hegel represents the becoming of absolute spirit in Gothic and phantasmagorical terms, we will turn to the third part of Hegel's *Encyclopedia of the Philosophical Sciences*, which was published as the *Philosophy of Spirit*. There, in a section on the "feeling soul," Hegel engages in a detailed discussion of supernatural agency and ghostly visions. Elucidating the "marvelous" phenomena of somnambulism, animal magnetism, and clairvoyance, Hegel defines magic as the "unmediated action of one spirit on another."[83] Similar to Schopenhauer, he distinguishes between subjective hallucinations and objective "visions, which have something real for their content." The latter are based on an "unmediated knowing."[84] The "seeing soul" is no longer restricted to space and time as its forms of intuition and therefore is capable of "television" (*Fernsehen*).[85] While the vision's content is real, the "television" or "clairvoyance" of the soul occurs as a "subjective way of knowing...unmediated...without the aid of the eyes and without the mediation of light."[86]

Hegel also describes this "seeing knowledge" as "a knowing in the undivided substantiality of genius."[87] Its precarious status derives from not being bound to "the series of mediatory conditions, one external to another, which...cool reflection has to traverse in succession."[88] In this respect, the "seeing knowledge" (*schauendes Wissen*) of the feeling soul nearly coincides with "transcendental intuitive seeing" (*transzendentale Anschauung*) as defined by Hegel in his early text on Schelling and Fichte. There, Hegel had characterized philosophical speculation as a transcendental, rather than empirical intuition that overcomes the limits of understanding (*Verstand*).[89] In the *Encyclopedia of the Philosophical Sciences*, Hegel himself acknowledges the proximity of somnambulist clairvoyance and speculative philosophy by conceding that as a result of "the visible liberation of spirit...from the limitations of time and space," such "magnetic phenomena...do have a kinship with philosophy."[90] But Hegel hastens to add that the seeing of clairvoyant somnambulists should not be equated with philosophical speculation. According to Hegel, universal theoretical cognition is the exclusive domain of philosophy, whereas clairvoyance has to be considered a morbid, pathological condition—in Hegel's words: "But it is vulgar to treat the seeing of this state ... as a truer state, capable of conveying universal cognition."[91]

Hegel thereby seeks to uphold the distinction between the speculative knowledge of philosophy and the clairvoyance of somnambulists while simultaneously integrating the knowledge about these magnetic phenomena into his philosophical system. The "seeing knowledge" of the feeling soul does not constitute philosophy.[92] But taking note of its actuality instigates our insight into the limits of our empirical categories. Similar to Schopenhauer's invocation of the "facts of animal magnetism," Hegel presents clairvoyance as "a brute fact" that "necessitates the advance from ordinary psychology to the comprehensive cognition afforded by speculative philosophy."[93] The phenomena of magnetic clairvoyance thus constitute "factual" proof for the superiority of reason (*Vernunft*) over understanding (*Verstand*).[94] As Hegel asserts: "In order to believe in this realm even what one's own eyes have seen and still more to comprehend it, the first prerequisite is not to be bound by the categories of understanding."[95]

Hegel refers to contemporaneous theories of animal magnetism to corroborate the superiority of speculative reason over empirical understanding while striving to maintain the boundary between universal philosophical cognition and the "vulgar" clairvoyance of somnambulist mediums. Schopenhauer undertakes a similar attempt at introducing animal magnetism as factual evidence while dissociating philosophy from its less savory aspects. He predicts that the "experimental metaphysics" of animal magnetism will allow for the discovery of "truths at which we could not otherwise hope to arrive," but he warns against taking the "paltry" metaphysical statements of clairvoyant somnambulists for philosophical insights.[96] Schopenhauer consequently criticizes "the credulity of our otherwise estimable and meritorious Justinus Kerner,"[97] whose popular and widely read treatise *The Seeress of Prevorst* will be analyzed in Chapter 4.

Similar to Schopenhauer's *Essay on Spirit Seeing*, Hegel's *Encyclopedia* refers to the "brute fact" of magnetic clairvoyance as philosophical proof.[98] But Hegel's and Schopenhauer's specific modes of introducing contemporaneous scientific observations differ starkly. According to his biographer and friend Karl Rosenkranz, Hegel excerpted the books he read throughout his lifetime in the following manner: "Everything which seemed noteworthy to him...was written on a loose sheet of paper, which he marked at the top with the general subject heading under which the specific content had to be subsumed.... The sheets themselves were arranged alphabetically, and with this simple device he was able to use his excerpts constantly."[99] By erasing bibliographical references, Hegel's note cards constituted an archive of knowledge that allowed for easy retrieval while concealing its sources.[100] Hegel's *Phenomenology of Spirit* is a book without footnotes. Even Kant is mentioned only once by name in passing.[101] The *Encyclopedia of the Philosophical Sciences* does contain a small number of footnotes, which refer to books by other authors. But they were probably added by Hegel's editors. As a result, Hegel's borrowings and appropriations from contemporaneous science and spiritualism are rendered largely invisible in his philosophical writings.

Schopenhauer, by contrast, highlights his appropriation of media technologies, physiology, and spiritualism. Concomitantly, he always provides references to the scientific and historical works he has consulted. In his *Essay on Spirit Seeing* Schopenhauer quotes numerous treatises, which range from Ludwig Lavater's *De spectris* (1580), to Sir Walter Scott's *Letters On Demonology and Witchcraft* (1830), to Joseph P. F. Deleuze's *Mémoire sur la faculté de prévision* (1836).[102] Other sources explicitly cited include Dietrich Georg von Kieser's *Archive for Animal Magnetism* (1817–1824), Johann Heinrich Jung-Stilling's *Theorie der Geisterkunde* [Theory of a doctrine of spirits] (1808), and Chinese ghost stories in French translation, which were printed in Stanislas Julien's *Orphelin de la Chine, accompagné de nouvelles et de poesies* (1834).[103] Schopenhauer's *On the Will in Nature*, and his *World as Will and Presentation* similarly contrast with the works of Hegel, whose *Phenomenology* seeks to suppress the technical and cultural materialities that render possible his ostensibly universal theory of "absolute spirit."

The difference between Schopenhauer's highlighting and Hegel's concealing of bibliographical sources corresponds to Schopenhauer's overt and Hegel's surreptitious reliance on spiritualist notions. Unlike Schopenhauer, Hegel is reticent to acknowledge the connections between his philosophical system and contemporaneous theories of ghostly apparitions. Instead of referring to its material and contingent preconditions, the *Phenomenology of Spirit* presents itself as universal and absolute knowledge. Similarly, in his *Encyclopedia*, Hegel strives to maintain the boundary between speculative idealism and "vulgar" occultism. But his open admission of a "kinship" between magnetic clairvoyance and philosophical speculation provides us with a rare glimpse of the half-hidden appropriation and transformation of spiritualist terms that underlies Hegel's speculative philosophy.

A comparably surreptitious interrelation connects Hegel's philosophical writings with the literary genre of the Gothic novel and the visual medium of the phantasmagoria. Schopenhauer openly compares our intellectual faculties to contemporaneous optical instruments, adapting Kant's critical epistemology by describing a material apparatus of cognition. Hegel, by contrast, refrains from overt references to contemporaneous optical technologies. The *Phenomenology of Spirit* functions as a textual back projection, as it were, for it invokes a succession of ghostly images and emulates the use of the magic lantern in phantasmagorical projections without naming the optical instrument. Apart from a passing mention in his *Lectures on Aesthetics*, Hegel's only conspicuous reference to the magic lantern and the visual medium of the phantasmagoria is to be found in his Jena *Lectures on Nature and Spirit*.[104] These were given in the fall semester 1805–1806, while he was writing the *Phenomenology of Spirit*. It is there that, in an early passage that I have quoted before, the text suggests an analogy between the interior of "pure self" and the dark void in which Philidor and Robertson staged their phantasmagorical projections: "Man is this night, this empty nothing, which contains everything in its simplicity, an infinite wealth of presentations.... It is the night, the inner of nature that exists here—pure self. In phantasmagorical presentations it is night on all sides; here a bloody head suddenly surges forward, there another white form abruptly appears, before vanishing again ... it is the night of the world that presents itself here."[105]

Hegel posits a "pure self" that is unable to distinguish between internal presentations and external objects.[106] In doing so, he introduces a detailed description of the visual medium of the phantasmagoria and highlights the disorientation of its viewers who mistake sudden magnifications for a rapid approach of the projected ghostly shape. In his lectures, Hegel refers to these special effects to characterize a self that is marked by a lack of differentiation and unable to distinguish between inside and outside in this "night of the world." The analogy between "phantasmagorical presentations" and the "infinite wealth of presentations" in the pure self serves to represent a primary stage of consciousness, one that has to be overcome by the subject in its teleological progress toward knowing.

In the *Phenomenology of Spirit*, the appropriation of the phantasmagoria assumes a more oblique form. But it can be discerned within the final chapter where Hegel describes a moment of recognition that is crucial for bringing spirit's progression toward knowledge to a close. According to Hegel, the becoming of absolute spirit relies on an anagnorisis in which absolute spirit recognizes itself in its own earlier forms. This final sublation of difference presupposes an external temporality in which spirit manifested itself in various shapes. Hegel characterizes this "history" of spirit, its movement from subjective through objective to absolute spirit, as "a slow motion and sequence of spirits, a gallery of images, of which each [is] endowed with all the riches of spirit."[107] The closing pages of the *Phenomenology* thus invoke the succession of moving images in a phantasmagoria and the trope of the Gothic novel's hero gazing at a gallery of ancestral portraits in a medieval castle.

By representing the "slow motion and sequence of spirits" as "a gallery of images," Hegel alludes to Robertson's combination of movable glass slides with moving back projection.[108] The comparison of these phantasmagorical projections to the "night of the world" in Hegel's Jena lectures reappears in the final chapter of the *Phenomenology* as the "night of self-consciousness" in which spirit cognizes itself.[109] In its overcoming of difference, the oneness of absolute knowledge is strangely reminiscent of the initial stage of pure, undifferentiated self. But instead of introducing the phantasmagoria as a conceptual analogy, the conclusion of Hegel's *Phenomenology* abandons the "labor of the concept" and emulates the visual medium without naming it. In doing so, the text comes close to the "shrine of inner…intuitive seeing" that Hegel himself had attacked in the preface, an inadvertent replication of a rejected philosophical approach that becomes even more obvious in Hegel's *Lectures on the History of Philosophy*.

There, Hegel paraphrases the end of the *Phenomenology* one more time. Again he brings his text to a closure by characterizing his lectures as a summoning of spiritual forms, a textual invocation that produces in his listeners a mental image of the teleological progress of knowledge: "I have tried to develop and bring before your thoughts this procession of philosophy's spiritual forms, indicating their connection and progress. This series is the true realm of spirits, the only realm of spirits that exists—it is a series which is not a plurality, nor does it even remain a series as a succession; but in the very process of recognizing itself it is transformed into moments of one spirit, into one and the same present spirit. And this long procession of spirits is formed by the individual pulses which spirit employs in his life."[110]

Hegel emphasizes that the final self-recognition of absolute spirit sublates the "series" or "procession" of these spiritual forms into a unity of difference. But on the level of his linguistic description of this process, Hegel cannot avoid a proliferation of absolute spirit into a plurality of ghosts. Similar to the *Phenomenology*, Hegel's *Lectures on the History of Philosophy* summon a "long procession of *spirits*." Hegel hastens to add that the sequence of these spiritual shapes is not a "plurality" (*Vielheit*). But the grammatical plural undermines the alleged transformation of this multitude of spirits into moments of one and the same spirit. The philosophical invocation of a "true realm of spirits" remains tied to spiritualist terms. At the same time, the lectures strive for producing a series of phantasmagorical images in Hegel's audience: "I have tried to...bring before your thoughts this procession of philosophy's spiritual forms."

One further point of reference for the "gallery of images" described at the end of the *Phenomenology* is the contemporaneous Gothic novel. The narrative interest of this literary genre centered on the restoration of rightful genealogical succession, often confronting a protagonist with a gallery of ancestral portraits.[111] In Horace Walpole's *Castle of Otranto*, it is the restoration of rightful genealogical succession that brings the narrative to a close. From the very beginning, the resemblance between the protagonist Theodore and a picture of the founder of Otranto in the gallery terrifies and troubles the current inhabitants of the castle.[112] The novel ends when the magnified shape of the founder's ghost finally becomes visible as a whole and identifies Theodore as his rightful descendant: "The form of Alfonso, dilated to an immense magnitude, appeared in the centre of the ruins. Behold in Theodore the true heir of Alfonso! said the vision and having pronounced those words...it ascended solemnly towards heaven."[113]

In Hegel's *Phenomenology of Spirit*, the "gallery of images" that is crucial for the self-recognition of absolute spirit also constitutes a ghostly lineage and genealogy. Describing the temporal sequence of different spiritual shapes that allows for the becoming of absolute spirit, Hegel refers to a genealogical succession of inheritance: "The realm of spirits (*Geisterreich*) which is formed in this way in the outer being constitutes a succession in time in which one spirit relieved another of his charge and each took over the realm of the world (*Reich der Welt*) from his predecessor."[114] Even though Hegel had welcomed the French Revolution, this line of inheritance between different spiritual shapes suggests the presence of a genealogical, possibly even monarchical principle in his speculative philosophy.[115] Relying on a language that Nietzsche characterized as "Gothic,"[116] Hegel summons the "memory and Calvary of absolute Spirit, the reality, truth and certainty of his throne."[117]

Just three years after the beheading of Louis XVI in January 1793, Edmund Burke had denounced the "Republick of Regicide" as a "vast, tremendous, unformed spectre" and a "hideous phantom."[118] Thomas Carlyle similarly conceived of the history of the French Revolution as "a red baleful phantasmagory" that marches "towards the land of Phantoms."[119] Hegel's Gothic rhetoric in the closing chapter of the *Phenomenology of Spirit* overlaps with these conservative condemnations of the French Revolution. But unlike Burke and Carlyle, Hegel condones or even celebrates the "sacrifice"[120] and "Calvary" of absolute spirit. Schopenhauer praised Kant's critical epistemology for "disassembling and presenting piece by piece the whole machinery of our cognitive faculties that brings about the phantasmagoria of the objective world."[121] Hegel, by contrast, seeks to suppress the cultural and technical materialities that allow him to formulate his ostensibly universal theory of absolute knowledge. Nonetheless, his speculative philosophy remains bound to the language of the Gothic novel and of animal magnetism, and his textual invocation of a "realm of spirits" emulates the use of the magic lantern in phantasmagorical projections without naming the optical instrument.

The next two chapters shift the focus of analysis from optical media to a newly emerging popular print culture. But in examining ghost narratives, the literary genre of the Gothic novel, and case histories about animal magnetism and clairvoyance, I will also revisit the "historical" part of Kant's *Dreams of a Spirit Seer* and the interconnection between Hegel's and Schopenhauer's theories and these narratives and case histories.

CHAPTER THREE

Ghost Narratives and the Gothic Novel:

Print Culture and Reading Addiction

On a sudden we all felt, at the same instant, a stroke as of a flash of lightning, so powerful that our hands flew apart; a terrible thunder shook the house, the locks jarred; the doors fell shut; the cover of the silver box fell down and extinguished the light, and on the opposite wall, over the chimney piece, appeared a human figure in a bloody shirt, with the paleness of death on its countenance.
—Schiller, *The Ghost Seer*

My terror contained a kind of raging delight, a pleasure that may lie beyond the limits of humanity—I cannot think of anything more frightening than seeing this apparition for a second time; and yet I intentionally repeat for myself the shock, the numbing dread of this moment.
—Tieck, *William Lovell*

On August 10, 1763, three years before the publication of *Dreams of a Spirit Seer*, Immanuel Kant wrote to Charlotte von Knobloch, responding to an earlier inquiry of hers about the reality of spiritual visions and ghostly apparitions. The opening of the letter betrays a certain unease that is mixed with sexual gallantry: "Far too long have I denied myself the honor and pleasure of obeying the command of a lady, who is an ornament to her sex, through submitting the requested report. But I had deemed it necessary to engage in a more complete investigation of this matter. The content of the narrative that I am about to relate is altogether different from those that are supposed to have the license of penetrating the chambers of beautiful women in a graceful manner.... But even though these images incite the kind of shudder that is a repetition of early impressions of our education, I am certain that the enlightened lady who reads these words will nonetheless not miss the pleasure that may arise from using this notion correctly. Allow me to justify my proceeding in this matter, gracious lady, since it may look as though a common sort of mania had predisposed me to seek out such narratives and gladly accept them without careful examination."[1]

The following four pages of Kant's letter detail several incidents that speak to Emanuel Swedenborg's purported ability of ghost seeing. According to Kant, the occurrences had been confirmed by several independent witnesses, among them diplomatic ambassadors, as well as a friend and former student. Kant presents as particularly compelling one episode in which Swedenborg, during a visit to Göteborg, gave an accurate description of a fire that was raging at the same time in Stockholm, more than fifty miles away: "The following incident seems to me to have the greatest force of proof and really removes any conceivable doubt." Toward the end of his letter, the German philosopher goes so far as to announce that he awaits "with desire" (*mit Sehnsucht*) the publication of a book by Swedenborg in London, a phrase that extends the sexual frisson of ghostly narratives that "penetrate" the "chambers of beautiful women" to Kant himself.[2]

The previous two chapters explored the crucial role of optical media for the philosophical theories of Kant, Hegel, and Schopenhauer. Shifting to contemporaneous print culture, I will now analyze the various functions of ghost narratives in the late eighteenth century. In his letter to Charlotte von Knobloch, Kant contrasts his "careful examination" of narrative testimonies that seem to provide empirical evidence for spiritualist claims with the "common mania" (*gemeiner Wahn*) induced by the proliferation of ghost stories in an exploding print market of pamphlets, journals, and books. Closely linked to this scientific approach to ghost narratives is the second, "correct" use of ghost stories, which consists in providing instruction to an "enlightened" reader. As we will see in analyzing Friedrich Schiller's novel *The Ghost Seer*, this didactic function of the ghost

narrative frequently assumed the form of turning against superstition and credulity by telling a cautionary tale about the deceptive
power of optical media and an enthusiastic imagination. Kant also
describes a third function of ghost stories in suggestive terms that
imply a link between fear and pleasure. Even though Kant engages
in a "careful examination" of these narratives and reports them to
an enlightened reader, they nonetheless create a certain "shudder"
(*Schauder*). Within the realm of late eighteenth-century narrative
fiction, it is the Gothic novel that centers on this effect of the ghost
story. The new literary genre, whose German name is "novel of
shudders" (*Schauerroman*), adapted spiritual apparitions as a serial
device of shock and terror. But the immersive appeal of these popular tales also caused considerable alarm. Anxieties about its harmful
effects had accompanied the rise of the novel since its beginning. But
now, conservative critics warned of the dangers of "reading addiction" (*Lesesucht*) and "reading rage" (*Lesewut*), and they invoked a
pathological loss of reality as the inevitable consequence of reading
too many Gothic novels.

The Proliferation of Ghost Narratives in Popular Print Culture

Kant's letter alludes to all of these functions of the ghost story. But
in his *Dreams of Spirit Seer, Elucidated by Dreams of Metaphysics*, published three years later, it is the ostensibly empirical status of ghost
narratives as evidence and the proliferation of nonscholarly writings
in the medium of print that are at the center of the second, "historical" part. In the "preamble" to the text, which we have cited before,
Kant criticizes the popularity of supposedly authentic ghost stories,
which were intruding upon philosophical theory: "But why is it that
the popular tales which find such widespread acceptance ... circulate
with such futility and impunity, insinuating themselves even into
scholarly theories?"[3] Yet even though Kant seems to dismiss spiritual
apparitions as a subject worthy of philosophical investigation, he has
to concede that empirical claims cannot be refuted by appealing to
the certainties of scholastic metaphysics. He states: "What philosopher, torn between the assurances of a rational and firmly convinced

eyewitness, on the one hand, and the inner resistance of an insuperable skepticism, on the other hand, has not, on some occasion or other, created the impression of the utmost imaginable foolishness? Is he completely to deny the truth of all such apparitions? What reasons can he adduce to refute them? Is he to admit the probability of even one of these stories? How important such an admission would be! And what astonishing implications would open up before us, if just one such occurrence could be supposed to be proven!"[4]

Kant opens his treatise by emphasizing the limits of metaphysical deduction in countering assertions that are ostensibly based on experience—in Kant's words: "what reasons can [the philosopher] adduce to refute the truth of all such apparitions?" The first, "dogmatic" part of *Dreams* seeks to answer this question. But as we saw in Chapter 1, instead of resolving the uncertainty as to whether spiritual apparitions are real or not, Kant develops two diametrically opposed theories without clearly marking his own position. The surprising "metaphysical hypothesis" of genuine apparitions is thus followed by the aggressive denunciation of imaginary "brain phantoms."

That theoretical deduction cannot determine with certainty whether spiritual apparitions are real or not is also the conclusion of a text written by Friedrich Schiller's most influential teacher at the Hohe Karlsschule in Stuttgart, Jacob Friedrich Abel. In his *Philosophical Investigations into the Connection of Humans with Higher Spirits* (1791), Abel sought to reject the probability of spirit apparitions.[5] Nonetheless, he had to admit that the impossibility of an interaction between higher spirits and humans could not be deduced from philosophical reasoning: "Even though we cannot consider this connection and the means suggested for its preservation as probable, we are still too firmly convinced of our utter ignorance vis-à-vis the nature of spirits and their relationship toward us, as that we could, based upon philosophical reasons, dare to deny the possibility of such a connection; instead we readily admit that we are indeed unable to reach a decision about this."[6] The philosophically undecidable question as to whether spiritual communications are real or not leads Abel to an appeal for positive facts and an empirical investigation.

Echoing the preamble of Kant's *Dreams*, Abel concedes: "If there is merely one single fact that necessarily presupposes our connection with spirits, then suddenly all doubt has been removed, and we will gladly and with pleasure give up all of the arguments that we formulated against this connection."[7]

The difficulties of finding a compelling solution as to how the bodily and spiritual realms might interact with each other and the distinction between dogmatic theoretical deduction and empirical claims founded on experience were also central to Friedrich Schiller's *The Philosophy of Physiology* (1779).[8] Schiller opened his treatise on the mind-body problem by highlighting in Cartesian terms the difference between the impenetrable *res extensa* and the penetrable *res cogitans*. Yet according to Schiller, this gulf between the spiritual and material worlds is bridged by a "mediatory force" (*Mittelkraft*) that, while "altogether different" from spirit and matter, nonetheless allows for the interaction of both.[9] Schiller concedes the impossibility of conceptualizing an excluded middle that would have to be penetrable and impenetrable at the same time: "Is such an entity thinkable? Certainly not."[10] But the "nerve spirit," as Schiller called this interface of spiritual and bodily realms, constitutes an empirical fact that has to be accepted, even if it contradicts the established theoretical propositions of philosophy and science. In Schiller's words, which simultaneously describe the predicament of late eighteenth-century philosophical doctrine vis-à-vis an ostensibly genuine ghostly occurrence: "Experience proves its existence. How can theory reject it?"[11]

Schiller emphatically privileges empirical claims over dogmatic theoretical deduction. But within the discussion about the reality of ghostly visions, the "single fact" that would convert skeptics such as Kant and Abel consists of narrative testimonies. Therefore, the reliability of these ostensibly genuine ghost narratives becomes another, equally undecidable question. As Kant states in the preamble to *Dreams of a Spirit Seer*: "Is [the philosopher] to admit the probability of even one of these stories?" Similarly, Abel remarks, immediately after invoking the one verified occurrence that would resolve the uncertainty as to whether spirit apparitions are real or not: "Other cases indeed deserve closer examination. A spectre announces his impending death to Brutus; Schwedenborg [sic] converses with spirits, living and dead, as with his friends; may we, should we lend credence to these narratives?"[12]

In the "historical" part of Dreams, as well, Kant hints at the impossibility of ascertaining the veracity of these stories. Restating the dilemma described in the preamble, Kant again contrasts the deductive approach of scholastic metaphysics with the empirical investigation of positive facts. But this time, he introduces a further differentiation on the side of empirical evidence, for Kant now distinguishes between "the arguments of reason, on the one hand," and "real experience or narrative, on the other hand."[13] By dividing his treatise into a "dogmatic" and a "historical" part, Kant shifts from theoretical argumentation to an empirical investigation of ostensible facts. Yet by further differentiating between "real experience" and "narrative," Kant raises the question as to whether the circulating stories about allegedly genuine apparitions are fiction or fact. The investigation of "facts" holds out the promise of overcoming the limitations of metaphysical deduction. But the empirical evidence for the reality of a connection with the spiritual realm consists of narratives, which may be authentic or not.

Kant similarly alternates between skepticism and credence at the end of the first, "dogmatic" part of Dreams—after the authorial "I" has developed the metaphysical hypothesis of genuine apparitions and after the aggressive denunciation of imaginary brain phantoms. In a strangely contradictory passage, Kant concludes: "It is exactly the same lack of knowledge that leads me to dare a complete denial as to the truth of the many different ghost stories; but I dare so only with the ordinary yet outlandish reservation of casting doubt on each of these individual stories while ascribing some credence to all of them taken together. The reader is free to judge for himself. But for my part, the arguments adduced in the second chapter [that is, in Kant's metaphysical hypothesis of genuine spirit apparitions] are sufficiently compelling that I adopt an attitude of seriousness and indecision when listening to the various strange narratives of this kind."[14]

While stressing the cognitive limits of speculative deduction, Kant first announces a "complete denial as to the truth" of ghost narratives. But then he gives two different reasons for suspending his disbelief and for adopting an "attitude of seriousness and indecision." The first argument for lending "some credence" to these ghost stories is Kant's "metaphysical hypothesis" of genuine apparitions, which he developed in the second chapter of *Dreams*. Even though this speculative proposition cannot claim any empirical proof, it can be formulated without logical inconsistency. But Kant's contradictory statement also speaks to the cumulative power of the numerous ghost narratives published at the end of the eighteenth century. While casting doubt on "each of these individual stories," he paradoxically ascribes some credence "to all of them taken together."

It seems possible that Kant's suspension of disbelief is based on the assumption that a factual claim deserves to be taken more seriously if it is confirmed by several witnesses. But the sum of testimonies that support one specific claim is quite different from the aggregate of the various ghost narratives published at the same time. In a wider context, Kant's stance of doubting each individual story while lending some credence to all of them taken together may also testify to an idealized view of print as a medium of enlightenment. The second half of the eighteenth century witnessed a rapid expansion of the book market, with an increase in the number of scholarly treatises and with new journals such as the *Berlinische Monatsschrift*, which served as an important site of rationalist critiques of superstition and religious fanaticism after its founding in 1783.[15] Kant's own response to the question "What is enlightenment?" was first published in this journal and predicated on scholarly print culture. After famously defining "enlightenment" as "the emergence from our self-imposed tutelage," Kant presents the "public use of reason" as the primary agent of this process. Clarifying the meaning of "public," he writes: "By the public use of one's own reason I understand that which someone makes of it as a scholar before the entire audience of the world of readers."[16] For Kant, the public use of reason, which is the primary motor of enlightenment, conincides with academic publishing.

Akin to Kant's positive perspective on scholarly print culture, Josias Ludwig Gosch's treatise *Fragments on the Circulation of Ideas* (1789) praised "the invention of the art of printing books" for allowing easy access to classical authors and scholarly works. Gosch described the "circulation of ideas" as purely beneficial for the moral, economic, and intellectual welfare of society and as promoting "the gradual perfection of the human species."[17] In *Dreams of a Spirit Seer*, it may be this model of scholarly communication and an idealized view of print as a medium of enlightenment that underlies Kant's strangely illogical assertion that not all of the published ghost narratives can be wrong. This seems corroborated by his previous assessment of Swedenborg, which explicitly invokes scholarly print culture. In his 1763 letter to Knobloch, Kant presents one report about Swedenborg's purported ability to see ghosts as particularly compelling because one ambassador communicated the incident to another one in a letter meant "*for public use.*"[18] Characterizing Swedenborg as a "scholar," Kant seems to expect an answer to his unresolved questions from Swedenborg's next book, which "will make this whole remarkable affair public before the eyes of the world."[19] In *Dreams*, Kant's assessment of Swedenborg is far more negative. But his high esteem of the printed scholarly word, a medium that he later equates with the public use of reason, persists, and it may have led him to lend some credence to the currency of published ghost narratives.[20]

Yet in adopting this "ordinary yet outlandish" stance, Kant comes precariously close to the "common mania" from which he had sought to distance himself in his letter to Knobloch. For print functioned as a malleable medium, and in addition to an increase in scholarly treatises and journals, the print market of the second half of the eighteenth century also witnessed an explosion in esoteric and occultist pamphlets, flyers, novels, and treatises. The boundary between scholarly and spiritualist writings thus became increasingly permeable, or, to quote one more time from Kant's preamble:

"But why is it that the popular tales which find such widespread acceptance ... circulate with such futility and impunity, insinuating themselves even into scholarly theories?"[21]

At the beginning of the second, "historical" part of *Dreams*, Kant responds to the proliferation of ghost narratives in popular and nonscholarly print culture by deploring the "haunting circulation" of these stories.[22] Kant now adopts a position that stands in stark contrast to his previously suggested attitude of "seriousness and indecision" and to Gosch's positive view of the "circulation of ideas." He figures the medium of print and an exploding book market—without naming them—in dismissive notions of rumor and (female) credulity. It may appear far-fetched to link Kant's scathing critique of hearsay to popular print culture. But the fluidity of an expanding and largely unregulated book market allowed for the same narrative to be reprinted and excerpted in many different versions and contexts, and the sheer number of new published titles and their wide distribution led Herder to liken the printing press to Fama, the winged Roman goddess of rumor. In 1793, Herder wrote in his *Letters on the Promotion of Humanity*: "Now the letterpress was introduced and lent wings to rags which had been scrawled on. They fly into every corner of the world; with every year, with every hour of the day ... the wings of this literary Fama grow and fly to the end of the world. ... That which human voices keep silent about is talked and yelled about by molded types and mercantilic pamphlets."[23]

Akin to Kant, Herder switches to an oral register of "talking" and "listening" to criticize the negative aspects of commercial, popular print culture. Herder concedes that the "world of scholarly knowledge" (*Welt der Wissenschaften*) would be impossible without print. But Herder also anticipates current concerns about the Internet by warning against an information overload in which "everything" is being published.[24] Highlighting the negative effects of wide and easy access to print, Johann Heinrich Zschokke wrote in the early nineteenth century that "nowadays, simple print tools allow for the worst as well as the best work to be reproduced a thousand times with marvelous speed before being dispersed into the world. ...

From this stems the immense flood of literary works that openly carry the imprint of wretchedness, destined to communicate the errors and the spiritual and moral aberrations of their authors."[25]

In the second, "historical" part of *Dreams,* Kant anticipates these negative accounts of popular print culture by denouncing the proliferation of ghost narratives as based on hearsay and rumor. The same narratives about Swedenborg's spiritual visions that Kant had described as "beyond any conceivable doubt" in his letter to Knobloch he now introduces as having "no other testimony than that of common hearsay, which provides very dubious proof."[26] Kant expands upon the implied danger for scholarly, rationalist discourse by stating: "It has always been the case . . . that certain absurdities have found acceptance even among rational people for no other reason than that everybody talks about them."[27] He includes among these "absurdities" the assumption that the imagination of pregnant women leaves a bodily mark on their children, and he illustrates the power of rumor by invoking a case of media-induced frenzy in France: "By a great deal of hearsay children and women eventually induced a substantial number of intelligent men to take a common wolf for a hyena, and that in spite of the fact that any sensible person could see that there are not likely to be any African predators prowling around the forests in France."[28]

By contrasting children and women with "intelligent men," Kant seeks to uphold the demarcation between scholarly discourse and popular print culture. But he has to concede that the boundary between the two has become permeable, because even "rational people" and "intelligent men" fall prey to the haunting circulation of ghost stories. Kant himself is not immune to this dynamic, and he concedes that his own summary of Swedenborg's *Arcana coelestia* engages "in such a despicable business as that of spreading fairy tales abroad, which every rational being would hesitate to listen to with patience—and, indeed, not merely disseminating them but actually making them the text of a philosophical investigation."[29]

The publication of *Dreams of a Spirit Seer* inadvertently contributes to the "haunting circulation" of ghost narratives that it seeks to end.

Kant even warns, somewhat ironically, against an impregnation of his readers' minds by his treatise. As he writes, comparing his readers to a woman who may give birth to a disfigured child after seeing a monster during her pregnancy: "I am tired of reproducing the wild figments of the imagination of this worst of all enthusiasts...[and] I also have other reservations as well. The naturalist [who] displays monsters in his show cabinet...must be careful not to allow them to be seen by just anyone.... For among the curious, there may easily be pregnant women on whom they could make a bad impression. Taking ideal conception into account, some of my readers may also be expecting, and I should very much regret it if anything they read impressed them too strongly. However, since I have warned them from the very start, I disclaim all responsibility, hoping that the mooncalves to which their fertile imagination may give birth as a result of this circumstance will not be laid on my doorstep."[30]

This warning against the dangers of reading *Dreams of a Spirit Seer* provides a stark contrast to Kant's "What Is Enlightenment?" and its equation of the public use of reason with scholarly publishing. Thirty years after the publication of *Dreams*, Kant returned to a discussion of the sources of "mystical enthusiasm" in a letter in which he recommends "scornful silence," rather than "elaborate refutation," as the appropriate media strategy in responding to the proliferation of stories about the marvelous power of animal magnetism.[31] Yet *Dreams of a Spirit Seer* remains part of the medium it criticizes. The second, "historical" part of the treatise warns against the dangers of popular print culture, which it represents as rumor and hearsay. The numerous ghost narratives, which Kant previously presented as deserving "some credence" when "taken together," are therefore rejected as unreliable and misleading. But they are nonetheless reprinted and turned into the "text of a philosophical investigation."

Friedrich Schiller's Ghost Seer

The constitutive role of ghost stories for the scientific debate about spiritual communications and the (false) promise of resolving a metaphysical uncertainty by recourse to narratives are also crucial for Schiller's *The Ghost Seer* (1787–89). In its subtitle the novel presents itself as a history founded on fact, taken "From the Papers of Count O."[32] Its first edition was printed in six installments over the course of two years, from 1787 to 1789, in Schiller's journal *Thalia*. The text proved an instant and enormous success with late eighteenth-century readers, and Schiller published three different book editions—in 1789, 1792, and 1798—that were equally popular. However, Schiller never wrote the second and third volume that he originally announced. That he did not complete the work may speak to its diverging concerns: the text functions as a narrative essay that seeks to enlighten its readers by warning against credulity and religious fanaticism, but at the same time, Schiller's novel is also a fast-paced, sensational story that is built around a sequence of sudden and terrifying apparitions. In *The Ghost Seer*, spiritual apparitions serve as both a subject of theoretical debate and a serial, narrative device of shock and terror.

The novel opens with Count O's first-person narrative about an unnamed Prince who, during Carnival, stays incognito in Venice. One evening, the Prince and the Count are taking a stroll on Saint Mark's Square when they notice that they are being followed by a stranger: "The mask was an Armenian and walked alone."[33] As the Prince and the Count sit down on a bench, the mysterious foreigner takes a seat next to them, addresses the Prince with his real name, and announces ominously: "Congratulate yourself, my Prince...he died at nine."[34] After this enigmatic pronouncement, the Armenian disappears without a trace. Six days later, a sealed letter from Germany arrives, informing the Prince that a cousin of his, who preceded him in the ascendance to the throne, died the previous Thursday at nine, minutes before the Armenian's revelation. The seemingly inexplicable coincidence is commented on by the Prince with Hamlet's words: "There are more things in heav'n and earth than are dreamt of in your philosophy."[35]

During the following week, two further episodes suggest the intervention of an "invisible Being" in the affairs of the Prince.[36] Accordingly, the Prince, a "melancholy enthusiast" who has always dreamed of "communicating with the spirit world," discusses the "occult sciences" during a dinner at an inn.[37] Most of the guests exhibit either superstitious or blasphemous attitudes. The Prince, however, contends that one "ought to refrain from a judgment in these matters," thereby adopting the standpoint of "seriousness and indecision" suggested by Kant's *Dreams of a Spirit Seer*.[38] But in the diegetic world of *The Ghost Seer*, the undecidable philosophical discussion about the reality of spiritual apparitions is interrupted by a Sicilian, who offers a practical trial of his ability to raise a spirit. Eager to go beyond the cognitive limits of theoretical speculation, the Prince responds with the exhortation: "Let me see an apparition."[39]

After receiving a generous donation, the Sicilian necromancer agrees to summon the spirit of the Marquis de Lanoy, the Prince's deceased friend, who in dying could not finish his last sentence: "In a convent on the frontiers of Flanders lives a——." The preparation for the conjuring lasts several hours. Finally, the Prince, Count O, and several others are asked to enter a dark room with shuttered windows, dimly lit by a small fire burning in a silver capsula. The Sicilian awaits them among wafting clouds of incense, wearing an amulet and a white apron with Kabbalistic characters. In the middle of the room, on a carpet of red satin, stands an altar covered with black cloth. On top of it lie a human skull and an opened Chaldee Bible, next to a silver crucifix fastened to the altar. The sorcerer arranges the Prince, Count O, and the rest of the party in a half circle, asking them to join hands and to abstain from addressing the apparition directly. He then chants a magical formula in a foreign language before calling on the spirit of the Marquis de Lanoy to appear. After the third summons, he stretches his hand toward the crucifix on the altar in the middle of the room. As Count O recounts: "On a sudden we all felt, at the same instant, a stroke as of a flash of lightning, so powerful that our hands flew apart; a terrible thunder shook the house, the locks jarred; the doors fell shut; the cover of the silver box fell down and extinguished the light, and on the opposite wall, over the chimney piece, appeared a human figure in a bloody shirt, with the paleness of death on its countenance."[40]

The deceased, who speaks with a "hollow, hardly intelligible voice," is finally about to complete his last sentence: "In a convent on the frontiers of Flanders lives a——."[41] Yet suddenly, a second apparition disrupts the conjuring: "The house again trembled; a dreadful thunder rolled; a flash of lightning illuminated the room; the doors flew open, and another bodily form, bloody and pale as the first, but even more terrifying appeared on the threshold. The spirit in the box began to burn again by itself and the hall was lit as before.... The figure advanced with noiseless and majestic steps directly up to the altar.... The first apparition was seen no more."[42] The stunned necromancer tries in vain to shoot the uninvited second apparition and then faints. The Prince, by contrast, remains calm and now identifies the second apparition as the real ghost of his friend. In the following, Lanoy's spirit reveals that he has an illegitimate daughter who lives in a convent in Flanders. A clap of thunder accompanies the disappearance of the second, seemingly genuine apparition.

Immediately thereafter, a Russian officer who has observed the conjuring as a witness steps forward and accuses the Sicilian sorcerer of being a juggler and a fraud. The previously inconspicuous Russian instills a fear in the necromancer that is surprisingly similar to the terror inspired by the second apparition: "The Sicilian turned round, looked steadfastly in [the Russian's] face, uttered a loud shriek, and threw himself at his feet."[43] Even the Count and the Prince cannot repress a feeling of awe when they look more closely at their companion: "We looked all at once at the pretended Russian. The Prince instantly recognized the features of the Armenian.... We were all as petrified with fear and amazement. Silent and motionless, our eyes were fixed on this mysterious being."[44]

Officers of the Venetian police appear and arrest the Sicilian, while in the ensuing confusion, the Armenian again vanishes without a trace. In the subsequent installment, the incarcerated Sicilian gives a detailed explanation of how he staged the first apparition with a "magic lantern" hidden behind the window shutters and operated by an accomplice.[45] The phantasmagoric projection of the alleged spirit became visible as soon as the light in the room was extinguished, and the electrical shock "as of lightning" that accompanied the appearance of the ostensible ghost was administered by an electrical machine, concealed underneath the room's floor and connected to the silver crucifix that served as a "conductor."[46] The spirit's "hollow voice," in turn, belonged to a second accomplice of the Sicilian who was hiding in the chimney.

In accounting for every detail of the first apparition, the novel appropriates numerous late eighteenth-century treatises on how optical tricks and an enthusiastic imagination may deceive credulous or superstitious observers.[47] The electrical shock to which the Sicilian's audience is subjected may be modeled after the ghost shows of Paul Philidor (a.k.a. Phylidor or Paul de Philipsthal) in which Philidor arranged his viewers with joined hands in a human chain, electro-shocking them by means of a hidden Leyden jar in order to silence any disbelief.[48] But above all, Schiller's novel draws on the first volume of Johann Samuel Halle's *Magic, or the Magical Forces of Nature* (1784). This instructional text contained a chapter called "A Magical Ghost Solicitation" that resembles Schiller's novel in numerous details.

In an exposition similar to the course of events narrated in *The Ghost Seer*, Halle first describes the effects of a ghostly projection before giving a detailed technical explanation: "The ostensible magus leads the assembly of curious into a room whose floor is covered with black cloth and in which is an altar painted black and with two lights and a skull or a funerary urn on it. The magus draws a circle in the sand around the table or altar and asks the audience not to step outside this circle. He begins his conjuration reciting from a book of arbitrary characters and burns mastic for good and stinky things for evil spirits. Suddenly, the lights extinguish themselves with a loud bang, a strange rumbling arises, and in this moment, the solicited spirit appears, hovering in the air over the altar."[49] Under the heading "Apparatus," the subsequent four pages of Halle's treatise give a detailed technical and psychological explanation, accompanied by a drawn illustration (Figure 7), of how and why the viewers will mistake the ghostly projection for a genuine apparition: "Apparatus: Optical science teaches us that the light of the magic lantern and the

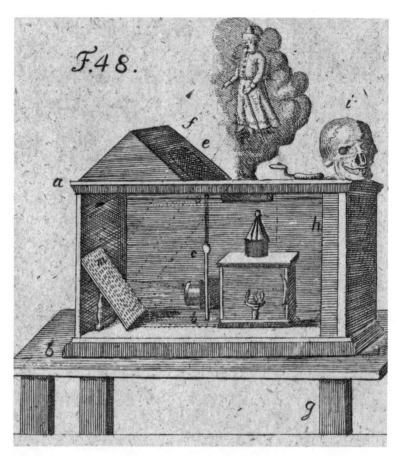

Figure 7. A phantasmagoric projection onto smoke by means of a magic lantern hidden inside an altar. Using a human skull as a theatrical prop appeals to the imagination of the conjuror's audience. From Samuel Halle, *Magie, oder die Zauberkräfte der Natur* (Berlin, 1784).

colors of the painted object can be projected onto a white wall or screen as well as onto smoke, be it from boiling water or dry smoke."

In giving a natural explanation to ostensibly supernatural phenomena, Schiller's novel adapts Halle's *Magic* and other contemporaneous treatises on natural magic and optical media.[50] In doing so, Schiller's text contrasts starkly with other Gothic novels, which delighted in shocking their readers with sudden apparitions of unambiguously real ghosts, such as Horace Walpole's *The Castle of Otranto* (1764) and Matthew Lewis's *The Monk* (1796). Yet following in the wake of *The Ghost Seer*, Cajetan Tschink's *The Victim of Magical Delusion* (1790–93) and Lawrence Flammenberg's *The Necromancer* (1792) similarly revealed ostensibly genuine spirit apparitions as produced by "a magic lanthorn" and "optical means."[51] In his preface to the 1811 edition of *The Castle of Otranto*, Sir Walter Scott commented on this split within Gothic fiction by praising Walpole's "bold assertion of the actual existence of phantoms," and he rejected the "attempt to reconcile the superstitious credulity of feudal ages with the philosophic skepticism of our own, by referring those prodigies to the operation of fulminating powder, combined mirrors, magic lanthorns, trap-doors, speaking trumpets, and such like apparatus of German phantasmagoria."[52]

Schiller's *The Ghost Seer*, which provides a detailed account of the Sicilian's "apparatus," seems prototypical of this "German phantasmagoria." The didacticism of the novel delivers what has been promised in its introduction. There, Count O aligns his report about the fate of the Prince with late eighteenth-century anthropological treatises, presenting the allegedly authentic story as a "contribution to the history of deception and the errors of the human intellect."[53] The narrator's introduction thus all but replicates the title of Johann Christoph Adelung's *History of Human Folly; or, Biographies of Famous Black Magicians, Alchemists, Necromancers, Prophets, Enthusiasts and Other Philosophical Villains*, an instructional textbook published in five volumes from 1785 to 1789.[54]

In the main narrative, the figure of the Sicilian also gives voice to the central arguments of these Enlightenment treatises, revealing how, in order to inflame the Prince's enthusiastic imagination, he staged several mysterious incidents in the days before the conjuring. The narrator's introduction to the second part of the novel expands on the didactic and anthropological interests of the case history by commenting on the detrimental effects of the Prince's upbringing, which rendered him susceptible to seeing ghosts. Count O indicts the Prince's "bigoted education," which imprinted "frightful images upon his tender brain," thereby transforming religious matters into an "enchanted castle into which one does not set one's foot without horror."[55] While thus alluding to the numerous Gothic novels in the wake of Walpole's *Castle of Otranto*, these remarks also repeat a skeptical warning against the deceptive power of an inflamed imagination from Schiller's early theoretical writings, which relate a false, feverish vision of "spirits expelled from their graves" to "images absorbed as a child."[56]

Yet instead of exorcizing the rhetoric of ghostliness, Schillers's *Ghost Seer* displaces its figures of supernatural agency onto the description of a vast hidden conspiracy, personified in the mysterious figure of the Armenian. The narrative does give a comprehensive account of how "fanatic enthusiasm" and optical media may lead a credulous spectator to mistake a phantasmagoric image for a real ghost.[57] However, even after the Sicilian's explanation of his fraudulent tricks, the language of the supernatural retains a central role, thereby allowing for further installments of the serial narrative. The Prince does give a short hypothetical account of how the Sicilian and the Armenian might have conspired in staging the sudden, "incomprehensible" appearance of the second specter.[58] But the details of how the Armenian's "invisible hand" might have achieved this remain shrouded in obscurity, thereby leaving room for the possibility of a genuine spiritual occurrence.[59]

The Repetition of Shock: Seriality and Reading Addiction
We have seen how this ambiguity corresponds to the undecided position of Kant's and Schiller's theoretical writings about spiritual visions. But in addition to drawing on the philosophical debate

about the possibility and reality of ghostly apparitions, Schiller's novel also deploys spiritual occurrences as a serial narrative device of shock and terror. The electrical shock, felt by Count O and the Prince when the apparition of the first Lanoy becomes visible—"On a sudden we all felt, at the same instant, a stroke as of a flash of lightning, so powerful that our hands flew apart"—also stands in for the novel's nearly bodily effect on its readers, an effect that the text aims for time and again. In the contemporaneous visual medium of the phantasmagoria, the viewer's disorientation in darkness and the use of black background slides allowed for frightening special effects. To quote Hegel's Jena lectures one more time: "In phantas-magorical presentations it is night on all sides; here a bloody head suddenly surges forward, there another white form abruptly appears, before vanishing again."[60] Comparable effects of disorientation and terror are central to Schiller's sensational novel and its serial narra-tion of unexpected ghostly apparitions. As in the sequence of sud-den optical magnifications that assault the phantasmagoria's viewer, Schiller's *The Ghost Seer* administers a series of shocks to its pro-tagonist and to its readers. In the diegetic world of the narrative, one sudden, unexpected appearance is always followed by another: immediately after the apparition of Lanoy's first specter, the text introduces a second ghost, "bloody and pale as the first, but even more terrifying." The Sicilian's fainting then serves as an embodied representation of horror before the unveiling of the Armenian's real identity leaves the Prince and the Count "petrified with fear and amazement."

This narrative structure of seriality and repetition also applies to the second of the six original installments, which features an unre-liable narrative told by the incarcerated Sicilian to the Prince and Count O about a previous encounter with the elusive Armenian five years earlier.[61] The Sicilian relates that back then, he was the guest of a bereaved family who remained in uncertainty about the fate of Jeronymo, a son, brother, and fiancé possibly abducted by pirates and missing for years. The false necromancer gives "lectures" on "the intercourse of men with higher beings" and finds a receptive audience in Jeronymo's "credulous" father and his fiancée, a "young Countess whose mind since the loss of her lover had been more occupied in the world of spirits than in that of nature, and who had, moreover, a strong shade of melancholy in her composition."[62]

Employing his hidden "machinery," the Sicilian finally stages a false apparition of the missing Jeronymo.[63] The somewhat tedious passages on how melancholy "enthusiasm" may lead to credulity and superstition appropriate a treatise on the notorious Cagliostro, published by one of his former victims.[64] But again, the enlightenment of the reader remains incomplete, for the text substitutes violent shock and narrative suspense for its initial didacticism.

The Sicilian's optical simulation of Jeronymo's ghost persuades the Countess that her fiancé has passed away, and she agrees to marry his brother. But the wedding celebration is disrupted by a second, ostensibly genuine apparition. The groom is asked to bring a toast to his departed sibling when Jeronomy's real ghost suddenly reveals his death as fratricide: "'That was my murderer's voice!'—exclaimed a terrible figure, which appeared suddenly in the midst of us, covered with blood and disfigured with horrible wounds."[65] Once again, the unexpected and shocking appearance of a second, seemingly genuine ghost is placed next to a lengthy psychological and technical explanation of a false spiritual vision.

A narrative interest in shock and repetition can also be observed in contemporaneous British Gothic fiction. The length of Ann Radcliffe's novels and their focus on sensibility and sentiment differ considerably from Schiller's fast-paced and comparatively short text. But *The Mysteries of Udolpho* (1794) also indulges in a textual representation and production of "terror."[66] The novel's villain, Montoni, holds the heroine, Emily, captive in Castle Udolpho, where a veiled picture may hold a clue to the identity of its legitimate owner. But when Emily finally seizes a long-desired chance to examine the portrait, she gains fear, rather than knowledge: "Emily ... hastily entered the chamber, and went towards the picture, which appeared to be enclosed in a frame of uncommon size, that hung in a dark part of the room. She paused again, and then, with a timid hand, lifted the veil; but instantly let it fall—perceiving that what it had concealed was no picture, and, before she could leave the chamber she dropped senseless on the floor."[67]

The fainting spell of the protagonist serves as an embodied representation of shock, while the reader's suspense is heightened even further by the novel's silence about the source of Emily's terror. We get to know only that what the veil had concealed "was no picture." The gap in the narrative thus follows Edmund Burke's appraisal of obscurity as a necessary condition of dread: "To make any thing very terrible, obscurity seems in general to be necessary."[68] Four hundred pages later, after a happy end is secured and when the information is no longer relevant, the reader does find out what was behind the curtain. This delay in explaining the supernatural markedly contrasts with the narrative structure of Schiller's Gothic novel, where the Sicilian's detailed account of how he staged the apparition of the first Lanoy comes shortly after the appearance itself. But similar to *The Ghost Seer*, Radcliffe's novel also aims for a repetition of the jolting moment of fright. Immediately after describing Emily's fainting, the text continues: "When she recovered her recollection, the remembrance of what she had seen nearly deprived her of it a second time." The text thereby strives for a repetition of the puncturing moment of shock and terror, which has disrupted the normal flow of time by creating a void of pure horror, one in which the past and future have become irrelevant: "Horror occupied her mind, and excluded, for a time, all sense of past, and dread of future misfortune."[69]

Radcliffe's borrowings from the sentimental novel set her novels apart from more violent tales such as Matthew Lewis's *The Monk* and Charles Maturin's *Melmoth, the Wanderer*. But the repetition of shock seems to be a shared structural quality of these texts,[70] one that can be traced back to Walpole's *The Castle of Otranto*, which opens with Conrad, Manfred's son, "being dashed to pieces" by a giant helmet unaccountably falling from the sky.[71] In *The Castle of Otranto*, the subsequent course of events comes close to abandoning narrative coherence. The storyline can be read as undoing the usurpation of the castle by Manfred's ancestors. But Walpole himself described the novel's "principal engine" as "terror,"[72] and indeed, the initial shock is followed by a succession of Gothic effects—the appearance of yet more outsized body parts—until Alfonso, the founder of Otranto, becomes visible as a whole.

A serial succession of ghostly appearances is also central to the second part of Schiller's *Ghost Seer*, which is no longer a first-person narrative, but composed of letters written by Baron F to Count O. The language of the supernatural is here applied to visions of a Greek woman whose "apparition" (*Erscheinung*) is described in two consecutive stories.[73] The Prince encounters the female figure in an empty chapel, where she is perfectly lit by the setting sun entering through a single window, and he responds to this sighting with "terror," a reaction more appropriate to the sublime than to the beautiful.[74] As a result, Baron F questions the Prince about his vision in terms that suggest a ghostly manifestation: "But this figure, your highness? Are you certain that it was something living, something real, and not perhaps a mere picture, or an illusion of your fancy?"[75] As the story progresses, the Greek woman turns out to be German, and the intensity of the Prince's reaction to her appearance is given a natural explanation—a painting of the Madonna has left a lasting imprint on the Prince's imagination.[76] But the equivalence between her appearance and that of a ghost is also corroborated by the fact that Schiller suggested two images for the frontispiece of the first book edition of *The Ghost Seer*: either the apparition of Lanoy's second specter or the Prince's vision of the Greek woman in the church (Figure 8).[77]

The parallel between seeing the Greek woman and seeing a ghost becomes even more pronounced in a story told by a new friend of the Prince, Civitella, who has previously observed the same woman with a telescope and who describes her as "a supernatural being."[78] Again the novel draws on contemporaneous warnings against the deceptive power of an enthusiastic imagination and optical effects: "Was it the play of my imagination, or the magic effect of lighting?"[79] The "angelic brightness of [the Greek woman's] look" pales, however,

Figure 8. Frontispiece of the 1792 book edition of Schiller's *The Ghost Seer*: the Prince sees a Greek woman whose appearance fills him with "terror."

once Civitella shifts his focus to the mysterious foreigner standing next to her, who turns out to be the Armenian.[80]

In recounting two sightings of the Greek woman, first as seen by the Prince and then as seen by Civitella, Schiller's novel repeats the serial narrative structure of the first part. At the same time, Civitella's vision suggests a contiguity between a ghostly "supernatural being" and the Armenian, whereas the Prince's vision is actually arranged by the latter. While staying out of sight, the Armenian thereby ignites the passions of the Prince and prevents him from leaving Venice. Baron F naïvely hopes that this new "apparition" will awaken the Prince from his "metaphysical dreams," but the opposite comes true.[81] It is the death of the Greek woman, real or simulated, that in the end drives the Prince into "the arms" of the Armenian, causing his final conversion to Catholicism and murder.[82]

This conclusion of *The Ghost Seer*, however, was hastily patched together in the final paragraph of the 1789 book edition, which was originally meant to be only the first of several volumes. In his letters, Schiller always distanced himself from his most popular and successful work, an unease that highlights the difference between a fast-paced sensational novel and Schiller's later poetics of Weimar Classicism, which was predicated on slow and repeated readings of canonical tragedies and poems. At the same time, Schiller's difficulties in completing *The Ghost Seer* also speak to the diverging concerns of the text. In addition to providing didactic instruction, the narrative also is engaged in the serial representation and production of shock. Concomitantly, the novel's representation of the mysteriously omnipresent Armenian partook in the rise of the "secret society novel" (*Geheimbundroman*), a specifically German genre that centered on the machinations of unseen conspiracies.[83]

The at times incongruous copresence of philosophical reflection and suspenseful narration in *The Ghost Seer* resurfaces in the second part, which relates not only the Prince's and Civitella's sightings of the Greek woman, but also a lengthy "Philosophical Dialogue" between Baron F and the Prince. The Prince, whose Pietist education had turned religious matters into an "enchanted castle," now undergoes a period of skeptical agnosticism—under the influence of "the most modern books," which lie beyond his understanding and which shatter his beliefs with a "dazzling style" and "captious sophisms."[84] Turning against the projection of a human "purpose onto an imagined deity," he goes so far as to assert: "What has already happened to me, and may still follow, I look upon as two black impenetrable curtains hanging over the two extremities of human life and not drawn aside by any mortal."[85] This emphatic invocation of the limits of human knowledge can be read as a very loose adaptation of Kant's insistence on the limits of philosophical knowledge.[86] But the Prince's statement also draws on the language of the Gothic novel, all but anticipating Radcliffe's heroine lifting a veil from what turns out not be a picture.[87] Right after this extended philosophical discussion, which was shortened in later editions, Count O writes in an editorial note: "I also ask my readers for forgiveness that I have copied the good Baron F so faithfully.... [He] could not foresee to what extent the Prince's philosophy would shape his future fate, but I know about it.... The reader who hoped to see ghosts here may rest assured that they are still to come."[88]

Schiller himself did not fulfill this promise of more ghosts still to come, for he never completed *The Ghost Seer*. It thus fell to sequels and spin-offs by other authors to capitalize on the serial structure of the narrative. Cajetan Tschink's *History of a Ghost Seer* (1790–93), translated into English as *The Victim of Magical Delusion*, made the Armenian part of a patriotic conspiracy that uses deception for noble purposes. Lorenz Flammenberg's *The Necromancer* copied the plot of *The Ghost Seer* while changing the names of its protagonists, and its second part even plagiarized Schiller's narrative "The Criminal from Lost Honor."[89] Other authors presented their books as a "counterpart" to *The Ghost Seer*, a marketing strategy adopted in *Ghost Stories Revealed, as an Instruction and Entertainment for Everybody: A Counterpart to Schiller's Ghost Seer*, anonymously published in 1797, and in Johann Jakob Brückner's *Angelika, Daughter of the Great Bandit Odoardo, Prince of Peschia from the House of Zanelti: A Counterpart to Schiller's Ghost Seer*.[90] Further popular titles in the wake of Schiller's

The Ghost Seer include *The Painting with the Blood Stains: A Ghost Story Based on a True Anecdote* (1800), by Ignatz F. Arnold; *Ghost Apparitions in the Tomb of the Scipios: From Papers Found on Hill Esquiline* (1816), by H. Krappe; *The Female Ghost Seer* (1794–98), by Karl August Gottlieb Seidel; *The Old One—Everywhere and Nowhere: A Ghost Story* (1803), by Christian Heinrich Spiess; *The Conjuration of the Devil* (1791), translated into English as *The Sorcerer: A Tale*, by Leonhard Wächter; and *Ghosts and Ghost Seers, or, Life and Premature Death of a Necromancer: A Warning Anecdote of our Times* (1789), by Johann Heinrich Zschokke.[91] The unimportance of a classical author function for these serial representations of spiritual and supernatural occurrences also comes to the fore in the most popular edition of *The Ghost Seer*, which combined Schiller's text with a continuation by Ernst Friedrich Follenius.[92] The compilation went through numerous reprints throughout the nineteenth century, and its English translation came forth in 1800 as *The Armenian; or the Ghost Seer: A History Founded on Fact.*

Carl August Grosse's *Der Genius: Aus den Papieren des Marquis C* von G*** (1791–95), which also cites Schiller's novel in its subtitle, came to be one of the most widely read literary texts in eighteenth-century Germany.[93] In 1796, the novel was published in two English versions—*The Genius: or, The Mysterious Adventures of Don Carlos de Grandez* and *Horrid Mysteries: A Story.*[94] It comes as no surprise that it was the second, more sensationalist title that made the list of "horrid" novels in Jane Austen's parody of Gothic fiction, *Northanger Abbey* (1798). There, the protagonist, Catherine, indulges in "the luxury of a raised, restless, and frightened imagination over the pages of *Udolpho*," and her friend Isabella exhorts her to continue thereafter with "*The Italian, Castle of Wolfenbach, Clermont, Mysterious Warnings, Necromancer of the Black Forest, Midnight Bell, Orphan of the Rhine,* and *Horrid Mysteries*."[95] The list reads like a parody, but all of these titles were actually published in the late eighteenth century, when Gothic novels appealed to a mass audience that conservative critics described as susceptible to "reading addiction."

As if lending credence to contemporaneous warnings against the dangerous allure of these popular tales, it is not only Austen's protagonist, Catherine, who starts seeing ghosts after reading too many Gothic novels; in 1792, the later Romantic author Ludwig Tieck also suffered a nervous breakdown after reading aloud with two friends the first two parts of Grosse's *Der Genius*. Beginning at four in the afternoon, Tieck and his friends, Schmohl and Schwinger, took turns reciting from the text. But even though his friends fell asleep around midnight, Tieck seemed unwilling or unable to stop. As he wrote in a letter: "I continued reading, always with the same enthusiasm, with the same persistent zeal; after two o'clock I was done with the book. A short break in which I could not speak or think; all scenes repeated themselves before my eyes.... I was alone...standing thoughtfully with my arm resting on a chair...rose-colored images swirled around me with blue butterfly wings—when suddenly—I still shudder when thinking about it—all of these sensations sank down in me like in an earthquake, all the beautiful blossoming hills, all the flowery valleys went suddenly under, and black night, the silence of death, dreadful rocks rose in a severe and dreadful manner.... Terror enveloped me, shudders, the most dreadful ones, were breathing at me, everything around me came to life, horrifying shadows hunted each other around me; my room and I seemed to fly into a black infinity."[96]

The letter continues to describe Tieck's hallucinations until they come to a frightful climax that is shaped by his readings of Gothic fiction and Shakespeare: "The horses tore the carriage forward relentlessly, I felt how my hair stood on end, I rush into the chamber and scream. They [Tieck's friends, Schmohl and Schwinger], believing I intend to terrify them, also scream, when suddenly the chamber expands as if to a wide hall; in it two giant beings, large and monstrous, unknown to me; their face is like a full moon (only now do I understand this admirable description in King Lear); I felt as if I was going to fall down, fear and rage shook all of my limbs; I would have stabbed both of them, had I had a rapier. For several seconds I was truly insane."[97] According to his letter, Tieck continued to scream and almost fainted before he gradually apprehended his friends and his environment. But even then, he was still so frightened by the white color of Schmohl's sleeping gown that his friend had to don an overcoat. After he had been put to bed, Tieck remained for another hour in a state of terror, picturing himself as lying in a coffin, before he finally fell asleep.

The episode constitutes an extreme example of what was called "reading rage"—*Lesewuth*—around 1800 in texts that criticized "reading addiction," the practice of reading too much and too fast.[98] Johann Gottfried Hoche published a treatise on the subject, defining "reading addiction" as a "misguided and pernicious abuse of an otherwise beneficial practice, a truly large evil as contagious as the yellow fever in Philadelphia." As Hoche continued: "one reads everything without purpose, without any order, one does not appreciate anything and devours everything; nothing is understood properly, and everything is given only a cursory reading and then forgotten right away, which is, however, quite good for most of what was read."[99]

Without taking these conservative lamentations at face value, one can read them as responding to a profound change of print culture in the second half of the eighteenth century, when reading was no longer restricted to religious and scholarly purposes, but also a practice of leisure and entertainment.[100] The rise in popular literacy, the emergence of the lending library and reading societies, as well as the availability of affordable reprints, pamphlets, and journals increased the number of readers.[101] Concomitantly, the book market saw an astonishing proliferation of Gothic, knight, and robber novels. While the number of German-language novels published between 1750 and 1760 was 73, the equivalent number for the 1790s grew to an astonishing 1,623 published novels.[102] The rise of immersive reading practices, which were so alarming to Hoche and others, was part of this newly emerging popular print culture.

Women and adolescents were deemed especially vulnerable to "reading addiction," an argumentative strategy reminiscent of Kant's distinction between "intelligent men" and women and children in his discussion of rumor and hearsay in *Dreams of a Spirit Seer*.[103] Hoche's simile of a contagious disease—"a truly large evil as contagious as the yellow fever in Philadelphia"—is also invoked

by Kant in a 1790 letter that addresses the sources of "the current prevalence of mystical enthusiasm." There, Kant characterizes
"reading addiction" as "the carrier which spreads this illness [and]
the miasmic poison which produces it."[104] In terms that come close
to Schiller's representation of the Prince being led astray by "the
most modern books," Kant condemns readers from the "wealthy
and higher classes" who, instead of pursuing the "thorny path of
thorough learning," attempt to "skim off the cream of scholarly
knowledge" by consulting "indexes and summarizing excerpts."
Kant describes such cursory readings as resulting in a "loquacious
ignorance" (*redselige Unwissenheit*) in which "things are presented as
facts even though only a lofty possibility of them can be conceptualized." In his 1790 letter, Kant thereby reintroduces the oral register
that underlies his indictment of hearsay in *Dreams*.[105]

As the only cure for this malady, Kant recommends a radical
change of school curricula: the substitution of "learning cursorily too
many diverse subjects with learning thoroughly the little that counts,
thereby channeling the desire to read into a purposeful habit rather
than exterminating it completely."[106] In the same way, Johann Georg
Heinzmann advocated slow and repeated readings of valuable texts
as a remedy against the pernicious effects of the rapid "devouring" of
fashionable novels.[107] Seen in this context, the inaccessible, "thorny"
terminology of Kant's critical writings and the high poetic register
of Goethe and Schiller's Weimar classicism become discernible as
distinct, yet parallel attempts at demarcating a small set of canonical
texts to be read repeatedly with care and scrutiny, in contrast to the
"flood" of popular material intended for fast consumption.[108]

Kant's letter criticized abridged textbooks, summaries, and
indexes, all of which excerpted and popularized scholarly knowledge—the CliffsNotes of the eighteenth century, as it were. But in
his *Anthropology*, he also warned against "the reading of novels" for
making "distraction habitual."[109] Johann Adam Bergk's *The Art of
Reading Books* (1799) condemned sensationalist narrative fiction in
even stronger terms: "A person who reads many ghost novels runs
the danger to lose the correct, if not all, use of reason.... Ghost

novels always keep our expectation under suspense; one impossibility after another one becomes real, one strange apparition follows the next one, and what human beings cannot accomplish is carried out by ghosts; we therefore consider nothing impossible anymore."[110]

According to Bergk, Gothic novels destroy the reader's sense of reality. Instead of educating, they appeal to our "natural inclination to the marvelous and the supernatural." Bergk expands on this by invoking contemporaneous visual media, warning that the reader's "imagination basks in an enchanted world, while his reason goes to sleep...when new, extraordinary, and strange apparitions constantly pass by, as in an optical box."[111] Exempting *The Ghost Seer* from his critique, Bergk described Schiller's novel as "a product of genius and taste" that stood in stark contrast to its many "imitations" by providing "entertainment and instruction."[112] In doing so, Bergk paid tribute to Schiller's status as a canonical author. But Bergk's critical account of how the ghost novel's reader is kept "under suspense" by "one strange apparition follow[ing] the next one" serves as an apt description of both *The Ghost Seer* and the numerous sequels and spin-offs written by other authors. Denouncing the monstrous "disfigurations" following in the wake of Schiller's narrative, Hoche commented on the repetitive structure of these narratives in nearly identical terms: "One spirit follows another spirit, and one devil another devil."[113]

It is this serial iteration of shock and terror that lent these texts the addictive quality that was so alarming to conservative critics such as Bergk and Hoche. Another contemporaneous text about the pernicious effects of reading sensationalist fiction put its focus on young women to conclude that novels "incite the inclination toward the marvelous and extraordinary while instilling disgust toward the normal course of things. Common chores, in which maidens are supposed to educate themselves to grow into women, become intolerable and produce boredom, to be overcome only by new shocks which shatter the imagination."[114] While figuring the addicted reader of the Gothic novel as adolescent and female, this exaggerated warning against the harmful power of narrative fiction rightly emphasizes the repetition of terror and shock in the Gothic novel. Its readers can always expect more ghosts still to come.

In addition to undergoing an episode of "reading rage" that followed his immersion into the fictional world of Grosse's *Horrid Mysteries*, Tieck also represented the dangers of fanatic reading in his novel *William Lovell* (1795). There, the melancholy enthusiast Balder sees a ghost walking through his room after he reads, in the middle of the night, the first scene of Shakespeare's *Hamlet*: "A marvelous imaginary play began in my head at the line.... *Peace, break thee off; look, where it comes again....* I saw the wild night.... Horatio listening with utmost suspense to the strange narrative of his friend—and now suddenly the ghost enters, slowly and silently, hovering, a black shadow.... I felt a shiver that drove its cold hand over my neck to the spine, the silence around me became more and more deathlike, I retreated further into my inner self and with terrified delight I observed the apparition in my innermost fantasy, lost to the external world. Suddenly I heard a long, quietly drawn step through the room, and looked up again—a man walked behind my back toward the door of my bedroom.... I clearly apprehended the white hair on his head; the shadow on the wall followed after him, distorted in a terrifying manner."[115]

The novel describes an external hallucination that rises from Balder's inner visualization of the first scene of *Hamlet*. Tieck thus represents Shakespeare's tragedy as producing the same "terrified delight" that was crucial for the enormous success of the contemporaneous Gothic novel.[116] Texts such as Schiller's *Ghost Seer* and Grosse's *Horrid Mysteries* engendered dread and delight by representing and administering a sequence of shocks. As if describing a reader immersed into sensationalist fiction, one who is subject to "reading addiction" and who longs for the next shock that will shatter his or her imagination, Tieck's narrator recounts: "My terror contained a kind of raging delight, a pleasure that may lie beyond the limits of humanity—I cannot think of anything more frightening than seeing this apparition for a second time; and yet I intentionally repeat for myself the shock, the numbing dread of this moment."[117]

CHAPTER FOUR

Romanticism and the Marvelous Facts
of Animal Magnetism and Clairvoyance

One year after undergoing an episode of frightening hallucinations that followed his ten-hour recitation of Grosse's Gothic novel *Horrid Mysteries*, Ludwig Tieck published an essay entitled "On Shakespeare's Treatment of the Marvelous" (1793).[1] The text presents itself as a study of the representation of ghosts and supernatural agency in Shakespeare's plays.[2] But while Tieck formulates astute and detailed observations of *Hamlet*, *Macbeth*, and *The Tempest*, the essay can also be read as an early programmatic outline of the literary poetics of German and European Romanticism. The central notion of the "marvelous" (*das Wunderbare*) is no longer discussed within a metaphysical or epistemological framework that has its focus on the possibility or reality of genuine spirit apparitions. Instead, Tieck introduces the marvelous as an aesthetic category that does away with classicist rules of verisimilitude, similar to the inversion of Horace's *Ars poetica* in the epigraph of Walpole's *Castle of Otranto*. Tieck's disregard for the constraints of classical form is announced at the beginning of the essay, where he praises Shakespeare for his ability to induce a suspension of disbelief in his audience. According to Tieck, the "genius" of Shakespeare consists in his "engaging our fantasy, even against our will, to such an extent that we forget the rules of aesthetics and all notions of our enlightened century.... Our soul willingly lends itself to being enchanted one more time, and no sudden or adverse surprise awakens our playing fantasy from its dreams."[3]

The Marvelous, Shock, and the Novella

Transforming Shakespeare into a theorist and practitioner of Romantic poetics, Tieck thus hints at the difference between a primordial belief in actual ghosts and a temporary forgetting of "all notions of our enlightened century." The Romantic suspension of aesthetic rules and rationalist notions presupposes an originary belief in spirits and magic, but one that has been dispelled by the doctrines of eighteenth-century enlightenment. Only after this skeptical repudiation of common ghost belief can we experience a second, momentary reenchantment in the aesthetic realms of the theater and fiction. As Tieck puts it, describing the appeal of Shakespeare's plays to our fantasy: "our soul lends willingly itself to being enchanted one more time." The marvelous and its central role in the poetics of Romanticism presuppose and turn against a disenchantment that has already taken place.[4] Tieck therefore highlights scenes in Shakespeare's work that stage the limitations of skepticism. He writes: "Only Macbeth sees Banquo's ghost; likewise, Hamlet's mother does not perceive her poisoned husband; she believes the apparition to be born from her son's heated fantasy; Macbeth's friends also adhere to this belief. The audience finds their belief quite natural, but the poet places it *above* this enlightenment, as it were; it sees their disbelief founded in their closed eyes, they are blind to what the audience and Macbeth see."[5]

In placing the audience of Shakespeare's plays "*above* this enlightenment, as it were," Tieck comes close to likening the theatrical illusion to the spiritualist assumption of actual ghosts. Both Macbeth and the audience see Banquo's apparition. In discussing *The Tempest*, Tieck similarly identifies the duration of the theatrical illusion with the duration of the audience's belief in supernatural agency: "only when the curtain falls, do we stop to consider Prospero a magician and ourselves to be inhabiting a world of fairies."[6] Shakespeare is presented as a "poet of his nation" who, in writing "for his people," appropriated ordinary folklore of magic and specters to transform it into an aesthetic simulacrum.[7] In Tieck's words: "he refined...common superstition into the most beautiful poetic fictions, putting aside all childish and vulgar elements while preserving the strange and the adventurous without which the spirit world would come too close to ordinary life."[8]

In emphasizing this transformation of popular ghost belief into poetic fiction, the essay introduces a demarcation between the literary representation of fictional revenants and the spiritualist belief in genuine apparitions. At the same time, Tieck's notion of the marvelous testifies to the continuity between the emerging movement of European Romanticism and the Gothic novels analyzed in the previous chapter. The essay's central technical question concerns the various ways in which Shakespeare's audience is tricked into accepting the supernatural, and Tieck describes these modes of representing the marvelous in terms that invoke late eighteenth-century narrative fiction. Shakespeare's comedies resemble "the enchanted world" of pleasant dreams and fairy tales, which engage our fantasy without interruption: "we lose for an extended period the analogy of our notions and create a new one that corresponds completely to these newly acquired notions."[9] The tragedies, by contrast, overwhelm our disbelief by sudden shock and terror—a strategy that Tieck characterizes as if referring to the Gothic novel and the literature of the fantastic: "the marvelous here is relegated to the background; like a flash of lightning it then suddenly rushes to the fore, and it is this suddenness that makes the poet's art of lending it the semblance of truth less necessary; he needs only to ensure that its occurrence shocks and terrifies, thereby winning our illusion completely, for the terror that we feel silences reason and its judgments."[10]

By emphasizing the startling and disorienting effects of the marvelous in Shakespeare's tragedies, Tieck conceptualizes the bodily terror and shock created by Gothic novels such as Schiller's *Ghost Seer* and Grosse's *Horrid Mysteries*.[11] It comes as no surprise, then, that Tieck draws on the same metaphors and categories that are deployed in Adam Bergk's *The Art of Reading* (1799), a treatise that warns against the pernicious effects of reading sensationalist narrative fiction. For Tieck, the poetic reenchantment of the marvelous "captivates our fantasy," while our "stricter reasoning is put to sleep."[12] Bergk relies on similar, but negative terms in criticizing literary texts that manipulate our "natural inclination to the marvelous and the supernatural."[13] Describing a reader who frequently indulges in "ghost novels," Bergk writes that he "runs the danger to lose the correct, if not all, use of reason...his imagination basks in an enchanted world, while his reason falls asleep on the pillow of the inexplicable."[14] Bergk conceives of the literary representation of apparitions not as an aesthetic device of shock and suspense, but as engendering a belief in actual ghosts. Tieck's essay, by contrast, replicates and undermines contemporaneous warnings against the pathology of "reading addiction," analyzing the marvelous in Shakespeare in terms that simultaneously celebrate the enchanting power of Romantic fiction.

The late eighteenth-century wave of Gothic novels and fantastic tales is once explicitly invoked in Tieck's essay—when Tieck sets out to highlight Shakespeare's remarkable skills in overcoming the technical impediments of rendering the marvelous visible on stage. Juxtaposing the medium of theater with narrative prose, Tieck writes: "In narrative fiction, the poet will far more easily succeed in transporting the reader into a supernatural world: he can rely on descriptions and poetic characterizations that prepare the soul for the marvelous; one sees apparitions first through the author's eyes, and the illusion is not encumbered by too many difficulties.... One believes the narrative poet on his word, as it were, if he only puts some artistic effort into lending probability to this marvelous world."[15]

The capacity of novels to reenchant their readers can therefore have wide-reaching effects. Tieck differentiates between the temporary suspension of disbelief and the complete loss of rational faculties that conservative authors such as Bergk considered a likely result of reading Gothic novels. Nonetheless, the essay on "Shakespeare's Treatment of the Marvelous" also introduces a pathological example of how immersive reading practices may distort the perception of reality. In his 1792 letter to Heinrich Wackenroder, Tieck represented the hallucinations that followed his ten-hour recitation of Grosse's *Horrid Mysteries* in strangely Shakespearean terms. The letter recounts the episode in a hectic staccato of short sentences that build up to Tieck storming into the room of his screaming friends, perceiving them as "two giant beings, large and monstrous...their face is like a full moon." But the frightening climax of Tieck's sensational account is interrupted by an unexpected reflective parenthesis that invokes Shakespeare's tragedies: "(only now do I understand this admirable description in King Lear)." Tieck then resumes his story to relate how close he came to killing his companions, concluding: "for several seconds I was truly insane."[16]

Not only is Tieck's account of his own immersion into the ghostly diegetic universe of Gothic fiction shaped by his readings of Shakespeare's work but the momentary loss of reason experienced by Tieck after his intense, ten-hour-long recitation of Grosse's *Horrid Mysteries* conversely serves as an unspoken, yet crucial point of reference in his essay on Shakespeare. There, one passage introduces a curious parallel to the suspension of disbelief and the loss of rational notions in the audience of Shakespeare's *Tempest*. Tieck writes: "The marvelous that is never interrupted here places the spectator in a disposition that is for a few hours what Don Quixote's insanity is for several years, and to a higher degree. The latter is never shaken in his belief in the most implausible tales of knightly adventures because his fantasy constantly creates the persons and incidents that he is seeking. All objects that he sees correspond to ones he has read about, for he transforms huts into castles, windmills into giants, and stewards into magicians."[17]

As in Tieck's perception of his friends as giant, monstrous beings, Don Quixote apprehends reality according to the diegetic world of novels he has read. Contemporaneous anxieties about the pathological effects of "reading addiction" and "reading rage" thus serve a surreptitious, yet constitutive role for Tieck's analysis of the marvelous in Shakespeare's plays. Tieck distinguishes between "common superstition" and "poetic fiction." But he also introduces Don Quixote as a reader who mistakes the diegetic universe of marvelous tales for reality, thereby blurring the boundary between literary ghosts and genuine apparitions. This oscillation between the fictional and the factual is reminiscent of the "historical" part of *Dreams of a*

Spirit Seer, where Kant alternates between considering ghost narratives as genuine evidence or unsubstantiated hearsay. But as we will see in the course of this chapter, a similar tension persisted within Romantic science and literature, particularly in narratives about the marvelous "facts" of animal magnetism and clairvoyance.

Whereas the previous chapter analyzed ostensibly authentic ghost narratives and the literary genre of the Gothic novel, we will now shift our focus to medical case histories and to the novella. Goethe famously defined the latter as based on a "real unheard-of incident"—"eine sich ereignete unerhörte Begebenheit"— emphasizing the novella's mixed status of factuality and sensational novelty.[18] Similarly, Tieck asserted in a late text from 1829 that the novella narrates an "incident [*Vorfall*] that—as easily as it can occur—is nonetheless marvelous, possibly singular."[19] Tieck furthermore hints at the importance of shock for the novella, emphasizing its "strange [and] remarkable turning point [*Wendepunkt*] that distinguishes it from all other narrative genres."[20] In his 1793 essay on Shakespeare, Tieck also takes note of the novella's affinity to the marvelous, highlighting the prominence of "incidents that are extraordinary and that approach the marvelous" in *The Merchant of Venice*, and he suggests that *The Tempest* may be based on an unidentified Italian novella or on an "ordinary incident that the poet transformed, by several degrees, into an extraordinary and marvelous one."[21]

The "unheard-of" sensational qualities of the marvelous are also constitutive of Goethe's *Conversations of German Emigrants*, a novella collection that was first published in 1795, two years after Tieck's essay on Shakespeare. As in the framing device of Boccaccio's *Decameron*, Goethe's text is structured by the "conversations" (*Unterhaltungen*) of the protagonists, who have been displaced by the revolutionary wars and who "entertain" each other by telling stories. In addition to a fairy tale, these diverting narratives also include two ghost stories that are based on allegedly real events, one about a female singer who is haunted by the sonic specter of a rejected lover whom she refused to visit on his deathbed and another about aural phenomena that occur regularly at midnight. Yet instead of remaining restricted to the diversion of these interior tales, the shock of the marvelous also intrudes upon the narrative frame. A loud blast, as if from an explosion, suddenly interrupts the narrator of the second ghost story. A careful investigation into the origins of the sound suggests that a mysterious sympathetic action at a distance must have destroyed the lid of a writing desk at the very moment when its "twin" desk, which was built by the same craftsman from the same materials, went up in flames on the other, revolutionary side of the Rhine.[22]

Without undertaking a more detailed analysis of Goethe's intricate text, it may suffice here to state that the anthology testifies to the renewed popularity of novella collections at the end of the eighteenth century and that its sequence of stories functions as a serial production of shocks.[23] In its mode of addressing its readers, the anthology thus resembles the Gothic novels analyzed in the previous chapter, even though Goethe's text is marked by an increased textual complexity as the parallels and differences between the various interior tales are commented upon by the narrators. In June 1800, Tieck proposed a similar book project, entitled *Phantasus*, to Goethe's and Schiller's publisher Goeschen in Weimar, pitching a "collection of several independent fairy tales and novellas, which together form another whole."[24] But Tieck did not succeed in securing a lucrative contract and postponed work on this project for a decade, until it finally came out in three volumes between 1812 and 1816.[25]

At that time, E. T. A. Hoffmann also published the first of his novella collections, *Fantasy Pieces in the Manner of Callot* (1814–15).[26] The four volumes made him one of the most widely read authors in the German-speaking countries, earning him a nickname—"Ghost Hoffmann" (*Gespenster Hoffmann*)—that highlighted the role of supernatural and occult incidents in his fantastic tales. Focusing on similar themes, but switching to a different genre, Hoffmann also wrote a Gothic novel, *The Devil's Elixirs* (1815), which reworked and complicated the story line of Matthew Lewis's *The Monk*.[27] But in 1817, he returned to the format of the novella collection with *Night Pieces*, an anthology that included Hoffmann's famous narrative "The Sandman."[28]

Prior to this literary career, Hoffmann himself had employed a hidden magic lantern in order to stage a private phantasmagoria in the home of an uncle in Berlin.[29] His fantastic tales testify to the persistence of this preoccupation, for they are predicated on the same bodily shock effects that were at the center of Philidor's and Robertson's ghost shows and that guaranteed, in the literary realm, the popular success of the Gothic novel. In Schiller's *Ghost Seer*, the protagonists' electrical shock stands in for the novel's sudden sensational impact on its readers, and Hoffmann aimed for similar effects in his novellas. "The Sandman," the first and programmatic tale of *Night Pieces*, thus contains a metafictional passage in which the narrator of the "strange and marvelous" story longs for a "first word" that would "jolt" his audience "like an electrical shock."[30] The same poetological model is to be found in the previously quoted passage from Tieck's essay on Shakespeare where Tieck invokes an electrical jolt to explain how the sudden impact of the marvelous in Shakespeare's tragedies suppresses our rational faculties by directly affecting our corporal sensations "like a flash of lightning."[31] The poetological appropriation of a contemporaneous technology that Philidor deployed for electroshocking the audience of his phantasmagoric projections can also be observed in Hoffmann's first anthology. In "The Golden Pot" (1814), initially published as the third volume of *Fantasy Pieces*, one passage directly addresses the reader. Seeking to incite the terror that the reader would have felt in witnessing the protagonist's encounter with an old witch, the narrator summons "an electrical jolt that shook through all of your fibers and nerves."[32]

E. T. A. Hoffmann's "The Magnetizer"

The narrative representation and production of shock is also central to "The Magnetizer: A Family Incident" (1814), a novella from the second volume of *Fantasy Pieces*. Hoffmann himself characterized the text in a letter from 1813 as "unveiling a side [of animal magnetism] that has not yet been treated poetically—its night side."[33] The comment alludes to the title of Gotthilf Heinrich Schubert's *Views of the Night Side of the Natural Sciences* (1808), which contained two lectures on "animal magnetism."[34] But Hoffmann's adaptation of contemporaneous scientific theories of mesmerism occurs in a complex literary text with multiple narrative layers. The novella has its focus on the abuse of animal magnetism in order to gain complete and absolute control over another human being, a theme that is the common concern of three different story lines. But even though these stories converge on one central subject, the novella's intricate temporal and narrative structures feature various frames and interior tales, which renders the text somewhat disorienting.

The novella's first and longest segment, "Dreams Are Froth," presents a conversation about the significance of dreams, an issue that is discussed by the old Baron, his son Ottmar, and a painter called Bickert. A fourth figure, Maria, the Baron's daughter and Ottmar's sister, listens and responds to the arguments and stories related by the three men. The Baron, who gives voice to the philosophical doctrines of the late Enlightenment, criticizes his son's "ebullient enthusiasm for the marvelous."[35] He dismisses dreams repeatedly as "froth," or unimportant.[36] But he nonetheless relates, as a first-person narrative, a story about his youth that one could describe, borrowing Tieck's terms, as placing the reader "*above* this enlightenment, as it were." In his youth, the Baron served as a cadet under a cruel Danish major whose "burning gaze" held a mysterious power over people around him.[37] The young cadet is simultaneously attracted and repulsed by the major, to whom he feels drawn by an "irresistible compulsion." One night, he dreams that the Danish officer steps next to his bed, calling himself the cadet's "Master and Lord." As a visible sign of his power, the major proceeds to drive a "pointed, glowing instrument into [the cadet's] brain." Awakening from this dream, the Baron hears and sees the officer leaving the compound in the middle of the night. The Baron and his alerted fellow cadets check on the major's chamber, which is locked from the inside. When its door is forced open, the major is found lying dead on the floor—with bloody "froth" around his mouth.[38]

Maria, the Baron's daughter, responds to the narrative with terror, announcing that she sees the frightening Danish major standing before her, "his gaze rigidly fixated on [her]."[39] The painter Bickert, however, rejects any deeper significance of the story, developing a materialist, enlightened theory of dreams by comparing them to a "concave mirror" that reflects and distorts physical reality.[40] He tries to corroborate this doctrine by relating several humorous dreams of his own that were based on real, external impressions. The Baron's son, Ottmar, by contrast, had characterized dreams as allowing us to dwell in a "higher life in which we not only surmise but truly apprehend all appearances of the spirit world, a life in which we hover above time and space."[41] Anticipating Schopenhauer's *Essay on Spirit Seeing*, Ottmar's stance also resembles the notion of an "inner life" in which one can perceive the spiritual realm formulated in Justinus Kerner's *The Seeress of Prevorst* (1829).[42] Ottmar's father, the Baron, had criticized this view by accusing his son of channeling his friend Alban—"it is as if I hear your friend Alban speaking," he says.[43] This charge seems now confirmed by the fact that Ottmar counters Bickert by relating, in a third-person narrative, an "incident" (*Begebenheit*) reported to him by Alban.[44]

While studying at the university of J____, Alban has entered into a close friendship with Theobald, who had responded eagerly to the "revival of interest in animal magnetism." After reading everything written on the subject, Theobald has come to reject the materialist explanation of mesmerist phenomena as based on a "physical medium," embracing instead the "profound notion of natural forces that act in a purely psychical manner." Hoffmann's novella ascribes this doctrine to "Barbarei's followers" and the "older school of spiritualists," misspelling the name of the Chevalier de Barbarin, who discarded with Franz Anton Mesmer's use of material instruments such as wands and *baquets* and who merged magnetic practices with Swedenborgian spiritualism.[45] Influenced by his lively discussions with Theobald, Alban now modifies his previous materialist stance, which was based on Mesmer's notion of an invisible fluidum. He adopts the theories proposed by the "newer school" of magnetism, which is described in Hoffmann's narrative as blending psychical and physical notions.[46] Hoffmann's literary text thereby adapts contemporaneous German treatises such as Carl A. F. Kluge's *Attempt at Presenting Animal Magnetism as a Curative Force* (1811) and Ernst Bartels's *Outlines of a Physiology and Physics of Animal Magnetism* (1812). Summarizing and modifying the various French theories of mesmerism and animal magnetism from the 1780s and 1790s, these German books from the 1810s were part of a second wave of scientific interest in animal magnetism, which lent the subject renewed legitimacy.[47] The episode related by Ottmar is presented as an ostensibly factual case history and highlights the curative and the pernicious power of animal magnetism.

After completing his studies at the university of J___, Theobald returns to his hometown and finds his fiancée, Auguste, in a somnambulist state: an Italian officer had passed through town and mesmerized the young woman in just a few days. Auguste, who had grown up with Theobald, does not even recognize her fiancé. Instead, she is in sympathetic rapport with the distant Italian officer.[48] Day and night she is tormented by the image of the Italian, who is bleeding on the battlefield, calling out to her in his last moments. With her mother's permission, Theobald starts treating the sleeping Auguste, who cries out, time and again, the Italian's name. Fixating his willpower and gaze on Auguste, Theobald lays his hands on her, calming her down by quietly and repeatedly pronouncing his own name.[49] He proceeds through several nights with this magnetic treatment and then turns to reawakening and reenacting old childhood memories shared by the two. After reliving an episode that had cemented the intense bond between the two children, Auguste remembers and recognizes Theobald while awake. She now describes herself as liberated from a "foreign power" that had taken control of her.[50] Ottmar is just about to reach the end of his story when Maria suddenly faints, immediately followed by the unexpected appearance of Alban. Prescribing a medication for the young woman, who is mistaken for dead by her father, Alban correctly predicts the precise time at which she will awake from her unconsciousness the next day.

Alban leaves, and Bickert compares his mysterious entrance and disappearance to Swedenborg and Cagliostro.[51] The Baron regrets that he previously allowed Alban's magnetic cure of a nervous disorder exhibited by Maria, and he remarks upon the "striking similarity" between Alban and the Danish major. Bickert responds by characterizing animal magnetism as a "cutting instrument" about which we know very little.[52] The subsequent part of the novella—a letter written by Maria to the sister of her fiancé—reveals that Maria fainted after momentarily recognizing the similarity between her own situation and that of Auguste in Ottmar's story. The letter shows Alban to be in complete control of Maria's thinking and writing. Recounting her fainting spell, Maria, who is again under Alban's spell, is now ashamed that she suspected Alban of using "secret, diabolical means" to make her his "slave,"[53] similar to the way in which the Italian officer gained power over Auguste in Ottmar's story.

Maria also relates to her friend how she encountered Alban for the very first time and immediately felt as if she "had to do, unconditionally, everything that he would command."[54] Now that Maria has been treated by Alban for a considerable period of time, the magnetic rapport between them has grown so strong and compelling that she can no longer imagine a life independent from him. Her loss of free volition and agency goes so far as to render Maria's letter a piece of writing under the dictation of a foreign will. As Maria puts it: "I realize that Alban is thinking these divine ideas into me, for he himself is in my mind, like a superior stimulating spark.... Only ... with *Him* and in *Him* can I truly live.... Indeed, in writing this, I feel only too clearly that only *He* lends me the words to allude to my existence in him."[55]

This hint at Maria's letter being written under the control and command of Alban is corroborated by his previous announcement that a "pressing correspondence" will keep him in his room for the rest of the day—a statement that refers not only to the third part of the novella, an excerpt of a letter written by Alban to Theobald, but also to Maria's letter, which is in reality authored by Alban.[56] It comes as no surprise, then, that Maria refers to Alban as her "Master and Lord," repeating the phrase used by the Danish major before inserting a glowing instrument into the Baron's brain.[57]

Alban's own letter confirms his use of animal magnetism to gain absolute control over Maria. He confides in Theobald that he has been seeking to "draw Maria into myself, weave her whole existence, her very being, so completely into mine that to separate herself from me would necessarily annihilate her."[58] Before revealing these disturbing fantasies of unlimited power over another human being, Alban describes the kinship of humans, animals, and plants in terms that read like a parody of contemporaneous Romantic philosophies of nature.[59] But in contrast to Theobald, who chooses contemplation as a path to knowledge, Alban seeks to use animal magnetism as a tool of dominion that penetrates the inner "secrets of nature."[60]

The fourth part of the novella is set three years later and describes the funeral of the painter Bickert from the perspective of an unnamed first-person narrator. A short excerpt from Bickert's diary and an unsent note by the anthology's editor close the novella. The excerpt from Bickert's diary details Maria's death at her wedding altar, a disaster that occurs not too long after her fainting spell and that testifies to the success of Alban's diabolical schemes. What follows is the complete annihilation of the family: Ottmar kills Maria's fiancé in a duel before seeking his own death on the battlefield, and the bereaved Baron dies in the arms of his friend Bickert.

By juxtaposing the stories of the Danish major, the Italian officer, and Alban, Hoffmann's "The Magnetizer" replicates the complex structure of the novella collection within one single textual body. The following chart may facilitate an overview of the somewhat disorienting sequence of interior tales and text segments that are part of the narrative frame.

1. "Dreams are Froth": conversation about the significance of dreams between the Baron, Ottmar, and Bickert; Maria listens and responds to the following stories:

   a. The Danish major, first-person narrative told by the Baron
   b. Bickert's theory of dreams as a "concave mirror"

c. Theobald's and Alban's studies of animal magnetism; story of the Italian officer, Auguste, and Theobald (told by Ottmar as a third-person narrative; reported to Ottmar by Alban)

Maria faints, Alban appears

II. Maria's letter to her fiancé's sister: Alban as her "Master and Lord"

III. Alban's letter to Theobald: animal magnetism as a tool to penetrate the secrets of nature and to annihilate Maria's independence

IV. "The Lonely Castle": first-person narrative by an unnamed narrator who attends Bickert's funeral three years later

V. "From Bickert's Diary": Maria's death, annihilation of the family

VI. Editorial note

Similar to Schiller's *Ghost Seer*, "The Magnetizer" is a hybrid of theoretical treatise and sensational narrative. The text outlines possible perspectives on the significance of dreams and gives a theoretical explication of animal magnetism. At the same time, it represents and administers a sequence of shocks: the insertion of a glowing pointed instrument into the Baron's brain; the death of the Danish major; Maria's fainting, which serves as the turning point of the novella; and Maria's death. The final outcome of the story clearly refutes the skeptical and rationalist arguments put forward by the Baron and Bickert, who belong to an older generation. But while the reader is placed "*above* this enlightenment," the text simultaneously vindicates Bickert's account of animal magnetism as a "cutting instrument." Alban's practice of magnetizing trees and his megalomania are represented as both delirious and dangerous. The night side of animal magnetism, however, is not restricted to the various story lines of the Danish major, the Italian officer, and Alban. The transformation of the seemingly sane and healthy Ottmar and Maria into docile mouthpieces of Alban incorporates the coercive power of animal magnetism into the narrative structure of the novella itself. Ottmar's story as well as Maria's letter provide a sinister confirmation of the Baron's initial dismissal of his son's enthusiasm: "It is as if I hear your friend Alban speaking."

One could even go so far as to raise the question whether the compelling power of animal magnetism also functions as a poetological model for an immersed reader who is mentally and physically affected by Hoffmann's narrative—similar to the literary representation and emulation of electrical shock in "The Sandman" and "The Golden Pot." Maria, who listens and responds to the stories of the Baron, Bickert, and Ottmar—"I can see the fearsome major in his Danish uniform standing before me, his gaze rigidly fixated on me"[61]—would then serve as an embodiment of how the reader is meant to respond to the text.[62] A similar parallel of animal magnetism and electricity is also suggested in Kluge's and Bartels's scientific treatises, which describe both natural forces as "modifications" of a single principle.[63] But in contrast to other texts by Hoffmann, "The Magnetizer" does not contain a direct, immediate interpellation of the reader. One can state with certitude, however, that the "pointed, glowing instrument" inserted by the Danish major into the Baron's brain does serve as a drastic literalization of Bickert's abstract description of animal magnetism as a "cutting instrument." In the diegetic world of Hoffmann's novella, Alban's mouthpiece, Ottmar, presents the marvelous phenomena of mesmerism as allowing for a "higher life" in which we hover above time and space and are capable of a true apprehension of the spiritual world. But the text has its focus on how animal magnetism transforms the relationship of magnetizer and somnambulist into one of unilateral dominance and control.

Justinus Kerner's The Seeress of Prevorst: The Narration of "Pure Facts"

A much more idealized account of animal magnetism and the access it allegedly provides to the world of the beyond is to be found in *The Seeress of Prevorst*, a text by the Swabian physician and folk poet Justinus Kerner. This medical case history was published in 1829 with the subtitle *Revelations on the Inner Life of Man and the Intrusion of the Spirit World upon Our Own*.[64] In it, Kerner gives a detailed account of a former female patient, Friederike Hauffe, or, as Kerner calls her, "Mrs. H." who, for seven years, was in a state of magnetic clairvoyance. Previously, in 1824, Kerner had written a related treatise entitled *History of Two Somnambulants*, and he continued his exploration of animal magnetism and the supernatural in *Histories of Possession in More Recent Times* (1834) and *Somnambulant Tables: A History and Explanation of the Phenomenon* (1853).[65]

The first printing of Kerner's *The Seeress of Prevorst* was highly successful, and in subsequent years, the book went through numerous new editions. These grew more and more voluminous, since Kerner included lengthy excerpts from positive book reviews while trying to refute critical objections.[66] The central argument of the book revolves around the precarious liminality of the somnambulist clairvoyant, who is caught between the material and the immaterial worlds. In Kerner's words: "If we seek to compare her to a human being, then we can say: she was a human being arrested by some fixation in the moment of dying between life and death, a human being already more capable of seeing into the world before her than into the one behind her."[67]

By describing the seeress as arrested in the moment of dying, Kerner appropriates and revises arguments that were at the heart of the philosophical and scientific debate about ghostly apparitions in the second half of the eighteenth century. In *Dreams of a Spirit Seer*, Kant had described the soul as partaking in both the bodily and the spiritual worlds: "the human soul, already in this present life, would therefore have to be regarded as being simultaneously linked to two worlds."[68] But Kant also asserted that the soul's spiritual dimension eludes our bodily perception. A "clear intuition" or "view" of the spirit world (*das klare Anschauen*), which in mesmerism came to be called "clairvoyance," could be achieved only in the afterlife.[69] Kant's *Lectures on Metaphysics*, which were given in the 1780s, but published posthumously, similarly characterized death as a transition from physical to spiritual modes of perception.[70] Yet in contrast to his metaphysical hypothesis of genuine apparitions from *Dreams*, Kant's lectures categorically denied the possibility of spiritual visions while being alive. Kant thus claimed that "when I still have a sensory intuition (*Anschauung*) in this world, I cannot at the same time have a spiritual intuition (*Anschauung*). I cannot be at the same time in this and also in that world."[71]

Kant's rejection of the excluded middle, however, gradually was undermined in early nineteenth-century treatises on animal magnetism and clairvoyance. These texts conceived of somnambulism as a liminal state between two worlds. Carl A. F. Kluge's *Attempt at Presenting Animal Magnetism as a Curative Force* described "magnetic sleep" in the following terms: "Having stepped out of life in external things and focused on his inner self, man stands here at the boundary of two very different worlds, at the dark gate of transition to a higher, better being."[72] Kluge's metaphor of a "dark gate of transition" suggests a proximity of animal magnetism and dying, one that is also central to the storyline of Hoffmann's "The Magnetizer," where Alban's magnetic treatment of Maria literally brings about her death. And in his *Views of the Night Side of the Natural Sciences*, Schubert went beyond a rhetorical or narrative contiguity by explicitly asserting a "kinship of animal magnetism with death that . . . deserves the most acute attention." Schubert continued: "Magnetism, which often brings about a stiffening of members and other related symptoms as in death, is in this and other respects in small what death is in large and in a perfect manner."[73] Schubert comes close to the French notion of orgasm as *petite mort*, ascribing a "feeling of ecstasy" (*Wonnegefühl*) to both death and somnambulism.[74] The Romantic poet Jean Paul similarly emphasized the "pleasing similarities between dying and magnetism."[75]

Kerner's treatise *The Seeress of Prevorst* draws on this tradition, but it describes Friederike Hauffe's "seven-year magnetic life" as an extended ordeal that is marked by extreme suffering.[76] In her magnetic trances, the ganglionic nervous system of the seeress enters into a connection with her "inner life." Yet according to Kerner, this "inner life" manifested itself only as a "disease of individuals" in early nineteenth-century Europe—in contrast to the "Orient," where the "cradle of mankind once stood" and where "whole tribes" still partook in it.[77] Kerner does not conceive of Friederike Hauffe's somnambulism in analogy to death, but emphasizes that the seeress was indeed, for the duration of seven years, "in the moment of dying between life and death." He thereby contends that Mrs. H. was at the same time in this and also in the other world, inhabiting a position that is described as a logical impossibility in Kant's *Lectures on Metaphysics*. After characterizing the somnambulist clairvoyant as "arrested by some fixation in the moment of dying," Kerner continues: "This is not a merely poetic expression but literally true. We see that human beings in moments of death often already look into another world and give news of it; we see how their spirit, as if already stepping out of its body, is able to manifest itself at distant places while it has not yet left its husk completely. If we can think of a person as arrested for years in these moments (which in the dying are often like mere lightning flashes), then we have the exact picture of this seeress; and in this I see only the *literal* truth and no poetic fiction."[78]

Kerner not only insists on the literal truth of his account, he denies that there are any rhetorical or narrative qualities of his case history, which he presents as a pure documentation of facts. Ending the introduction to his treatise on the seeress of Prevorst, he reaffirms: "What arose from such a bodiless life … some premonition of an inner life of man and of an intrusion of the spirit world upon our own … is the further content of these pages. I give here *pure facts* and leave their explanation to the reader's discretion."[79]

The subtitle of E. T. A. Hoffmann's "The Magnetizer" presents the text as based on a "Family Incident," but the final editorial note makes it very clear that the novella is nothing but a literary fiction.[80] In *The Seeress of Prevorst*, by contrast, Kerner emphatically asserts the "pure" factuality of his text. In this respect, the medical case history is quite typical of how early nineteenth-century treatises on animal magnetism and mesmerism emulated scientific positivism. The second part of Kerner's book consists of chapters entitled "Facts," which are arranged according to time and place of their occurrence: the first two are entitled "Facts at Oberstenfeld," where Mrs. H. lived before she arrived in 1826 as "a picture of death" in Weinsberg to enter into Kerner's treatment.[81] Then follow the "Facts at Weins-berg": "First Fact," "Second Fact," "Third Fact," and so on, up to the "Twenty-Second Fact" at Weinsberg and finally her death in August 1829 in Löwenstein. Introducing this series of facts, Kerner further-more points to another scientific treatise of his, which allegedly describes a phenomenon in the night realm of nature "without any theory, purely according to the facts."[82] Kerner conceives of himself as merely observing and witnessing the recorded events: "Most of these facts were witnessed and observed by myself."[83] This insistence on the accuracy and pure factuality of the case history also comes to the fore in how Kerner chooses to conclude his documentation of Friederike Hauffe's passion and dying: "And thus I have given to you, dear reader, these facts without any addition, in naked fidelity, the way I received them and partially witnessed them myself."[84]

In equating his case history with naked facts, Kerner sets out to conceal his own role as narrator and author of the case history. In the second edition of his treatise, Kerner rejects the charge that his own magnetic treatment and his "manic desire to see ghosts" had "put these ghosts into Mrs. H. in the first place."[85] Instead of acknowl-edging that it might have been his own observation that altered or even produced the observed facts, Kerner claims unconvincingly and in diametrical contrast to Hoffmann's representation of animal magnetism as an instrument of control and coercion: "But Mrs. H. was self-contained and not in any way comparable to a somnambulist who is dependent on the will of a magnetizer."[86]

In her visions, the seeress speaks an "inner language" that cor-responds to the original language of mankind (Figure 9), and she relays detailed information about seven solar circles, the different qualities of spirits, and the relation of soul, spirit, and body. Seeking to buttress the credibility of these revelations, Kerner highlights Friederike Hauffe's lack of formal education. In addition to describ-ing her as "self-contained," he presents the unadulterated clairvoyant as in a state of natural purity, emphasizing that she "never learned a foreign language" and that she was not "artificially educated or trained" in history, geography, or physics.[87]

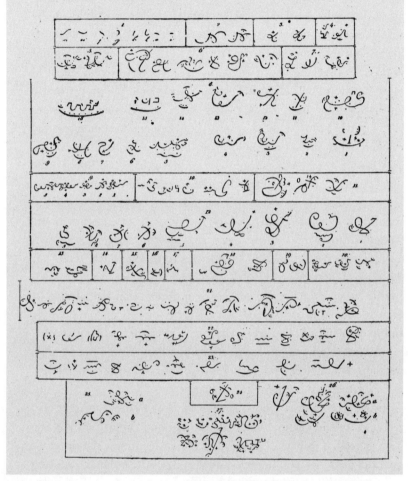

Figure 9. Sample of Mrs. H.'s "inner writing," which ostensibly corresponds to the original human language and the first writing system. From Justinus Kerner, *Die Seherin von Prevorst* (Stuttgart, 1829).

Even though he treated his patient for several years, Kerner denies any role of his own that would go beyond merely witnessing and documenting Mrs. H.'s "inner life" and her visions. In this respect, his treatise *The Seeress of Prevorst* parallels *The Dolorous Passion of Our Lord Jesus Christ: According to the Contemplations of the God-Blessed Anna Katharina Emmerich* (1834). The Romantic poet Clemens Brentano published that text after he had spent several years, from 1817 until her death in 1824, at the bedside of the stigmatized nun. In daily visits interrupted only by a short interval, Brentano took detailed notes of her visions, which provided a picture of Jesus's final days and of Mary's life.[88] Mel Gibson's *The Passion of the Christ*, released in 2004, draws on Brentano's account of Emmerich's visions as its main source, while Kerner's claim of giving a purely factual description of Hauffe's visions is upheld in a 1958 reissue whose ninth edition is still in print in Germany today. In its introduction, the editor justifies the abridgments of the original text by stating: "The revised edition at hand aimed for separating the story of the 'seeress' from all time-bound thoughts and speculations, thereby allowing for a pure presentation of the facts observed."[89]

In the early to mid-nineteenth century, treatises such as Chauncy H. Townshend's *Facts in Mesmerism* (1840) made similar claims of factuality, claims that were also upheld in philosophical texts by Fichte, Schelling, and Hegel.[90] In 1836, Schopenhauer published *On the Will in Nature* with the immodest, but telling subtitle *A Discussion of the Corroborations from the Empirical Sciences That the Author's Philosophy Has Received Since Its First Appearance*. The fifth and longest chapter introduces mesmerism and animal magnetism as factual proof of his metaphysical theory of the will.[91] In the opening pages of his *Essay on Spirit Seeing*, Schopenhauer likewise asserted: "A person who nowadays doubts the facts of animal magnetism and its clairvoyance is not incredulous but ignorant."[92] Yet in elucidating the assumption that at a dying person can appear before various absent friends in different places at the same time, Schopenhauer likens fact and storytelling by affirming: "The case has been narrated and verified so often and from such different sources that I accept it without hesitation as founded on fact."[93]

This reliance on narration as tantamount to empirical proof is constitutive of how Schopenhauer corroborates his metaphysical claims. What a skeptical reader might interpret as adherence to the generic conventions of the ghost story—"the perfect resemblance in the wholly characteristic course of events and in the nature of the alleged apparitions"[94]—serves for Schopenhauer as a marker of truth. Instead of engaging in a protostructuralist analysis of a literary genre, he draws on this "perfect resemblance" in order to extrapolate general characteristics of a ghostly apparition as such. Schopenhauer concedes that his empirical basis consists of a "few cases and ghost narratives...which have become typical through endless repetition."[95] But he never doubts the factuality of these stories. In *Dreams of a Spirit Seer*, Kant had criticized the intrusion of ghost narratives upon the discursive realm of academic philosophy, denouncing the "haunting circulation" of these tales as hearsay and rumor. Schopenhauer, by contrast, adopts a thoroughly positive perspective on contemporaneous print culture and its repetition of these narratives in pamphlets, journals, anthologies, and monographs. Similar to Gosch in *Fragments on the Circulation of Ideas* (see Chapter 3), Schopenhauer therefore praises steamships and railways as new modes of communication that promote an "exchange of ideas" and thereby serve as a means of enlightenment.[96]

In presenting "the facts of animal magnetism and its clairvoyance" as beyond any doubt, Schopenhauer comes surprisingly close to Kerner's equation of storytelling with pure factuality. Schopenhauer even goes so far as to describe animal magnetism as an experimental science that provides new and valuable data: "From the philosophical point of view...animal magnetism is the most significant of all the discoveries that have ever been made.... It is...a kind of experimental metaphysics."[97] Yet even though he invokes this parallel between animal magnetism and experimental physics, Schopenhauer simultaneously upholds the importance of philosophical reflection: "Even in mere physics the experiments

THE MARVELOUS FACTS OF ANIMAL MAGNETISM

and facts are far from providing us with a real insight, but we need their correct interpretation for this, which is often very difficult to attain. How much more will this be the case with the mysterious facts of a metaphysics that manifests itself empirically! Rational or theoretical metaphysics will therefore have to keep up with it so that the treasures discovered here may be unearthed. But a time will come when philosophy, animal magnetism, and the natural sciences, which have made unparalleled progress in all branches, will shed so bright a light on each other that truths will be discovered at which we could not otherwise hope to arrive."[98] Similar assumptions were formulated at the end of the nineteenth century by authors such as Carl du Prel, who imagined a collaboration of occultists, scientists, and engineers as leading to the invention and construction of new technical devices. (See Chapter 5.) But Schopenhauer never elucidated in more detail what experiments he considered as conducive of this kind of synergy between philosophy, animal magnetism, and the natural sciences.

In his *Essay on Spirit Seeing*, Schopenhauer replicates Kerner's equation of narrative with "pure facts," and he quotes several times from *The Seeress of Prevorst* as providing a factual corroboration of his philosophical claims.[99] Yet immediately after invoking the "new truths" that will be discovered through a cooperation of experimental and theoretical philosophy, Schopenhauer seeks to demarcate his notion of "experimental metaphysics" from more popular authors who expect the solution of metaphysical problems from somnambulist clairvoyants: "Yet in this connection we should not pay any attention to the metaphysical utterances and doctrines of somnambulists. For these are almost always miserable views which have sprung from dogmas learned by the somnambulist and mixed with what she happens to find in the mind of her magnetizer; they are therefore not worthy of our attention. Through magnetism we also see the way opened up to information concerning spirit apparitions. Nonetheless...this path...must lie midway between the credulity of our Justinus Kerner, so estimable and meritorious in other respects, and the view...which admits of no other order of nature than a mechanical one."[100]

By formulating this critique of Kerner's credulity, Schopenhauer implicitly casts doubt on Kerner's description of Friederike Hauffe as "self-contained" and independent from his thoughts and expectations, for Hauffe's metaphysical revelations can also be characterized as "dogmas learned by the somnambulist and mixed with what she happens to find in the mind of her magnetizer." The distinction between a proper and a trivial notion of experimental metaphysics serves to segregate Schopenhauer's acceptance and philosophical interpretation of the "facts of animal magnetism" from the replication of worn-out metaphysical doctrines in Kerner's *The Seeress of Prevorst* or other contemporaneous treatises, such as Alphonse Cahagnet's *The Celestial Telegraph; or, The Secrets of the Life to Come, Revealed Through Magnetism* (1851).[101]

Kerner himself similarly feels compelled to assert time and again that his account of Mrs. H. is based on "pure facts" whose explanation is left to the reader's discretion and that his description of the seeress as caught in the moment of death is "the literal truth and no poetic fiction." But even though he distinguishes between his own text and the figurative discourse of literary fiction, Kerner nonetheless introduces a thought experiment into his ostensibly pure and factual case history when he writes: "If we can think of a person as arrested for years in these moments (which in the dying are often like mere lightning flashes), then we have the exact picture of this seeress." As we will see in the following, it is this thought experiment inherent to and constitutive of Kerner's presentation of "pure facts" that lends itself to a literary, fictional adaptation of the case history, one that imitates and undermines Kerner's claims by pretending to be real.

Edgar Allan Poe's "The Facts in the Case of M. Valdemar"

In a literary text first published in December 1845, Edgar Allan Poe transformed Kerner's documentation of the "Facts at Weinsberg" into a narrative entitled "The Facts in the Case of M. Valdemar." In May 1843, Margaret Fuller, the American Transcendentalist and women's rights advocate, had written a letter to Ralph Waldo

Emerson in which she praised *The Seeress of Prevorst* as "a really good book."[102] Fuller's *Summer on the Lakes* (1844) also contained a summary of the case history and a translation of various passages from Kerner's treatise.[103] In March 1845 an abridged translation of Kerner's *The Seeress* by Catherine Crowe came out in London and in New York under the title *The Seeress of Prevorst: Being Revelations Concerning the Inner-Life of Man and the Inter-Diffusion of a World of Spirits in the One We Inhabit.*[104] The American edition was advertised in *The Broadway Journal*, a weekly edited by Edgar Allan Poe, on August 2, 1845, as on sale for twenty-five cents.

The proximity of Poe's "The Facts in the Case of M. Valdemar" to Crowe's abridged translation of Kerner's case history earned Poe the accusation of plagiarism in a text published anonymously in 1855.[105] But the literary scholarship on Poe has either ignored Kerner's *The Seeress of Prevorst* or restricted its focus to how Kerner and Poe describe the final moments of Friederike Hauffe and Valdemar.[106] However, viewed more broadly, we now can see how Poe's ostensibly scientific, documentary mode of narration emulates Kerner's emphatic claim of documenting "pure facts" and how the storyline of Poe's novella is built on giving an unexpected twist to Kerner's account of Mrs. H. hovering between life and death.

Introducing the novella, the unnamed narrator presents his minutes on the case of Valdemar as a reaction to the circulation of distorted and exaggerated rumors, rumors that he intends to correct by a factual and accurate report: "It is now rendered necessary that I give the facts."[107] But in adapting Kerner's claim of giving pure facts, Poe's narrative transforms Kerner's account of Hauffe's spiritual visions into a disturbing story about physical decay. In Catherine Crowe's translation, the seeress of Prevorst is characterized in the following manner: "We know that men, in the moment of dying, have often glimpses of the other world, and evince their knowledge of it. We see that a spirit partially leaves the body, before it has wholly shaken off its earthly husk. Could we thus maintain any one for years in the condition of a dying person, we should have the exact representation of Mrs. H—'s condition. And this is not the language of fiction, but of simple truth."[108] At the beginning of the second part of the text, we furthermore read: "We have seen in the former part of this volume, how this nerve-spirit—arrested, as it were, in the act of dying—became sensible of the spiritual properties of all things."[109] Margaret Fuller similarly defines the liminal state of the somnambulist clairvoyant in her *Summer on the Lakes*: "She was, as Kerner truly describes her, like one arrested in the act of dying and detained in her body by magnetic influences."[110]

Yet in Poe's narrative, any figurative quality of "as it were" or "like one" has disappeared. The narrator literally arrests Valdemar in the act of dying and detains him in that state by putting him into a magnetic trance. As we have seen, Kerner himself had introduced a thought experiment into his ostensibly factual description of Mrs. H.: "If we can think of a person as arrested for years in these moments (which in the dying are often like mere lightning flashes), then we have the exact picture of this seeress." The American edition of the case history renders this sentence as: "Could we thus maintain any one for years in the condition of a dying person, we should have the exact representation of Mrs. H—'s condition." Crowe's transformation of "if we can think" into "could we thus maintain" suggests the possibility of implementing Kerner's thought experiment in the real world. But Crowe's statement is still in the modality of the subjunctive: "*Could* we thus maintain...."

In the diegetic universe of Poe's novella, by contrast, we encounter an actual, real-life experiment that is meant to generate new knowledge. The narrator's scientific curiosity leads him to identify a gap in previous research into animal magnetism. He therefore envisages and enacts an experiment that has not been undertaken before: "My attention, for the last three years, had been repeatedly drawn to the subject of Mesmerism; and, about nine months ago, it occurred to me, quite suddenly, that in the series of experiments hitherto, there had been a very remarkable and most unaccountable omission:—no person had as yet been mesmerized *in articulo mortis*. It remained to be seen...to what extent or for how long a period, the encroachments of Death might be arrested by the process."[111]

Not only has Kerner's thought experiment, already closer to its practical implementation in Crowe's translation, morphed into an actual, real-life experiment in Poe's novella, but Poe's text further adapts Kerner's account of Mrs. H.'s liminal position between life and death. In *The Seeress of Prevorst*, Friederike Hauffe arrives as a "picture of death" in Weinsberg, and she remains for seven years "arrested by some fixation...between life and death." Yet Kerner's case history implies that she is detained on the threshold *to* or *before* death in a state of suffering and misery. In Poe's text, by contrast, the test subject, Valdemar, who suffers from tuberculosis and who has been magnetized just in time by the narrator, truly dies. The tale represents the boundary between life and death as being crossed at the very moment in which "a marked change" comes over the face of the sleeping Valdemar and his lower jaw suddenly falls open to reveal a swollen and blackened tongue.[112] The ostensibly abolished binary opposition between life and death is thereby reintroduced into the diegetic universe of the story. At the same time, Valdemar's death functions as the turning point of the novella, similar to Maria's fainting spell in Hoffmann's "The Magnetizer." The narrator builds suspense and announces the catastrophic shift of events after this moment by declaring: "I now feel that I have reached a point of this narrative at which every reader will be startled into positive disbelief."[113]

After this turning point, Valdemar's vital functions have ceased. He no longer breathes, and the blood in his body no longer circulates. Only Valdemar's tongue transmits messages from the beyond, like "the trembling tongue of steel" of the contemporaneous needle telegraph.[114] Cahagnet's mesmerist treatise *The Celestial Telegraph* promised revelations about the afterlife in its subtitle, *The Secrets of the Life to Come, Revealed Through Magnetism*. But the narrator's minutes of the facts in the case of M. Valdemar do not provide any positive account of what to expect in the beyond. Poe's tale "The Mesmeric Revelation" (1844), which had been published one year earlier, consisted of a long dialogue between the narrator and a magnetized somnambulist named Vankirk. In it, Vankirk reiterates

Schubert's account of magnetic trance as analogous to death by pronouncing: "The mesmeric condition is so near death as to content me."[115] Before he passes away, still in a state of somnambulism, Vankirk also makes detailed and stereotypical declarations about God, spirit, ether, and matter. "Mesmeric Revelation" thereby comes close to the "metaphysical utterances of somnambulists" denounced by Schopenhauer as "miserable views" in his *Essay on Spirit Seeing*. The narrator's account of Valdemar's case, by contrast, withholds any information about the spiritual realm of the beyond. In lieu of relaying information about the other world, Valdemar responds to the question whether he is still sleeping with the laconic statement: "Yes; —no;—I *have been* sleeping—and now—now—*I am dead*."[116]

Kerner's ostensibly factual documentation of how the spiritual world intrudes upon our own is thus transformed into a pseudomedical case history. Apart from the fainting of the medical student and note taker Mr. L——l, the experiment produces the following result: "It was evident that, so far, death (or what is usually termed death) had been arrested by the mesmeric process."[117] And while Friederike Hauffe is arrested for seven years between life and death, Valdemar is detained in this state for seven months before the narrator wakes him from his magnetic trance—with the unintended consequence that his body decomposes before the narrator's eyes: "As I rapidly made the mesmeric passes, amid ejaculations of 'dead! dead!' absolutely bursting from the tongue and not from the lips of the sufferer, his whole frame at once—within the space of a single minute, or even less, shrunk—crumbled—absolutely rotted away beneath my hands. Upon the bed, before that whole company, there lay a nearly liquid mass of loathsome—of detestable putridity."[118]

The accelerated, gory conclusion is the last in a sequence of shocks administered by Poe's narrative. In a comparable focus on ghastly detail, the narrator earlier indulges in a lengthy description of how Valdemar's swollen and blackened tongue becomes visible in his moment of death before he announces: "I presume that no member of the party then present had been unaccostumed to death-bed horrors; but so hideous beyond conception was the appearance of M.

Valdemar at this moment, that there was a general shrinking back from the region of the bed."[119] Under the guise of providing detailed scientific information, the text aims for the production of terror and shock in the reader. Commenting on Valdemar's declaration "I *have been* sleeping—and now—now—*I am dead*," the narrator himself characterizes "these few words" as "well calculated to convey" terror. The fainting of the medical student and note taker L——l thus stands in as an exaggerated version of the reader's intended response to the horrifying and revolting story.

Although the narrator announces "a point of this narrative at which every reader will be startled into positive disbelief," and although the tale does have a startling and unsettling impact, its sensational shock effects actually serve to suppress a skeptical reaction of "disbelief." The narrator's pseudoscientific invocation of sudden, accelerated physical decay comes close to emulating Tieck's account of how the marvelous subdues our rational faculties: "it is this suddenness that makes the poet's art of lending [the marvelous] the semblance of truth less necessary; he only needs to ensure that its occurrence shocks and terrifies, thereby winning our illusion completely, for the terror that we feel silences reason and its judgments."

Poe's masterful production of terror and disgust, the careful avoidance of worn-out metaphysical doctrines about the beyond, and the ostensibly factual mode of narration led many readers to consider the text an authentic account of real events. The tale was first published in the December issue of *The American Review*, where it was printed between an article about the "positions and duties" of the Whig Party and a poem entitled "The Flight of Helle."[120] That the end of Poe's story and the beginning of the poem were placed on the same page could be taken as implying that both texts belong to the realm of aesthetic literature. But the journal did not provide any explicit heading or marker that indicated the status of the narrative. On December 20, 1845, the story was reprinted in the *Broadway Journal*, a weekly magazine edited by Poe himself, where the following remarks introduced the text: "*The Facts in the case of M. Valdemar*. An article of ours, thus entitled, was published in the last number of Mr. Colton's 'American Review,' and has given rise to some discussion—especially in regard to the truth or falsity of the statements made. It does not become us, of course, to offer one word on the point at issue. We have been requested to reprint the article, and do so with pleasure. We leave it to speak for itself. We may observe, however, that there are a certain class of people who pride themselves upon Doubt, as a profession."[121]

In its next number, the *Broadway Journal* published an excerpt from a letter sent to Poe by Robert H. Collyer, a medical doctor and expert in mesmerism, who wrote from Boston: "Your account of M. Valdemar's Case has been universally copied in this city, and has created a very great sensation. It requires from me no apology, in stating, that I have not the least doubt of the *possibility* of such a phenomenon." Soliciting further information about the case, Collyer hoped to counter "the growing impression that your account is merely a splendid creation of your own brain, not having any truth in fact." But Poe's printed editorial response stated: "the truth is, there was a very small modicum of truth in the case of M. Valdemar."[122] Nonetheless, the narrative was reprinted in Philadelphia and in Baltimore and, in January 1846, in London.[123] There, the *Sunday Times*, the *Morning Post*, and the *Popular Record of Modern Science* published the narrative in under the title "Mesmerism in America: The Death of M. Valdemar of New York," introduced by various editorial disclaimers that described *The American Review* as a "respectable periodical" before leaving it to the readers' discretion whether to take the narrative as genuine or not.[124] In being placed next to factual stories, Poe's novella thus renewed the genre's claim to be reporting "news" that is based on a real, unheard-of incident.

In late January 1846, the text then came out as a pamphlet under the title *Mesmerism "in articulo mortis": An Astounding & Horrifying Narrative, Shewing the Extraordinary Power of Mesmerism in Arresting the Progress of Death.*[125] The actual story was again preceded by an editorial announcement: "The following astonishing narrative first appeared in the *American Magazine* [sic], a work of some standing in the United States, where the case has excited the most intense interest.... The narrative, though only a plain recital of facts, is of so extraordinary a nature as almost to surpass belief. It is only necessary to add, that credence is given to it in America, where the occurrence took place."

The editorial note enacts the power of print to produce "credence" in a self-referential gesture. It cites the *American Review*, which is wrongly named the *American Magazine*, as "a work of some standing in the United States" before unequivocally stating that the occurrence did take place in America. In April 1846, the *Popular Record of Modern Science* revealed that the story was only fiction after it had received a letter from Poe to that effect. But the pamphlet edition continued to circulate, inciting one faithful reader in November 1846 to write a letter to Poe in order to ascertain the factuality of the narrative. Despite his belief in the veracity of print and in the theories of animal magnetism, Poe's correspondent, Archibald Ramsay, a Scottish pharmacist, was uncertain about whether to take the narrative as fiction or fact: "As a believer in Mesmerism I respectfully take the liberty of addressing you to know, if a pamphlet lately published in London ... under the authority of your name & entitled *Mesmerism, in Articulo-Mortis*, is genuine. It details an account of some *most extraordinary circumstances*, connected with the death of a M M Valdemar under mesmeric influence, *by you. Hoax* has been emphatically pronounced upon the pamphlet by all who have seen it here, and for the sake of the Science and of truth a note from you on the subject would truly oblige."[126]

Poe's response, on December 30, 1846, went like this: "'Hoax' *is* precisely the word suited to M. Valdemar's case. The story appeared originally in 'The American Review,' a Monthly Magazine published in this city. The London papers, commencing with the 'Morning Post' and the 'Popular Record of Science' [*sic*], took up the theme. The article was generally copied in England and is now circulating in France. Some few persons believe it—but *I* do not—and don't you."[127]

Poe's letter may serve as a fitting coda to our investigation of ghost narratives and their circulation in eighteenth-century and nineteenth-century print culture. Kant opened his *Dreams of a Spirit*

Seer by turning against the intrusion of ostensibly authentic ghost narratives upon the discursive realm of academic philosophy, deploring the "haunting circulation" of these tales. Referring to contemporaneous print culture in more positive terms, Schopenhauer conceded in his *Essay on Spirit Seeing* that the empirical foundation of his metaphysical claims consisted of a "few ghost narratives" that had "become typical through endless repetition." But Schopenhauer upheld his belief in the "facts of animal magnetism," and he praised the new communication technologies of railways and steamships, technologies that also allowed for the rapid transatlantic dissemination of Poe's narrative, as promoting an "exchange of ideas" and as a means of enlightenment. Poe's letter, by contrast, undermines any simple equation of print culture with enlightenment by giving an account of how the seemingly genuine narrative is printed and reprinted in numerous journals and newspapers. Even after Poe had explicitly declared that the story was not authentic, readers such as Archibald Ramsay remained in doubt as to whether the narrative was based on fact or fiction. The persistence of this fallacy speaks to a belief in the veracity of the printed word that was not easily shattered, even though the wide dissemination and durability of pamphlets and journals did not imply that their content was factual. In the late eighteenth century, Herder already had taken note of this phenomenon by comparing the medium of print to rumor and by describing the printing press as "giving wings to rags that have been scrawled on."

In "The Facts in the Case of M. Valdemar," it is also the allure of the ostensibly scientific, documentary mode of writing by Poe's narrator that produces readings of the narrative as based on fact.[128] In a letter from April 1846, the contemporaneous British poet Elizabeth Barrett remarked upon how Poe's narrative was "going the rounds of the newspapers." But Barrett focused on Poe's narrative mode of producing reality effects, explicitly comparing "The Facts in the Case of M. Valdemar" to the "ghost story," which also throws its readers into "dreadful doubts as to whether it can be true." In terms that resemble Ludwig Tieck's in his essay "Shakespeare's Treatment of the Marvelous," Barrett concluded: "The certain thing in the tale in question is the power of the writer and the faculty he has of making horrible improbabilities seem near & familiar."[129]

In his letter to Archibald Ramsay, Edgar Allan Poe described "The Facts in the Case of M. Valdemar" as a "hoax." But the tale is a surprisingly complex appropriation of Kerner's *The Seeress of Prevorst*, one that emulates and undermines Kerner's and Schopenhauer's acceptance of the marvelous facts of animal magnetism.

CHAPTER FIVE

Psychic Television

Much of what the old fairytales promised has been delivered by the latest technology: radio brings distant voices into a room where no-one is speaking; even television is becoming thinkable, which, in the midst of the soberest scientific worldview, takes us into the realms of the magic mirror.

—Ernst Bloch, *The Anxiety of the Engineer*

The occultist can reveal to the engineer the problems of the future; he can change the blind finder of technology into a purposeful inventor. But it is the engineer who can offer the occultist a scientific explanation for human beings' magical faculties.

—Carl du Prel, *Magic as Natural Science: Part 1 — Magical Physics*

On March 8, 1929, Germany's state postal agency presented its first wireless television broadcast. The medium-wave transmitter at Berlin-Witzleben relayed a number of moving and still images—a man smoking, a pair of pliers opening and closing, letters of the alphabet—that were received in various parts of the city. The picture quality was poor. Because the transmitted images consisted of just thirty lines, only close-ups were recognizable on the tiny four-square-inch screens. In addition, technical limitations permitted the transmission of only twelve and a half images per second. The images appearing on viewers' screens therefore flickered considerably. Nonetheless, the first television broadcast in Germany appeared promising.

Three months later, Robert Bosch GmbH, Zeiss Ikon, and the British company Baird Television founded Fernseh AG (Television

Ltd.). During the following years, this new company, along with its competitor Telefunken and the state postal agency itself, attempted in vain to establish the television set as a profitable mass product. Early models from this period included devices such as Denes von Mihaly's Volksempfänger (People's Receiver) and John Logie Baird's Televisor. On September 30, 1929, the British Broadcasting Corporation began the regular transmission of an experimental television program that would be interrupted only by the Second World War. Using the Baird system, a medium-wave transmitter in London broadcast five days a week for half an hour. Since both image and sound still had to be relayed on the same frequency, their transmission was at first possible only in alternating two-minute cycles. In the imagination of contemporaneous engineers, however, this technical limitation had long since been overcome: they emphasized that at the same time as the sound film was expanding the previously silent cinema, television offered the prospect of "extending the purely acoustic radio into the optical realm." As Hans Bredow announced: "Film and radio both stand on the verge of a new and important stage of their development. While film has hitherto merely transmitted sense impressions to the eye, now the ear, too, will play a part in receiving sound films.... In contrast, while [radio] was solely directed toward the ear, television will in the future appeal to the eyes of a previously 'sound-only' audience."[1]

The hybridity of image and sound also characterized the film clip *Weekend*, recorded toward the end of 1929 and later to become a model for early German television.[2] The film showed two young women, Schura von Finkelstein and Imogen Orkutt, singing a German folk song, "Listen to What's Coming in from Outside."[3] For the medium of television, the words "Look what's coming in from outside" would of course have been more appropriate, all the more so because the film strip's repeated broadcasts took place without any accompanying soundtrack. But the wording of the song's opening lines deserves to be taken seriously, since the focus on what was coming "from outside" into the living room also shaped cultural perceptions of the new medium, often designated "home cinema"

(*Heimkino*). In April 1929, the magazine *At Home: A German Family Paper* published an article entitled "Telecinema in Your Home," beginning with the words: "Things which we had to run after, now come to us at home."[4] Also in 1929, in the magazine *Broadcast*, Eduard Rhein noted: "The world will be brought to us in our own room."[5] Rhein, later to found the enormously successful radio and television magazine *Listen* (*Hör zu*), continued euphorically: "Everything that interests us will be made visible on a little screen in our own home.... Our wildest dreams are now becoming marvelous reality." In an essay on the future of radio, Warschauer similarly contended: "Of all inventions of our time, wireless television is perhaps not only the most magical, but also the most consequential.... By this means, a selection of the whole world will be delivered to our homes."[6]

It was with nearly identical terms, however, that authors such as Ernst Bloch and Eugen Diesel conjured the sinister side of the newly emerging medium in "The Anxiety of the Engineer" and "The Uncanny of the Technological Age," both dating from 1929. While Bloch compared television's "latest technology" with the "realms of the magic mirror," Diesel wrote: "What was hitherto seen only in dreams or belonged to the realm of the miraculous is now available in everyday experience."[7] In a vague reference to Sigmund Freud's essay from 1919, the son of the famous inventor defined the uncanny as "a sudden, ghostly appearance."[8] Apart from a "mechanical uncanny," arising "directly from the machine in itself," he further described an "uncanny 'of the second kind'... dissolving old measures of time and space."[9] According to Diesel, in this way, "a whole new artificial world" was coming into being, a world "in which nothing could be certain," because material reality appeared only as a ghostly phantom on the screen or magic mirror in the living room.[10]

Television in 1929 was thus regarded as the uncanny (*unheimlich*) occurrence of the supernatural or marvelous in one's own living room. Evidence for this is not limited to contemporaneous advertisements depicting television sets as magical crystal balls (Figure 10). In the same year, 1929, the spiritualist *Journal for Psychic Research*

Figure 10. Advertisement in *Television* (September 1934).

printed an article entitled "Domestic Phenomena" next to other pieces such as "Metaplasma Phenomena," "Phenomena of Possession," and an obituary for Albert von Schrenck-Notzing, a famous German spiritualist and physician who had died in February.[11] After a short digression on occult "clairvoyance" (*Hellsehen*), the author, a retired justice named Driessen, outlined various supernatural phenomena, including "nocturnal wall inscriptions," "inexplicable light apparitions," and "knocking sounds." These manifestations had taken place in Driessen's own "solidly built 1903 family house," located not in Berlin-Witzleben, but in Witzenhausen, a small town by the river Werra in Hesse. Without explicitly referring to electrical television, the article specified a "small cupboard bearing family portraits" in a corner of the living room as the "main location" of these phenomena.[12]

The coincidence of texts from 1929 describing occult "domestic phenomena" and the magical properties of the new technology in one's own home can be related to a structural and mutually constitutive interrelation of television and clairvoyance. Walter Benjamin understood spiritualism and occultism to be the "flip side" (*Kehrseite*) of technological development.[13] However, spiritualist research into the psychic television of somnambulist mediums functioned as a necessary, but not sufficient condition for the invention and implementation of the technological medium. Spanning from the late nineteenth century into the first decades of the twentieth century, television's gradual emergence relied not only on technical, but also on cultural materialities. The slow accumulation of technical and physical knowledge, beginning around 1890, accelerating in the 1920s, and enabling the first wireless transmissions of moving pictures in the last years of that decade was intimately linked to ostensibly marginal cultural contexts that have been ignored within the history of technology. Occultist studies of psychic "clairvoyance" (*Hellsehen*) and "television" (*Fernsehen*), carried out in the same period by spiritualists who emulated the rules and procedures of science thus played a constitutive role in the technological inventions and developments of electrical television.

143

Placed in a larger theoretical context, such an approach to the archaeology of media addresses the complex relation between technology and culture by avoiding a simple determinism that, in its focus on a technological a priori, threatens to reduce culture to a mere epiphenomenon. The influential media theorist Friedrich Kittler has provided us with important insights into how new information technologies give rise to cultural change. But in defining the materiality of a medium, Kittler adopts an exclusive focus on hardware and technology. As a result, he asserts that "literatures or fantasies are...irrelevant" for the conception of television.[14] In Kittler's view, it is technology that generates spiritualism, not the other way around. A more circumspect analysis, however, reveals the interdependence of electrical and psychic television as presupposing each other. The archaeology of the medium therefore testifies to a reciprocal interaction between the cultural and the technical materialities of television as a newly emerging medium. Or to put it in terms of classical logic: while spiritualism serves as a necessary (but not sufficient) condition for the invention of electrical television, the emerging technology simultaneously fulfills the very same function for spiritualist research on psychic telesight.

The notion that the concept of television emerged from a two-directional exchange between occultism and technology immediately gains plausibility when recalling equivalent coinages such as "telegraphy," "telepathy," "telephony," "telekinesis," and "teleplasty."[15] Even the German term *Fernsehen* ("television," or "remote viewing"), which, according to recent studies, was employed for the first time in Raphael Eduard Liesegang's 1891 book *The Phototel: Contributions on the Problem of Electrical Television*, appeared in the same year in Charles Richet's *Experimental Studies in the Field of Thought Transmission and So-Called Clairvoyance.*[16] The author, a French physician who would receive the Nobel Prize for Medicine in 1913, also wrote novels on demonic possession under the pseudonym Charles Epheyre. His spiritualist study was published under his own name with a prestigious medical press and examined "psychic actions at a distance" such as "telepathy," "telaesthesia," "clairvoyance,"[17] as well as "television."[18] In numerous supposedly scientifically verified experiments conducted by Richet, his sensitive clairvoyants were able to transcend space and time, describing remote buildings or objects in such detail that it was as if "they had the room and the objects in question before their eyes."[19] The mediums thus functioned like a psychic equivalent to a technical apparatus for the transmission of images registered by Paul Nipkow as the "electrical telescope" at the German Imperial Patent Office in January 1884 and intended "to make visible at any arbitrarily chosen point B an object located at point A."[20]

Nipkow's device was based on the segmentation of an image into individual lines, a principle first devised in 1843 by Alexander Bain, a Scottish inventor whose model for the transmission of images already contained the idea of scanning two-dimensional surfaces line by line. However, since Bain could not satisfactorily resolve the problems associated with synchronizing sender and receiver, his image telegraph was rarely put to practical use.[21] Forty years later, Nipkow's electrical telescope depended upon a revolving disk with holes arranged in a spiral around its edge. As the disk rotated, light passing through the holes rendered it possible to scan an object point by point and line by line.[22] The spatial contiguity of individual picture elements was thereby transformed into a temporal sequence of electrical signals to be transmitted by wire before being reassembled into a coherent picture by the receiver.

Prior to being supplanted in the 1930s by the electronic tube systems of Vladimir Kosma Zworykin and Manfred von Ardenne, nearly all of the early electromechanical television devices from the late nineteenth and the early twentieth centuries relied on selenium. This chemical element, discovered by Jöns Jacob Berzelius in 1817, owed "its significance to a marvelous property by which its resistance drops considerably under the influence of light."[23] Its photosensitivity was discovered by chance in 1873 by the British engineer Willoughby Smith and his assistant, Joseph May, during the laying of transatlantic undersea telegraph cables. Two years later, Werner von Siemens constructed the first selenium cell, which, like the subsequent photocell, allowed for the "conversion of an optical into an electrical image."[24]

Translating images into signals that can be relayed and reconverted into images—this principle was outlined in comparable form in those spiritualist texts that formulated a theory of psychic television. A number of works in the field of electrical engineering, such as Liesegang's *The Phototel*, Benedict Schöffler's *Phototelegraphy and Electrical Television* (1898), and Fritz Lux's *The Electrical Televisor* (1903), described devices, frequently interrelated and based on each another, that depended on the use of selenium and employed mechanical systems, akin to the Nipkow disk, for the scanning and generation of images.[25] At the same time, a theory of occult messages or "dispatches" (*Depeschen*)[26] was being developed in texts such as Carl du Prel's *The Discovery of the Soul by Means of the Secret Sciences, Vol. 2: Television and Action at a Distance* (1895), Walter Bormann's *The Norns: Inquiries into Television in Space and Time* (1909), and J. Körmann-Alzech's *Marvels and Secrets from throughout the Ages Revealed–Vol. 4: Telepathy, Thought Transmission, Thought Reading, Cumberland, Television, Action at a Distance, Second Sight* (1904).[27] Just as in electrical television, the signals of these occult broadcasts were "transformed by the terminal station [*Endstation*] into perceptible images [*anschauliche Bilder*]."[28] Walter Bormann similarly describes "subjective visions" in which "the telepathically affected receiver converts the message into a perceptible image."[29]

One of the most prolific of these spiritualist authors was du Prel, who, in addition to publishing numerous essays and books, edited part of Kant's metaphysical lectures in 1889. Du Prel, drawing on the philosophical theories of Kant and Schopenhauer, defined "television" as a function of the "transcendental subject."[30] In his 1895 treatise *The Discovery of the Soul*, he describes "television" as "a viewing of images" (*ein bildliches Schauen*).[31] Moreover, in contrast to many spiritualist authors, du Prel distinguishes between "clairvoyance" (*Hellsehen*) and "television" (*Fernsehen*) according to the distance between sender and receiver. Whereas clairvoyance takes place only "at close range," television allows "distances of many miles" to be overcome.[32] In the latter case, "a perceptible image" (*ein anschauliches Bild*) enters the mind of the somnambulist medium and reveals "the finest details," corresponding "precisely to reality."[33] Of course, du Prel adds, it is not a matter of "seeing in the physiological sense" when "one sees an event taking place at a distance of many miles."[34] "Telesight" (*Ferngesicht*) is thus not based "on peripheral stimulation of the optic nerves," but arises from "brain presentations" (*Gehirnvorstellungen*), which are then transformed into "images existing in space" and projected towards the exterior.[35] According to du Prel, the brain cannot actively create this "telesight." Instead, it can only "passively receive such impressions, which are then transformed into perceptible images, by way of the brain's normal functioning."[36]

In an effort to designate the material medium carrying these wireless transmissions, psychical researchers referred to various categories borrowed from the natural sciences. Cesare Lombroso invoked the concept of radioactivity, which had emerged subsequent to the discoveries by Antoine Henri Becquerel and Marie Curie in 1896. William Crookes considered X-rays, first observed by Wilhelm Röntgen in 1895 and not integrated into the electromagnetic wave spectrum until 1912, as the medium underlying the "transmission of . . . images from one mind to another, without the agency of the recognised organs of sense."[37] The spiritualist Lazar von Hellenbach named the "ether" and Carl du Prel the "od" as the bearer of wirelessly transmitted messages.[38]

In particular, the belief in an all-pervasive "ether," a material, yet weightless substance that was often invoked in idealist and mesmerist theories around 1800, appears to have gained renewed scientific respectability at the end of the nineteenth century. After discovering the electromagnetic wave spectrum in 1887–88, Heinrich Hertz stated: "It is thus certain that all space of which we have knowledge is not empty, but rather is filled with ether, a substance capable of propagating waves."[39] He was not alone in adhering to this assumption. Among English physicists, particularly among the followers of James Clerk Maxwell, Hertz's proof that "there are electrical or magnetic waves that radiate in the same way as light waves" was also taken to confirm the mysterious medium's reality.[40] This belief was retained even after Einstein formulated his special theory of relativity, which in 1905 stringently refuted the existence of ether and therefore at first met with substantial opposition.[41] The category of ether, oscillating across the borderlines between occultism and physics, thus continued to serve as "scientific" authentication for a variety of theories that described occult mental rays—or for the postulation of "od vibrations" connecting transmitter and receiver by a "psychomagnetic band."[42]

Yet it was not only the notion of "ether waves" that linked representations of psychic and technical television. In addition, spiritualist texts introduced the concepts of "sympathy" or "psychophysical attunement" between transmitter and receiver to address the often difficult synchronization of image scanner and image generator.[43] Electrical television could produce a clear picture only if sender and receiver were precisely tuned to each other, a problem that August Karolus circumvented by mounting two Nipkow disks on a single axis when demonstrating his television system at the University of Leipzig in 1924.[44] In parallel fashion, spiritualist texts indicated that occult television could take place only if a strong "personal involvement" joined the somnambulist medium with the transmitting psyche. Such an involvement might occur at the death of a close relative or at the moment of an accident, bringing about a synchronous "oscillation" of sending and receiving souls and thereby providing the basis for occult television.[45]

In the work of physicists and electrical engineers, references to occult and psychical research remained—with occasional exceptions—mostly implicit. Spiritualist authors, however, aggressively appropriated technical and physical concepts in order to confirm and legitimize the possibility of psychic actions at a distance. In 1896, Marconi's first successful experiments with wireless telegraphy were immediately cited as establishing the possibility of telepathy and thought transmission. The psychical researcher Körmann-Alzech put it succinctly: "Since Marconi invented telegraphy without wires, even the most determined opponents of telepathy must allow for its possibility."[46] In similar terms, Bormann represented the "teleaesthetic band" between transmitter and receiver as "corresponding to wireless telegraphy."[47]

Yet as early as 1895—that is, one year before Marconi's first successful experiments with wireless telegraphy—a model for the wireless transmission of electrical signals can be found in spiritualist texts. In his *The Discovery of the Soul*, Carl du Prel wrote: "Natural science is already on the verge of providing a proof for the possibility of such an action at a distance, a proof based on the transmission of electricity through space without connecting wires. It is obvious that this works by means of the wave movements in the ether. The fact that this wave motion gets through to its target in the case of human action at a distance has at present no other explanation than that the human agent is also capable of television."[48]

Du Prel thus refers to scientific knowledge before its successful technological implementation. But spiritualist theories of thought transmission also appear to have functioned as a cultural blueprint for electrical wireless transmissions. In his 1892 article "Some Possibilities of Electricity," William Crookes, a chemist, physicist, and occultist, had already pointed out that Hertz's discovery of previously unknown electromagnetic waves might render possible the wireless transmission of Morse signals: "Whether vibrations of the ether, longer than those which affect us as light, may not be constantly at work around us, we have, until lately, never seriously enquired. But the researches of Lodge in England and Hertz in Germany give us an almost infinite range of ethereal vibrations or electrical rays.... Here is unfolded for us a new and astonishing world—one which it is hard to conceive should contain no possibilities of transmitting and receiving intelligence. Rays of light will not pierce through a wall.... But the electrical vibrations of a yard or more in wave-length...will easily pierce such mediums.... Here, then is revealed the bewildering possibility of telegraphy without wires, posts, cables or any of our costly appliances. Granted a few reasonable postulates, the whole thing comes well within the realms of possible fulfillment."[49]

According to Crookes, the necessary preconditions for wireless telegraphy included an apparatus to create electrical waves of the desired frequency, sensitive receivers that could be tuned to a particular wavelength, and some method of concentrating electromagnetic waves at a target point in order to facilitate their reception.

The question of whether the first wireless transmission of electrical signals was actually achieved by Marconi in 1896 or whether this already had been accomplished in 1894 by the English physicist and spiritualist Oliver Lodge is therefore of lesser importance in analyzing the relation between occult and technical television.[50] In fact, Lodge closely collaborated with Crookes and, alongside his studies in physics, conducted research into "sympathetic communication between places as distant as India... and England."[51] His texts, apparatuses, and experiments highlight with unusual clarity the reciprocal interaction between occultism and the natural sciences that characterized the cultural construction of new technological media in the late nineteenth century. Both Lodge, an acknowledged physicist at the center of Maxwellian electrodynamics, and Crookes, possibly the most important British chemist of his time, served for several years as presidents of the spiritualist Society for Psychical Research, which in the United States counted William James among its members. Both scientists developed their theories in close connection with their occultist studies.[52] In the same article in which he outlined a research program for the realization of wireless telegraphy, Crookes also referred to experiments with telepathy and thought transmission: "In some parts of the human brain may lurk an organ capable of transmitting and receiving electrical rays of wave-lengths hitherto undetected by instrumental means. These may be instrumental in transmitting thought from one brain to another. In such a way the recognised cases of thought transference and the many instances of 'coincidence' would be explicable."[53]

However, the role of spiritualist theory in the invention of modern communication technologies was not restricted to describing invisible psychic "organs," thereby engendering insight into the possibility of functionally equivalent technical devices. Even in terms of material components, devices developed in occult research played a constitutive role in the emergence of radio and television. Thus, in 1879, Crookes developed the Crookes tube—an early cathode-ray tube intended to prove that "radiation" is the "fourth state of matter."[54] In 1897, Ferdinand Braun transformed Crookes's tube into a measuring instrument,[55] while in 1906, his assistants Max Dieckmann and Gustav Glage registered the first patent to use this "Braunian tube" as an "image writer" (*Bildschreiber*). Also in 1906, Robert von Lieben and Lee de Forest developed the triode, which was likewise based on a vacuum tube and first employed in image telegraphy and radio for the purpose of amplifying electrical signals before and after their transmission by wire or electromagnetic waves.[56] On the level of the material apparatus, one indispensable precondition of technical television—the possibility of amplifying electric signals—can thus be traced back to an electrical device invented by Crookes, who explicitly pointed to the "connexion" between his spiritualist research and his work in the natural sciences.[57] Furthermore, spiritualist theory anticipated this principle of amplification on the discursive level as early as 1894, when du Prel asserted: "By its very nature, television would be made easier if the od radiation were artificially amplified (*verstärkt*)."[58]

In drawing attention to such texts as Liesegang's *Contributions on the Problem of Electrical Television* (1891), Kerstin Bergmann and Siegfried Zielinski have noted: "Everything that in the twentieth century evolved into the media system we have grown accustomed to had already been outlined by the end of the nineteenth century."[59] Yet this conclusion about the archaeology of television should include more than electrical engineering, physics, and science fiction novels such as Albert Robida's *The Twentieth Century*, which in 1883 described televisionlike devices to be used for live transmissions of wars and political assemblies.[60] In addition, the theories and conceptions of electrical television also presupposed contemporaneous spiritualist research into psychic telesight that was linked to the emerging technology in a relation of reciprocal and constitutive exchange. Often taking place unbeknownst to individual researchers, this exchange encompassed discursive figures, concepts, and theories, as well as technical components. Hence, a determinist approach to the history of television can only strive in vain to locate its "origin" in one single domain of knowledge, be it electrical engineering, physics, or occultism. Instead, it is the interaction of these ostensibly strictly separated spheres that marks not so much the "invention" as the gradual emergence of the medium known as television.

The interrelation of occult and technical telesight also comes to the fore in the appropriation of a highly influential treatise by the philosopher Ernst Kapp, who in 1877 defined technology as "organ projection." Kapp's anthropocentric theory, still living on in Marshall McLuhan's notion of media as "an extension of man," was originally taken up in both electrical engineering and occultism. Liesegang opens his *Contributions on the Problem of Electrical Television* with a reference to Kapp's *Outlines of a Philosophy of Technology*, according to which "almost all tools, machines, etc. are unconscious copies that imitate parts of the human being."[61] Liesegang, for whom the Morse telegraph corresponded to the human sense of touch and the telephone to the ear, thus understood his "instrument for the telegraphing of lens-produced images" as "imitating the sense of sight."[62] In this context, Liesegang not only quotes Crookes, but alongside the model of the human eye, he also invokes the "archetype" (*Muster*) of the fairytale's "magic mirror"—a figure that, in addition to shaping the technology's cultural reception in the late 1920s, already had surfaced in most of the early writings on television from the late nineteenth century on: "Mirrors in which we can see distant objects can be found in the fairytales of all countries. Faust saw Helena in such a mirror. The mirrors of Amamterasu, Dschemschid, Agrippa and Nostradamus all had the same marvelous property."[63]

The double model for imagining technical television—the human eye *and* the magic mirror—can also be observed in Fritz Lux's *The Electrical Televisor*. Lux at first refers to nature's "marvelous and perfectly realized creations," before he goes on to describe his apparatus as the technological projection of a magical process: "In very many inventions of recent years, we see the realization of thoughts and ideas that have often occupied the human mind for centuries. In the phonograph, we can see Münchhausen's post horn, from which could be heard the sound of beautiful melodies and songs played long ago. Likewise, in television we can see the fairytale's magic mirror, the gift of a good fairy, which enables us to observe the deeds of people far away."[64]

The engineers Liesegang and Lux understood their inventions as ways to make these tales into reality, but did not go more deeply into television's magical models. The spiritualist du Prel, by contrast, explained mirror magic and "medieval crystal ball gazing" as corresponding to psychic television, which by his own account takes place as the outward projection of internally received images: "The crux of the matter is this: under the influence of narcotic substances or due to the exhaustion of the optical nerves when looking at a reflective surface, a condition arises in which autosuggestion or external suggestion can bring about television, thereby projecting the image onto the mirror's surface."[65]

Du Prel did not consider the magical process of psychic television to be supernatural, however; rather, he thought it operated in accordance with natural laws as yet unknown to contemporaneous physics. Thus, it is not altogether surprising that he also refers back to the principle of organ projection cited by Liesegang, additionally calling for the construction of technical devices that imitate occult human capabilities. In the first volume of his treatise *Magic as a Natural Science* (1899), du Prel writes: "In his *Philosophy of Technology*, Kapp demonstrates beautifully that our mechanical devices are merely unconscious copies that imitate organisms or parts of organisms. The camera obscura, for example, can be understood as a copy of the eye. This 'organ projection,' as he calls it, is of great philosophical and scientific interest.... The philosophical engineer won't waste his time on random speculations on aviation, but will instead say that nature has solved the problem in the wings of insects and birds and that ... the human mind must seek out the organ projection of the wing."[66]

Yet because magic is "nothing but unknown natural science," the principle of organ projection undergoes an "entirely unforeseen expansion" in du Prel's book.[67] Although occult human faculties such as telepathy or television may be "designated as magical, as long as the process is not clear to us," they are in fact based on natural processes. Hence, he claims, it should also be possible to project these magical capabilities as "technological copies."[68]

According to du Prel, examples of such technical devices that imitate magical processes are already at hand: wireless telegraphy is a projection of telepathy; the X-ray apparatus corresponds to clairvoyance. For du Prel, the productiveness of any future collaboration between occultism and the natural sciences is therefore obvious: "In place of their perpetual division, natural scientists and occultists should complement each other. Researchers in the natural sciences should translate occult functions into technologies, while the occultist converts technical functions into psychic ones." Du Prel would also integrate physiology, psychology, and anatomy into this program of how technology and spiritualism should mutually advance each other: "Engineers, physiologists, anatomists, psychologists, and occultists are . . . by nature reliant on each other. The occultist can reveal to the engineer the problems of the future; he can change the blind finder of technology into a purposeful inventor. But it is the engineer who can offer the occultist a scientific explanation for human beings' magical faculties."[69]

Of course, this wishful fantasy of a "purposeful" inventor attempts to negate the contingency that marks the cultural construction of a new medium. Thus, du Prel scripts a teleological narrative onto a gradual emergence of knowledge that is in fact both contingent and dependent on cultural imaginations. Even today, this teleology underlies numerous works on the history of technology, which retrospectively reconstruct a medium's "prehistory" from the vantage point of a cultural realization and appropriation that could easily have assumed quite different forms. Nonetheless, du Prel's text can also be read as an astonishing metareflection on the reciprocal interaction in which spiritualism and technology partially constitute each other. Du Prel's imagining of an engineer trained in occultism and projecting a device that imitates the occult faculty of telesight thereby reveals with exceptional clarity to what extent the conception and construction of a technological medium may depend on seemingly marginal cultural materialities.

According to du Prel, such an engineer could have invented the wireless telegraph even before the discovery of the electromagnetic wave spectrum: "Our engineer, well versed in these matters and convinced that physical processes lie behind all magical capabilities, would have confronted the problem of wireless telegraphy and purposefully revealed the physical processes behind telepathy, even before the discovery of Hertz waves."[70] Moreover, an engineer proceeding from spiritualism would not have been limited to constructing a wireless telegraph: "His study of the occult would have taken him yet another step further. Specifically, telepathy frequently manifests itself in conjunction with acoustic phenomena. For instance, a subject in a state of considerable mental agitation who cries out a name may be *heard* by the physically remote addressee, who simultaneously *sees* the sender's phantom image as a telepathically transmitted hallucination."[71]

In du Prel's account, the alliance between technological and occult research not only could create an explanation for this magical process, but also function as if it were a blueprint for a technical copy supplanting the "psychic lever" (*psychischer Hebel*) of suggestion by means of a material apparatus: "For the engineer, the explanation of this phenomenon as caused by a psychic force is not sufficient. He would conceive of the subject's psychic excitation simply as a lever for unleashing a force that acts at a distance; but this force itself is of a physical nature. For exactly this reason, he would tell himself that this natural pattern must also be imitable. . . . Drawing on occultism, our engineer would in this way apply himself to the creation of an apparatus that would allow us . . . to see as well as to hear a theatrical production in our own living room."[72]

Here, in a text from 1899—thirty years before the first television broadcasts—du Prel imagines an apparatus for wireless image and sound transmissions into the domestic sphere. Thus, there are two modes of responding to du Prel's question: "How can we become televisionary?"[73] First, autosuggestion, which engenders psychic television, but occurs only at moments of great "personal involvement," can be replaced by the "lever of external suggestion."[74] Second, this lever will in the future itself be supplanted by the switch of a technical device: "The magnetizer [that is, the hypnotist] will hereafter be replaced by an apparatus," and "the magnetic capability will be projected as technology."[75]

Apart from the omnipresent categories of magic, du Prel's fantasy of projecting psychic organs as technical devices additionally introduces the figure of "hypnotic suggestion," which dominated early medical and psychological representations of cinema.[76] A spellbinding, irresistible influence was similarly ascribed to television during the 1950s, when the technology indeed became a mass medium, often labeled as the "hypnotist in your own living room."[77] Conversely, fifty years earlier, du Prel had already conceived of the television set as replacing the hypnotist, thereby testifying to how closely television's cultural invention and reception are connected to each other.

Furthermore, we can conclude that the technological television projects of the late nineteenth century, dismissed by Arthur Korn in the 1920s as unrealizable and "fantastical,"[78] were inextricably linked to the cultural fantasies that also pervaded the contemporaneous spiritualist theories of psychic telesight. The successful wireless transmission of moving images in 1929 is therefore by no means the implementation of a medium without discursive precedent that would have generated itself from its own technical parameters.[79] Instead, television gradually emerged from a surreptitious exchange across the permeable boundaries of such clearly demarcated spheres as electrical engineering, the natural sciences, and occultism. The texts, experiments, and technical devices of researchers such as William Crookes and Oliver Lodge merely provide us with an unusually clear glimpse of these often half-hidden borrowings, which did not unfold as "purposefully" as du Prel might have wished. Despite the cultural contingencies that undermine any teleological history of occult and technical television, or even because of these accidental coincidences, du Prel's metacommentary on the interrelation of occultism and technology may serve as an apt conclusion for this chapter. After all, du Prel succinctly captures spiritualism as an epistemic condition for the emergence of electric television. The interactions between occultism, the natural sciences, and technology point, however, to a mutually constitutive relationship in which psychic and technical television render each other imaginable. Thus, spiritualism, too, has no claim to any primacy as an all-encompassing origin: "But, alas, no such engineer, well versed in occultism, has been found.... Valuable time was lost because it was thought that occultism had nothing to do with technology, whereas in truth, it contains the very philosophy of technology."[80]

Acknowledgments

I would like to thank the Warner Fund at the University Seminars at Columbia University for supporting this publication. An early version of Chapter 1 was presented in the University Seminar "Theory and History of Media." The ensuing discussions there and at other institutions have been enormously helpful in sharpening the central arguments of this book, and I would like to thank Ken Alder, Friedrich Balke, David Bates, Kyung-Ho Cha, Peter Fenves, Rupert Gaderer, Michael Gamper, Lydia Goehr, Tom Gunning, Niklaus Largier, Rosalind Morris, Peter Schnyder, and David Wellbery for their invitations, questions, suggestions, and comments. Christoph Hoffmann helped me to get hold of a high resolution scan of a table from Georg Krünitz' *Oeconomisch-technologische Encyklopädie*. I would also like to acknowledge Thomas Weynants who generously granted the rights to reproduce images from his early visual media collection. Tyler Whitney, Brían Hanrahan, and Brook Henkel helped me with editing the text, locating English translations of German texts, and with verifying bibliographical references. During the last two years I have served as the chair of Columbia's Department of Germanic Languages and I am grateful to Bill Dellinger whose administrative skills made it possible to complete the book while being chair.

I was thrilled when Jonathan Crary indicated that Zone Books might be interested in publishing this book, and I would like to thank him for his unwavering support as my editor. Throughout the production of the book it has been a real pleasure to work with Meighan Gale. I am grateful to Julie Fry for the wonderful cover and design and to Bud Bynack for his careful and meticulous copyediting of the text. Mark Anderson, Kelly Barry, Jimena Canales, Bernhard Dotzler, Noam Elcott, Andreas Huyssen, Reinhold Martin, Harro Müller, Leander Scholz, and Oliver Simons read parts of the manuscript in early or late incarnations. I am grateful for their valuable feedback. I am especially indebted to Hubertus Breuer, Brian Larkin, and Dorothea von Mücke. Their friendship, encouragement, and advice were crucial. Over the years they commented on the whole manuscript, and I appreciate that they were willing to read parts of it more often than once.

I would like to thank my parents and my sister who have supported this project from afar and across a linguistic boundary. Finally, I am grateful to and for Alexander and Shiaolan. In profile Alex still looks like Casper the friendly ghost; his happiness is a daily inspiration. Shiaolan's love and energy have been at the center of my life as I was researching and writing these pages. I dedicate this book to her.

New York, Spring 2013
Stefan Andriopoulos

Abbreviations

CPuR.

Immanuel Kant, *Kritik der reinen Vernunft*, in vols. 3 and 4 of *Werkausgabe*, ed. Wilhelm Weischedel, 12 vols. (Frankfurt am Main: Suhrkamp, 1977); Kant, *Critique of Pure Reason*, trans. and ed. Paul Guyer and Allen W. Wood (Cambridge: Cambridge University Press, 1999).

CPrR.

Immanuel Kant, *Kritik der praktischen Vernunft*, vol. 7 of *Werkausgabe*, ed. Wilhelm Weischedel, 12 vols. (Frankfurt am Main: Suhrkamp, 1974); Kant, *Critique of Practical Reason*, trans. Mary Gregor (Cambridge: Cambridge University Press, 1997).

D.

Immanuel Kant, *Träume eines Geistersehers, erläutert durch Träume der Metaphysik*, in *Vorkritische Schriften bis 1768*, vol. 2 of *Werkausgabe*, ed. Wilhelm Weischedel, 12 vols. (Frankfurt am Main: Suhrkamp, 1977); Kant, *Dreams of a Spirit Seer, Elucidated by Dreams of Metaphysics*, in *Theoretical Philosophy 1755–1770*, trans. and ed. David Walford (Cambridge: Cambridge University Press, 1992).

"E."

Arthur Schopenhauer, "Versuch über das Geistersehn und was damit zusammenhängt" (1851), in *Parerga und Paralipomena: Kleine philosophische Schriften I*, vol. 4 of *Sämtliche Werke*, ed. Wolfgang Freiherr von Löhneysen, 5 vols. (Frankfurt am Main: Suhrkamp, 1986); Schopenhauer, "Essay on Spirit Seeing and Everything Connected Therewith," in *Parerga and Paralipomena: Short Philosophical Essays*, trans. E.F.J. Payne, 2 vols. (Oxford: Clarendon Press, 2000).

En.

> G. W. F. Hegel, *Enzyklopädie der philosophischen Wissenschaften: Die Philosophie des Geistes* (Frankfurt am Main: Suhrkamp, 1986); Hegel, *Hegel's Philosophy of Mind* [sic]: *Being Part Three of the Encyclopaedia of the Philosophical Sciences*, ed. J. N. Findlay, trans. William Wallace (Oxford: Clarendon, 1971).

G.

> Friedrich Schiller, *Der Geisterseher: Aus den Papieren des Grafen von O*, in *Historische Schriften und Erzählungen II*, ed. Otto Dann, vol. 7 of *Werke und Briefe* (Frankfurt am Main: Deutscher Klassiker Verlag, 2002); Schiller, *The Ghost-Seer, or Apparitionist*, ed. Jeffrey L. Sammons, trans. Henry G. Bohn, (Columbia, SC: Camden House, 1992).

"M."

> E. T. A. Hoffmann, "Der Magnetiseur: Eine Familienbegebenheit," in *Fantasiestücke in Callots Manier*, ed. Hartmut von Steinecke (Frankfurt am Main: Deutscher Klassiker Verlag, 1993); Hoffmann, "The Mesmerist" in *Fantasy Pieces in Callot's Manner*, trans. Joseph M. Hayse (Schenectady, NY: Union College Press, 1996).

Ph.

> G. W. F. Hegel, *Phänomenologie des Geistes* (Frankfurt am Main: Suhrkamp, 1986); Hegel, *Phenomenology of Spirit*, trans. A. V. Miller (Oxford: Oxford University Press, 1977).

Prolegomena.

> Immanuel Kant, *Prolegomena zu einer jeden künftigen Metaphysik die als Wissenschaft wird auftreten können* (1783), in *Schriften zur Metaphysik und Logik*, vol. 5 of *Werkausgabe*; Kant, *Prolegomena to Any Future Metaphysics*, trans. and ed. Gary Hatfield (Cambridge, Cambridge University Press, 1997).

WPP.

> Arthur Schopenhauer, *Die Welt als Wille und Vorstellung*, in *Sämtliche Werke*, ed. Wolfgang Freiherr von Löhneysen, 5 vols (Frankfurt am Main: Suhrkamp, 1986); Schopenhauer, *The World as Will and Representation*, trans. E. F. J. Payne, 2 vols. (New York: Dover, 1958).

Notes

Unless otherwise noted, all translations are mine. Throughout, where an existing English translation is cited, an asterisk * following the relevant page number indicates that the published translation has been modified. The first page number refers to the German original and the second to the English translation.

INTRODUCTION

1. The phrase is "Gestalten des Geistes." See G. W. F. Hegel, *Phänomenologie des Geistes* (Frankfurt am Main: Suhrkamp, 1986), p. 46; Hegel, *Phenomenology of Spirit*, trans. A. V. Miller (Oxford: Oxford University Press, 1977), p. 28*. Hereafter cited as *Ph*.

2. "Dies [ist] die Nacht, das Innere der Natur, das hier existiert—reines Selbst. In phantasmagorischen Vorstellungen ist es ringsum Nacht; hier schießt dann ein blutig[er] Kopf, dort ein[e] andere weiße Gestalt plötzlich hervor und verschwinden ebenso. Diese Nacht erblickt man, wenn man dem Menschen ins Auge blickt—in eine Nacht hinein, die furchtbar wird; es hängt die Nacht der Welt hier einem entgegen." G. W. F. Hegel, *Jenaer Realphilosophie: Vorlesungsmanuskripte zur Philosophie der Natur und des Geistes von 1805–1806*, ed. Johannes Hoffmeister (Hamburg: Felix Meiner, 1967), pp. 180–81.

3. For a Lacanian reading of this passage in terms of the fragmented body, see Slavoj Žižek, *The Ticklish Subject: The Absent Centre of Political Ontology* (London: Verso, 1999), pp. 29–30. Many of Žižek's arguments were previously formulated by Georges Bataille and Alexandre Kojève. See Alexandre Kojève, *Introduction à la lecture de Hegel* (Paris: Gallimard, 1947), p. 575; Georges Bataille, "Hegel, Death and Sacrifice" (1955), *Yale French Studies* 78 (1990), pp. 9–28. Already in 1988, Terry Castle had emphasized that the word "phantasmagoria" was coined to

163

describe the optical medium and only subsequently transferred to representations of inner mental images. See her "Phantasmagoria: Spectral Technology and the Metaphorics of Modern Reverie," *Critical Inquiry* 15.1 (Autumn 1988), pp. 26–61. According to Laurent Mannoni, the first usage of the term occurred in December 1792, when Paul Philidor, a precursor of Etienne-Gaspard Robertson, advertised his ghost shows in the daily newspaper *Les Affiches* as a "phantasmagoria"; Laurent Mannoni, "The Phantasmagoria," *Film History* 8 (1996), p. 393.

4. "I think the transcendental ideality, i.e. the *cerebral phantasmagoria*, of the whole thing here becomes uncommonly clear." Arthur Schopenhauer, "Vereinzelte, jedoch systematisch geordnete Gedanken über vielerlei Gegenstände" (1851), in *Parerga and Paralipomena: Kleine philosophische Schriften II*, vol. 5 of *Sämtliche Werke*, ed. Wolfgang Freiherr von Löhneysen (Frankfurt am Main: Suhrkamp, 1986), p. 51; Schopenhauer, "Stray Yet Systematically Arranged Thoughts on a Variety of Subjects," in *Parerga and Paralipomena: Short Philosophical Essays*, trans E. F. J. Payne, 2 vols. (Oxford: Oxford University Press, 2000), vol. 2, p. 40*.

5. Lorraine Daston once described historical epistemology as "transcending the history of ideas by asking the Kantian question about the preconditions that make thinking this or that idea possible." Daston, "Marvelous Facts and Miraculous Evidence in Early Modern Europe," in James Chandler, Arnold Davidson, Harry Harootunian (eds.), *Questions of Evidence: Proof, Practice, and Persuasion across the Disciplines* (Chicago: University of Chicago Press, 1994), p. 283.

6. Immanuel Kant, *Träume eines Geistersehers, erläutert durch Träume der Metaphysik*, in *Vorkritische Schriften bis 1768*, vol. 2 of *Werkausgabe*, ed. Wilhelm Weischedel, 12 vols. (Frankfurt am Main: Suhrkamp, 1977); Kant, *Dreams of a Spirit Seer, Elucidated by Dreams of Metaphysics*, in *Theoretical Philosophy 1755–1770*, trans. and ed. David Walford (Cambridge: Cambridge University Press, 1992). Hereafter cited as *D*. See *D* 950/328; for "real spiritual impression," see *D* 949/327*.

7. *D* 950/328.

8. For *Hirngespenster*, see *D* 953/330, 958/334, 959/335; for *Spectrum*, see *D* 955/332.

9. Immanuel Kant, *Kritik der praktischen Vernunft*, vol. 7 of *Werkausgabe*, A 255; Kant, *Critique of Practical Reason*, trans. Mary Gregor (Cambridge: Cambridge University Press, 1997), p. 117*. Hereafter cited as *CPrR*.

10. The phrase is "herumgehende Geistergeschichten," *D* 965/340*. The German *herumgehend* means both "haunting" and "circulating."

11. See, among others, Tom Gunning, "Phantom Images and Modern Manifestations: Spirit Photography, Magic Theater, Trick Films, and Photography's Uncanny," in Patrice Petro (ed.), *Fugitive Images: From Photography to Video* (Bloomington: Indiana University Press, 1995), pp. 42–71; Tom Gunning, "To Scan a Ghost: The Ontology of Mediated Vision," *Grey Room* 26 (Winter 2007): pp. 95–127; Wolfgang Hagen, *Radio Schreber: Der moderne Spiritismus und die Sprache der Medien* (Weimar: Verlag und Datenbank für Geisteswissenschaften, 2001); Jeffrey Sconce, *Haunted Media: Electronic Presence from Telegraphy to Television* (Durham: Duke University Press, 2000).

12. Friedrich Kittler, *Aufschreibesysteme 1800/1900*, 2nd ed. (Munich: Fink, 1987), p. 235; Kittler, *Discourse Networks 1800/1900*, trans. Michael Metteer with Chris Cullens (Stanford: Stanford University Press, 1990), p. 229.

13. "'Phantasmagoria,' a word that...is generally relieved of its literal sense which links it to speech and to public speech." Jacques Derrida, *Specters of Marx*, trans. Peggy Kamuf (New York: Routledge, 1994), p. 108. See also p. 142, where Derrida describes the "language act" of "*phantasmagoreuein.*"

14. Friedrich Kittler, "Romantik—Psychoanalyse—Film" (1985), in *Draculas Vermächtnis: Technische Schriften* (Leipzig: Reclam, 1993), p. 96; Kittler, *Literature, Media, Information Systems*, ed. John Johnston (Amsterdam: OPA, 1997), p. 95.

15. Friedrich Kittler, *Grammophon, Film, Typewriter* (Berlin: Brinkmann & Bose, 1985), pp. 22–23; Kittler, *Gramophone, Film, Typewriter*, trans. Geoffrey Winthrop-Young and Michael Wutz (Stanford: Stanford University Press, 1999), p. 12; Kittler, *Optische Medien: Berliner Vorlesung* (Berlin: Merve, 2002), p. 290; Kittler, *Optical Media: Berlin Lectures 1999*, trans. Anthony Enns (Malden, MA: Polity, 2010), p. 207*.

16. "There is an old and most likely irresolvable dispute—the question of whether technological innovations are a reflection of social or economic needs, or if they are not instead inductively developed from existing technical standards. As regards television at least, and indeed image transmission in general, factors immanent to the technology appear to have been the chief inspiration for thinking on the subject." Joseph Hoppe, "Wie das Fernsehen in die Apparate kam" [How television became an apparatus], in Wulf Herzogenrath, Thomas Gaethgens, Sven Thomas Hoenisch, and Peter Hoenisch (eds.), *TV-Kultur: Das Fernsehen in der bildenden Kunst seit 1879* [TV culture: Television in art since 1879] (Dresden: Verlag der Kunst, 1997), p. 26.

17. On the mixed status of the camera obscura as a material object and an epistemological figure see Jonathan Crary, *Techniques of the Observer: On Vision and Modernity in the Nineteenth Century* (Cambridge, MA: The MIT Press, 1990), pp. 30–31. On the camera obscura and the magic lantern see *ibid.*, p. 33: "The magic lantern . . . never occupied an effective discursive or social position from which to challenge the dominant model of the camera obscura." Don Ihde similarly focuses on the camera obscura as an "epistemology engine" without taking note of the specific change that occurred in the second half of the eighteenth century when the projective and deceptive capabilities of the magic lantern became a predominant model within critical epistemology. See Don Ihde, *Bodies in Technology* (Minneapolis: University of Minnesota Press, 2001), pp. 71–75.

18. On the use of the magic lantern in scientific lectures during the seventeenth and early eighteenth centuries, see Thomas Hankins and Robert J. Silverman, "The Magic Lantern and the Art of Demonstration," in Thomas L. Hankins and Robert J. Silverman (eds.), *Instruments and the Imagination* (Princeton, NJ: Princeton University Press, 1995), pp. 37–71. On the interrelation of the magic lantern to the occult in the seventeenth century see Koen Vermeir, "The Magic of the Magic Lantern (1660–1700): On Analogical Demonstration and the Visualization of the Invisible," *British Journal for the History of Science* 38 (2005), pp. 127–59.

19. *CPrR* A 255/117*.

20. The phrase is "Anzeige eines übersinnlichen Substrats." Immanuel Kant, *Kritik der Urteilskraft*, vol. 10 of *Werkausgabe* (Frankfurt am Main: Suhrkamp, 1996), B LVII, A LV; Kant, *Critique of Judgment*, trans. Werner S. Pluhar (Indianapolis: Hackett, 1987), p. 37*.

21. Arthur Schopenhauer, *Die Welt als Wille und Vorstellung I*, vol. 1 of *Sämtliche Werke*, ed. Wolfgang Freiherr von Löhneysen, 5 vols. (Frankfurt am Main: Suhrkamp, 1986), vol. 1, p. 567; Schopenhauer, *The World as Will and Representation*, trans. E. F. J. Payne, 2 vols. (New York: Dover, 1958), vol. 1, p. 420. Hereafter cited as *WWP*.

22. "Eine träge Bewegung und Aufeinanderfolge von Geistern, eine Galerie von Bildern, deren jedes mit dem vollständigen Reichtume des Geistes ausgestattet [ist]"; *Ph* 590/492*. In *Optical Media*, Friedrich Kittler drew attention to Hegel's *Phenomenology* sharing its title with an eighteenth-century treatise about various forms of semblance and illusion. See Johann Heinrich Lambert, *Phänomenologie oder die Lehre vom Schein: Neues Organon* [Phenomenology, or the doctrine of

semblance: New organon] ed. Günter Schenk, 2 vols. (1764; Berlin: Akademie-Verlag, 1990). But Kittler ignores the divergent modes in which Kant, Hegel, or Schopenhauer appropriate optical media, and he contends in a formulation whose argumentative overreach was silently corrected by his American translator: "German idealism, too, sprang from the history of optical media." (Auch der deutsche Idealismus ist der Geschichte der optischen Medien entsprungen); Kittler, *Optische Medien*, p. 123. Anthony Enns's translation softens Kittler's argumentative overreach: "German idealism also emerged from the history of optical media"; *Optical Media*, p. 96. While Enns's account of the relation between media and philosophical theory is less problematic than Kittler's, his translation is incorrect.

23. Lorraine Daston and Peter Galison, *Objectivity* (New York: Zone Books, 2007); on Crary's historical account of the "conditions of possibility" of a new discursive regime, see *Techniques of the Observer*, p. 85.

24. Diethard Sawicki, *Leben mit den Toten: Geisterglauben und die Entstehung des Spiritismus in Deutschland 1770–1900* [Living with the dead: Spirit belief and the emergence of spiritualism in Germany 1770–1900] (Paderborn: Schöningh, 2002), pp. 13–14. Sawicki gives a good overview of the late eighteenth-century debate about spirit apparitions, but, postulates for the period around 1800 a "split of the polysemous concept *spirit* into two homonymous concepts" (p. 14).

25. Moses Mendelssohn, "Kant's Träume eines Geistersehers" [Kant's *Dreams of a Spirit Seer*], in *Gesammelte Schriften: Jubiläumsausgabe*, ed. Eva J. Engel and Alexander Altmann, 39 vols. (Stuttgart: F. Frommann, 1971), vol. 5, pt. 2, p. 73.

26. For a poststructuralist reading of Kant's *Dreams of a Spirit Seer* that also has its focus on language, see Liliane Weissberg, *Geistersprache: Philosophischer und literarischer Diskurs im späten achtzehnten Jahrhundert* [Spirit language: Philosophical and literary discourse in the late eighteenth century] (Würzburg: Königshausen & Neumann, 1990).

27. Derrida, *Specters of Marx*, p. 190 n. 13.

28. "In der ganzen Ideologie [erscheinen] die Menschen und ihre Verhältnisse wie in einer Camera obscura auf den Kopf gestellt." Karl Marx and Friedrich Engels, "Die deutsche Ideologie," in Rolf Hecker and Richard Sperl (eds.), *Werke*, 43 vols. (Berlin: Dietz, 1958), vol. 3, p. 26; Marx and Engels, "The German Ideology," trans. William Lough, in *Marx and Engels: Collected Works*, 50 vols. (New York: International Publishers, 1976), vol. 5, p. 36. On Marx's use of the camera obscura metaphor see Sarah Kofman, *Camera Obscura: Of Ideology* (Ithaca, NY:

Cornell University Press, 1999); and W. J. T Mitchell, *Iconology: Image, Text, Ideology* (Chicago: University of Chicago Press, 1986), pp. 160–208.

29. Immanuel Kant, *Kritik der reinen Vernunft*, in vols. 3 and 4 of *Werkausgabe*, A 384; Kant, *Critique of Pure Reason*, trans. and ed. Paul Guyer and Allen W. Wood (Cambridge: Cambridge University Press, 1999), p. 433; hereafter cited as *CPuR*.

30. *CPuR* A 384/434*.

31. Karl Marx, *Das Kapital: Kritik der politischen Ökonomie. Band I: Der Produktionsprozeß des Kapitals* (1867/1872; Berlin: Ullstein, 1979); Marx, *Capital: A Critique of Political Economy, Volume 1*, trans. Ben Fowkes (London: Penguin, 1976). For "gegenständlicher Schein der gesellschaftlichen Arbeitsbestimmungen," see p. 61/176*; for "phantasmagorische Form," p. 52/165*; for "gespenstige Gegenständlichkeit," p. 20/128*.

32. On the Marxist appropriations of the term "phantasmagoria" see Margaret Cohen, "Benjamin's Phantasmagoria," in *New German Critique* 48 (Fall 1989), pp. 87–107; Tom Gunning, "Phantasmagoria and the Manufacturing of Illusions and Wonder: Toward a Cultural Optics of the Cinematic Apparatus," in Andre Gaudreault et al. (eds.), *The Cinema: A New Technology for the 20th Century* (Lausanne: Payot Lausanne, 2004), pp. 31–44.

33. See Reinhard Wittmann, "Was There a Reading Revolution at the End of the Eighteenth Century?," in Guglielmo Cavallo and Roger Chartier (eds.), *A History of Reading in the West*, trans. Lydia Cochrane (Amherst: University of Massachusetts Press, 1999), pp. 284–312. Kittler described immersive reading practices from around 1800 as an internal, "hallucinatory mediality." Kittler, *Aufschreibesysteme 1800/1900*; *Discourse Networks 1800/1900*, p. 129/123*. But Kittler's *Discourse Networks 1800/1900* presents a problematic typological periodization that describes literary Romanticism as prefiguring the advent of film. According to Kittler, the discourse network 1800 was characterized by a monopoly of the book in which readers hallucinated in a manner that would become technological reality in the medium of cinema around 1900. This juxtaposition of two centennial medial configurations ignores the cultural use of the magic lantern in the visual medium of the phantasmagoria. At the same time, it relies on a teleology in which the emergence of cinema becomes the goal or, in Kittler's term, the "implementation" of earlier discursive dreams. The teleology that underlies Kittler's *Discourse Networks 1800/1900* is even more evident in his shorter essay "Romanticism — Psychoanalysis — Film." There, Kittler interrelates Romanticism, psychoanalysis, and

early cinema in a teleological historiography that turns the emergence of cinema into the goal and fulfillment of a purposeful development. Kittler thus describes identificatory reading practices that lead to visions of a double as "clinically veri-fied" by psychoanalysis and "technologically implemented" by cinema (p. 95). In typological terms, one could summarize Kittler's thesis in the following manner: literary Romanticism around 1800 prefigures the advent of psychoanalysis and film around 1900 in a mode that structurally corresponds to the relation of Old and New Testament. Around 1900, furthermore, psychoanalysis functions as equiva-lent to John the Baptist, as it were, while the technology of cinema represents the word becoming flesh: "Silent films implement with technological positivity what psychoanalysis can only conceive of" (Stummfilme implementieren in technischer Positivität, was Psychoanalyse nur denken kann); Kittler, "Romanticism—Psycho-analysis—Film," p. 92; Kittler, "Romantik—Psychoanalyse—Film," p. 91.

34. In addition to interpreting identificatory reading practices as anticipating a technological media revolution that occurred one hundred years later, Kittler also presents a "general alphabetization" that is theorized in terms of maternal orality as a context contemporaneous with the alleged "monopoly of the book" around 1800.

35. "Will man sie mit einem Menschen vergleichen, so kann man sagen: sie war ein im Augenblicke des Sterbens, durch irgend eine Fixierung, zwischen Sterben und Leben zurückgehaltener Mensch, der schon mehr in die Welt, die nun vor ihm, als in die, die hinter ihm liegt, zu sehen fähig ist." Justinus Kerner, *Die Seherin von Prevorst*, in *Kerners Werke: Auswahl in sechs Teilen*, ed. Raimund Pissin, 6 vols. (Berlin: Deutsches Verlagshaus Bong, 1914), vol. 4, p. 58.

36. Carl du Prel (ed.), *Immanuel Kants Vorlesungen über die Psychologie: Mit einer Einleitung "Kants mystische Weltanschauung"* [Immanuel Kant's lectures on psychol-ogy: With an introduction on Kant's mystical worldview] (Leipzig: Ernst Günthers Verlag, 1889); du Prel, "Das Fernsehen in Zeit und Raum" [Television in time and space], *Sphinx* 14 (1892), p. 9; du Prel, "Fernsehen als Funktion des transzenden-talen Subjekts" [Television as a function of the transcendental subject], *Sphinx* 15 (1893), pp. 200–209, 305–16.

37. Carl du Prel, *Die Magie als Naturwissenschaft: Erster Theil: Die magische Physik* [Magic as natural science, pt. 1: Magical physics] (Jena: Hermann Costeno-ble, 1899), p. 23.

38. *Ibid.*, p. 22.

39. Frank Warschauer, "Rundfunk heute und morgen" [Radio today and tomorrow] (1928), in Ernst Glaeser (ed.), *Fazit: Ein Querschnitt durch die deutsche Publizistik* [On balance: A cross-section of German journalism] (Kronberg/Ts.: Scriptor, 1977), pp. 307–308.

CHAPTER ONE: THE MAGIC LANTERN OF PHILOSOPHY

An early version of this chapter was published under the title "Kant's Magic Lantern: Historical Epistemology and Media Archaeology," in *Representations* 115 (Summer 2011), pp. 42–70.

1. The following two editions lack an author's name: *Träume eines Geisterse-hers, erläutert durch Träume der Metaphysik* (Riga, Mietau: Bey Johann Friedrich Hartknoch, 1766); *Träume eines Geistersehers, erläutert durch Träume der Metaphysik* (Königsberg: Bey Johann Jacob Kantes, 1766).

2. Kant's *Dreams* already had this epigraph on the title page of the first edition, whereas the first edition of *The Castle of Otranto* was published as William Marshall's translation of an Italian text by Onuphrio Muralto and without epigraph.

3. "Credite, Pisones, isti tabulae fore librum / persimilem cuius, uelut aegri somnia, uanae / fingentur species, ut nec pes nec caput uni / reddatur formae" (Believe me, Pisones, very similar to such a painting would be a book whose...); Horace, *Epistles Book II and Epistle to the Pisones ('Ars Poetica')*, ed. Niall Rudd (Cambridge: Cambridge University Press, 1989), p. 58.

4. "Velut aegri somnia, vanae / finguntur species." Kant substitutes the present tense *finguntur* for the original future tense. The differing translation of "vanae species" as "empty semblances" derives from the fact that Kant, like Walpole, gives an unequivocal meaning to Horace's polysemous phrase.

5. "Vanae / fingentur species, tamen ut pes, & caput uni / reddanter formae."

6. Horace Walpole, *The Castle of Otranto: A Gothic Story*, ed. W. S. Lewis and E. J. Clery (Oxford: Oxford University Press, 1998), p. 112.

7. Walpole, "Preface to First Edition," *The Castle of Otranto*, p. 6.

8. Immanuel Kant, *Träume eines Geistersehers, erläutert durch Träume der Metaphysik*, in *Vorkritische Schriften bis 1768*, vol. 2 of *Werkausgabe*, ed. Wilhelm Weischedel, 12 vols. (Frankfurt am Main: Suhrkamp, 1977), p. 923; Kant, *Dreams of a Spirit Seer, Elucidated by Dreams of Metaphysics*, in *Theoretical Philosophy 1755–1770*, trans. and ed. David Walford (Cambridge: Cambridge University Press, 1992), p. 305. Hereafter cited as *D*.

9. See Immanuel Kant's letter "An Fräulein Charlotte von Knobloch 10. Aug [1763]," in Kant, *Briefe*, ed. Jürgen Zehbe (Göttingen: Vandenhoeck & Ruprecht, 1970), p. 24; Kant, *Correspondence*, trans. and ed. Arnulf Zweig (Cambridge: Cambridge University Press, 1999), p. 73. For a reading of this letter, in which Kant gives an assessment of Swedenborg that is far more positive than that presented in *Dreams of a Spirit Seer*, see Chapter 3. See also Liliane Weissberg, *Geistersprache: Philosophischer und literarischer Diskurs im späten achtzehnten Jahrhundert* [Spirit language: Philosophical and literary discourse in the late eighteenth century] (Würzburg: Königshausen & Neumann, 1990), pp. 55–57.

10. *D* 985/356*; *D* 983/354.

11. As early as 1804, Ludwig Ernst Borowski described the *Dreams of a Spirit Seer* as containing "the germ of the *Critique of Pure Reason*." Borowski, *Darstellung des Lebens und Charakters Immanuel Kants* [The life and character of Immanuel Kant] (Königsberg: F. Nicolovius, 1804), p. 66.

12. John H. Zammito has made the compelling suggestion that the text can be read, conversely, as an elucidation of metaphysical dreams by the dreams of spirit seeing. See Zammito, *Kant, Herder, and the Birth of Anthropology* (Chicago: University of Chicago Press, 2002), pp. 197 and 206. For further readings of Kant's text, see also Friedrich Balke, "Wahnsinn der Anschauung: Kants *Träume eines Geistersehers* und ihr diskursives Apriori" [Fanatic intuition: Kant's *Dreams of a Spirit Seer* and their discursive a priori], in Moritz Baßler, Bettina Gruber, Martina Wagner-Egelhaaf (eds.), *Gespenster: Erscheinungen—Medien—Theorien* [Specters: Apparitions—media—theories] (Würzburg: Königshausen & Neumann, 2005), pp. 297–313, and Sarah Pourciau, "Disarming the Double: Kant in Defense of Philosophy (1766)," *The Germanic Review* 81.2 (Spring 2006), pp. 99–120. Already in the 1980s, Hartmut and Gernot Böhme had emphasized that Kant's text shows "just how closely spirit seeing and speculative metaphysics are related to each other." Hartmut Böhme and Gernot Böhme, *Das Andere der Vernunft: Zur Entwicklung von Rationalitätsstrukturen am Beispiel Kants* [The other of reason: On the development of structures of rationality in the work of Kant] (Frankfurt am Main: Suhrkamp, 1985), p. 252. In contrast to them, I do not strive to "lend speech to the Other of reason" (p. 246), nor do I interpret Kant's relationship to Swedenborg as a "psychodynamic process" (p. 251).

13. *D* 982/354.

14. *D* 963/338. A spiritualist interpretation of the text can be found in Carl du

Prel's "Kants mystische Weltanschauung" [Kant's mystical worldview], in du Prel (ed.), *Immanuel Kants Vorlesungen über die Psychologie: Mit einer Einleitung "Kants mystische Weltanschauung"* [Kant's lectures on psychology: With an introduction on Kant's mystical worldview] (Leipzig: Ernst Günthers Verlag, 1889), pp. xv–lxiv. For a skeptical reading, see Robert Zimmermann, *Kant und der Spiritismus* [Kant and spiritualism] (Vienna: Gerold, 1879).

15. Jacob F. Abel, *Philosophische Untersuchungen über die Verbindung der Menschen mit höheren Geistern*, [Philosophical investigations into the connection of humans with higher spirits] (Stuttgart: Mezler, 1791), p. ii.

16. D 923/309.

17. D 935/315.

18. D 940/319. For Schiller's dissertations, see Friedrich Schiller, "Philosophie der Physiologie" (1779) and "Versuch über den Zusammenhang der tierischen Natur des Menschen mit seiner geistigen" (1780), in *Theoretische Schriften*, ed. Rolf-Peter Janz, vol. 8 of *Werke und Briefe in zwölf Banden*, ed. Klaus Harro Hilzinger et al., 12 vols. (Frankfurt am Main: Deutscher Klassiker Verlag, 1992), pp. 37–58 and 118–63; Schiller, "Philosophy of Physiology" and "Essay on the Connection between the Animal and Spiritual Nature of Man" in Kenneth Dewhurst and Nigel Reeves (eds.), *Friedrich Schiller: Medicine, Psychology, and Literature* (Berkeley: University of California Press, 1978), pp. 149–75 and 253–98.

19. D 940/319. The notes for Kant's *Lectures on Metaphysics*, which were given in the 1780s, but published posthumously, were not edited by Kant himself and are thus to be treated with considerable caution. Nonetheless, it is worth noting that in these texts, Kant describes the transition from physical to immaterial intuition in almost identical terms: "But when the soul separates itself from the body, then it will not have the same sensory intuition [*Anschauung*] of this world; it will not intuit [*anschauen*] the world as it appears, but rather as it is. Accordingly the separation of the soul from the body consists in the change of sensory intuition to spiritual intuition." Immanuel Kant, *Immanuel Kants Vorlesungen über die Metaphysik: Zum Drucke befördert von dem Herausgeber der Kantischen Vorlesungen über die philosophische Religionslehre*, ed. Karl Heinrich Ludwig Pölitz (1821; Darmstadt: Wissenschaftliche Buchgesellschaft, 1988), p. 255; Kant, *Lectures on Metaphysics*, trans. and ed. Karl Ameriks and Steve Naragon (Cambridge: Cambridge University Press, 1997), p. 104*. In describing the "other world," Kant here refers explicitly to Swedenborg: "The thought of Swedenborg is in this quite sublime" (257/105).

Yet in contrast to *Dreams of a Spirit Seer*, Kant categorically denies the possibility of spirit seeing in this life: "But one question still remains: whether the soul, which already sees itself spiritually in the other world, will and can appear in the visible world through visible effects? This is not possible, for only matter can be intuited sensorily and fall in the outer senses, but not a spirit.... When I still have a sensory intuition in this world, I cannot at the same time have a spiritual intuition. I cannot be at the same time in this and also in that world" (259/105–106*).

20. *D* 941/320*.

21. *D* 942/321*.

22. *Ibid.*; *D* 944/323*.

23. *D* 945/325*.

24. *D* 945/325 n.; *D* 944/323.

25. *D* 942/321.

26. *D* 943/322*.

27. See Stefan Andriopoulos, "The Invisible Hand: Supernatural Agency in Political Economy and the Gothic Novel," *English Literary History* 66.3 (1999), pp. 739–58.

28. *D* 943/322*.

29. The structural parallel between *Dreams of a Spirit Seer* and Kant's moral philosophy is also highlighted by Josef Schmucker and John H. Zammito. See Schmucker, *Die Ursprünge der Ethik Kants* [Origins of Kant's ethics] (Meisenheim: A. Hain, 1961), pp. 162–63 and 168–73, and Zammito, *Kant, Herder, and the Birth of Anthropology*, p. 205. A demonic version of being controlled by a foreign will is to be found around 1900 in debates about hypnotism and the agency of corporate aggregates. See Stefan Andriopoulos, *Possessed: Hypnotic Crimes, Corporate Fiction, and the Invention of Cinema* (Chicago: University of Chicago Press, 2008).

30. *D* 944/323.

31. See *D* 945/324* n.: "The reciprocal effects which take their origin from the ground of morality and which human beings and the members of the spirit world exercise upon each other in accordance with the laws of pneumatic influence—these reciprocal effects might be construed in the following terms: there naturally arises from these reciprocal effects a closer community between a good (or bad) soul and a good (or bad) spirit; as a result, the former associate themselves with that part of the spiritual republic which is consonant with their moral constitution." That any theory of the "spiritual republic" is simultaneously a theory

of the social can also be seen in F. W. J. Schelling's *Stuttgart Private Lectures*: "And just as the spirit world is joined to nature in general by a necessary *consensus harmonicus*, so too are the individual objects of the spirit and natural worlds. Thus there must be communities within the spirit world, corresponding to those on earth." Friedrich Wilhelm Joseph Schelling, "Gedanken über eine Philosophie der Geisterwelt" [Thoughts on a philosophy of the spirit world], in Manfred Schröter (ed.), *Werke: Nach der Originalausgabe in neuer Anordnung*, 6 vols. (Munich: Beck, 1927), vol. 4, p. 373 (original edition, vol. 7, p. 481).

32. *D* 942/321*; *D* 946/324*.

33. *D* 946/325*.

34. *D* 947/325.

35. *Ibid.*

36. *D* 947/325 n.*.

37. *D* 948/326; *D* 949/326–27*.

38. *D* 949/327.

39. *D* 949/327*.

40. *D* 950/328.

41. *D* 950/328*.

42. Immanuel Kant, "To Moses Mendelssohn [April 8, 1766]," in *Briefe*, p. 33/93*.

43. *D* 945/324.

44. *D* 942/321*.

45. *D* 950/328.

46. See *D* 972–73/346–47: "I declare . . . either that one must suppose that there is more cleverness and truth in Schwedenberg's writings than first appearances would suggest, or that, if there is any agreement between him and my system, it is a matter of pure chance. . . . Nonetheless, there prevails in that work such a wondrous harmony with what the most subtle ruminations of reason can produce on a like topic."

47. *D* 954/331.

48. On the Enlightenment and its turn against fanaticism, see also Lorraine Daston and Katharine Park, "The Enlightenment and the Anti-Marvelous," in Daston and Park, *Wonders and the Order of Nature, 1150–1750* (New York: Zone Books, 1998), pp. 329–64.

49. On the emergence of "projection" as a psychological and optical category

around 1850, see Jutta Müller-Tamm, *Abstraktion als Einfühlung: Zur Denkfigur der Projektion in Psychophysiologie, Kulturtheorie, Ästhetik und Literatur der frühen Moderne* [Abstraction as empathy: On the figure of projection in modern psychophysiology, cultural theory, aesthetics, and literature] (Freiburg im Breisgau: Rombach, 2005), p. 117. On the history of projection, see also Lorraine Daston, "Projection and Perfect Passivity," in Natascha Adamowsky, Robert Felfe, Marco Formisano, Georg Toepfer, and Kirsten Wagner (eds.), *Affektive Dinge: Objektberührungen in Wissenschaft und Kunst* [Affective things: Touching upon objects in science and art] (Göttingen: Wallstein, 2011), pp. 24–50.

50. *D* 954/331.

51. "Wir sehen ausser uns, was blos in unserem Kopfe spukt." Abel, *Philosophische Untersuchungen*, p. 116. The imagination is often described as the source of sensory delusions. See also Justius Christian Hennings, *Von Geistern und Geisterse-hern* [Of spirits and spirit seers] (Leipzig: Weygand, 1780), p. 8: "The imagination is the first and comprehensively fertile source of phantoms and deceptive sensations of all kinds." See also Gottfried Immanuel Wenzel, *Geist- Wunder- Hexen- und Zaubergeschichten, vorzüglich neuester Zeit, erzählt und erklärt von G. I Wenzel* [Tales of ghosts, miracles, witches, and magic, chiefly from our own time, narrated and explained by G. I. Wenzel] (Prague: Schönfeld, 1793), p. 55: "The cloud of smoke is there; now the *imagination* becomes sensation." John Ferriar refers to this kind of mental disorder as hallucination. See Ferriar, *An Essay Towards a Theory of Apparitions* (London: Cadell and Davies, 1813), p. 95: "In medicine, we have fine names, at least for every species of disease. The peculiar disorder, which I have endeavoured to elucidate, is termed generally HALLUCINATION, including all delusive impressions, from the wandering mote before the eye, to the tremendous spectre, which is equally destitute of existence."

52. *D* 960/336. For *Hirngespinste*, see *D* 954/331; for *Hirngespenster*, see *D* 953/330, 958/334, 959/335. A critical turn against "Hirngespenster" or "brain phantoms" is also to be found in Christoph Martin Wieland, *Euthanasia: Drey Gespräche über das Leben nach dem Tode* [Euthanasia: Three conversations on life after death] (Leipzig: Göschen, 1805), p. 10. Kant himself, in his *Versuch über die Krankheiten des Kopfes* [Essay on the diseases of the head] (1764), had already developed a similar explanation of pathological visions. See Kant, *Vorkritische Schriften bis 1768*, vol. 2 of *Werkausgabe*, p. 893. Furthermore, Kant's *Anthropology*, first published in 1798, formulated a similar model, according to which "man . . . takes

imaginations for sensations, or for inspirations [*Eingebungen*] caused by a different being that is not an object of the external senses; in these cases the illusion soon turns into enthusiasm or spirit seeing, and both are deceptions of the inner sense." Immanuel Kant, *Anthropologie in pragmatischer Hinsicht* (1798), in *Schriften zur Anthopologie, Geschichtsphilosophie, Politik und Pädagogik II*, vol. 12 of *Werkausgabe*, p. 457; Kant, *Anthropology from a Pragmatic Point of View*, trans. Mary Gregor (The Hague: Martinus Nijhoff, 1974), p. 39*.

53. *D* 954/331*; *D* 955/332. In 1802, Johann Gottfried Herder similarly invoked the medium of the magic lantern in order to describe Swedenborg's projection of his inner fantasies toward the external world: "Swedenborg's celestial secret was that he saw and believed the fantasies that had risen from his innermost being; this conviction gave reality to the appearances in his inner world, presenting them to his senses. Heaven and hell emerged from, and resided in his interior; a magic lantern of his own thoughts." Johann Gottfried Herder, "Emanuel Swedenborg, der größeste Geisterseher des achtzehnten Jahrhunderts," in Günter Arnold (ed.), *Werke in zehn Bänden*, 10 vols. (Frankfurt am Main: Deutscher Klassiker Verlag, 2000), vol. 10, pp. 567–68.

54. Bonaventure Abat, *Amusemens philosophiques sur diverses parties des sciences, et principalement de la physique et des mathématiques* [Philosophical amusements on various parts of sciences, chiefly physics and mathematics] (Amsterdam: J. Mossy, 1763); Edme Gilles Guyot, *Nouvelles récréations physiques et mathématiques* (Paris: Gueffier, 1769–1770). On the production of optical "spectres" with concave mirrors, see also Jurgis Baltrusaitis, *Der Spiegel: Entdeckungen, Täuschungen, Phantasien* [The mirror: Disoveries, deceptions, fantasies] (Gießen: Anabas, 1986), pp. 247–72.

55. Edme Gilles Guyot, *Neue physikalische und mathematische Belustigungen oder Sammlung von neuen Kunststücken zum Vergnügen mit dem Magnete, mit den Zahlen, aus der Optik sowohl, als auch aus der Chymie. Dritter Theil* [New physical and mathematical amusements, or a collection of enjoyable new tricks with magnets, numbers, optics, and chemistry. Third part] (Augsburg: Bey Eberhard Kletts sel. Wittwe, 1772), p. 159. On the description of concave mirrors, see also p. 142.

56. *Ibid.*, pp. 160–61.

57. *Ibid.*, p. 191.

58. On Robertson's phantasmagoria, see also Mervyn Heard, *Phantasmagoria: The Secret Life of the Magic Lantern* (Hastings, UK: Projection Box, 2006);

Tom Gunning, "Phantasmagoria and the Manufacturing of Illusions and Wonder: Toward a Cultural Optics of the Cinematic Apparatus," in Andre Gaudreault, Catherine Russell, and Pierre Veronneau (eds.), *The Cinema: A New Technology for the 20th Century* (Lausanne: Payot, 2004), pp. 31–44; Barbara Maria Stafford and Frances Terpak, *Devices of Wonder: From the World in a Box to Images on a Screen* (Los Angeles: Getty Center, 2001), pp. 79–90 and 134–37; Laurent Mannoni, "The Phantasmagoria," *Film History* 8.4 (1996), pp. 390–415; Marina Warner, *Phantasmagoria: Spirit Visions, Metaphors, and Media into the Twenty-First Century* (Oxford: Oxford University Press, 2006), pp. 146–58.

59. See Friedrich Schiller, *Der Geisterseher: Aus den Papieren des Grafen von O*, in *Historische Schriften und Erzählungen II*, ed. Otto Dann, vol. 7 of *Werke und Briefe* (Frankfurt am Main: Deutscher Klassiker Verlag, 2002), pp. 602–21; Schiller, *The Ghost-Seer, or Apparitionist*, ed. Jeffrey L. Sammons, trans. Henry G. Bohn (Columbia, SC: Camden House, 1992), pp. 8–24; Cajetan Tschink, *The Victim of Magical Delusion; or, The Mystery of the Revolution of P--L: A Magico-Political Tale*, trans. Peter Will, 3 vols. (London: Robinson, 1795). The German original was published as *Geschichte eines Geistersehers: Aus den Papieren des Mannes mit der eisernen Larve*, 3 vols. (Vienna: Kaiserer, 1790–93); Carl Grosse, *Der Genius: Aus den Papieren des Marquis C* von G***, ed. Hanne Witte (1791–95; Frankfurt am Main: Zweitausendeins, 1982). Grosse's novel appeared in two different English translations: *Horrid Mysteries: A Story*, trans. Peter Will, 3 vols. (London: William Lane, 1796), and *The Genius: or, The Mysterious Adventures of Don Carlos de Grandez*, trans. Joseph Trapp, 2 vols. (London: Allen and West, 1796).

60. See *Cagliostro: Dokumente zu Aufklärung und Okkultismus* [Cagliostro: Documents on enlightenment and occultism], ed. Klaus H. Kiefer (Munich: Beck, 1991). On Johann Georg Schröpfer, see Christian August Crusius, *Bedenken eines berühmten Gelehrten über des famosen Schröpfers Geister-Citieren* [Doubts of a famous scholar regarding the notorious Schröpfer's necromancy] (Frankfurt and Leipzig: n.p., 1775); Johann Salomon Semler, *Samlungen von Briefen und Aufsätzen über die Gaßnerischen und Schröpferischen Geisterbeschwörungen, mit vielen eigenen Anmerkungen* [Collection of letters and articles on Gaßner's and Schröpfer's conjuring of ghosts, with many additional remarks] (Halle: Hemmerde, 1776).

61. "§476...bei Betrug durch vorgegebene oder eingebildete Zauberey folgt eine Zuchthausstrafe von 6 Monaten bis zu 2 Jahren." Ernst Ferdinand Klein, *Grundsätze des gemeinen deutschen und preußischen peinlichen Rechts* [Foundations

of common German and Prussian penal law] (Halle: Bey Hemmerde und Schwetschke, 1796), p. 349.

62. Karl von Eckartshausen, *Aufschlüsse zur Magie aus geprüften Erfahrungen über verborgene philosophische Wissenschaften und seltne [sic] Geheimnisse der Natur* (Munich: Joseph Lentner, 1790). See also Johann Wallberg, *Sammlung natürlicher Zauberkünste oder aufrichtige Entdeckung viler [sic] bewährter, lustiger und nützlicher Geheimnüsse* [Collection of natural magic, or honest discovery of many worthwhile, amusing, and useful secrets] (Stuttgart: Metzler, 1768); Johann Peter Eberhard, *Abhandlungen vom physikalischen Aberglauben und der Magie* [Essays on physical superstition and magic] (Halle: Renger, 1778); Johann Christian Wiegleb, *Die natürliche Magie, aus allerhand belustigenden und nützlichen Kunststücken bestehend* [Natural magic, consisting of many kinds of amusing and useful tricks] (Berlin: Nicolai, 1780); Christlieb B. Funk, *Natürliche Magie oder Erklärung verschiedener Wahrsager und natürlicher Zauberkünste* [Natural magic, or an explanation of various soothsayers and natural conjuring tricks] (Berlin: Nicolai, 1783); Johann Samuel Halle, *Magie; oder, die Zauberkräfte der Natur, so auf den Nutzen und die Belustigung angewandt worden* [Magic; or, The magical powers of nature, applied for use and amusement] (Berlin: Joachim Pauli, 1783–1786); David Brewster, *Letters on Natural Magic* (London: J. Murray, 1832); Theodor Philadelphus, *Phantasmagorie oder die Kunst, Geister erscheinen zu lassen* [Phantasmagoria, or The art of making ghosts appear] (Leipzig: Basse, 1833).

63. Eckarthausen, *Aufschlüsse*, pt. 2, pp. 74–75.

64. *Ibid.*, pp. 67–68.

65. *D* 955/332.

66. *D* 949/327*.

67. *D* 942/321.

68. Eckarthausen, *Aufschlüsse*, pt. 2, pp. 64–65.

69. Eckartshausen describes a genuine spiritual manifestation as "an apparition [*Erscheinung*] different from normal appearances [*Erscheinungen*], yet equally real as what we normally conceive as reality." Simultaneously, he affirms that even the "normal kind of appearance" does not correspond to the "reality of things." *Ibid.*, p. 32.

70. *D* 983/354.

71. Immanuel Kant, *Prolegomena zu einer jeden künftigen Metaphysik die als Wissenschaft wird auftreten können* (1783), in *Schriften zur Metaphysik und Logik*, vol. 5

of *Werkausgabe*, A 13; Kant, *Prolegomena to Any Future Metaphysics*, trans. and ed. Gary Hatfield (Cambridge, Cambridge University Press, 1997), p. 10. Hereafter cited as *Prolegomena*.

72. Immanuel Kant, *Kritik der reinen Vernunft*, in vols. 3 and 4 of *Werkausgabe*, B XVI; Kant, *Critique of Pure Reason*, trans. and ed. Paul Guyer and Allen W. Wood (Cambridge: Cambridge University Press, 1999), p. 433. Hereafter cited as *CPuR*.

73. *CPuR* B XXI/112.

74. *CPuR* B XXIX/116.

75. *CPuR* B XXVI/115.

76. *Ibid.*, B XXVI/115*.

77. Kant, *Prolegomena* A 104/68*.

78. "Es folgt auch natürlicher Weise aus dem Begriffe einer Erscheinung überhaupt: daß ihr etwas entsprechen müsse, was an sich nicht Erscheinung ist, weil Erscheinung nichts vor sich selbst, und außer unserer Vorstellungsart sein kann, mithin, wo nicht ein beständiger Zirkel herauskommen soll, das Wort Erscheinung schon eine Beziehung auf etwas anzeigt." *CPuR* A 252/348*.

79. Kant's critical assumption is that "things" appear "as objects . . . that exist outside of us" by "affecting our senses." *Prolegomena* A 63/40*. See also A 105/68 on "the way in which our senses are affected by this unknown something." However this assumption remains as vague as Kant's earlier supposition of a "genuine spiritual influence." What Gerold Prauss would like to separate as "transcendent-metaphysical nonsense" from the "transcendental-philosophical sense" of the concepts *Erscheinung* and thing in itself is accordingly a constitutive part of Kant's critical philosophy. See Prauss, *Kant und das Problem der Dinge an sich* [Kant and the problem of things in themselves] (Bonn: Bouvier, 1974), p. 43. See also Prauss, *Erscheinung bei Kant: Ein Problem der "Kritik der reinen Vernunft"* [Appearance in Kant: A problem of the *Critique of Pure Reason*] (Berlin: de Gruyter, 1971), where Prauss distinguishes between empirical appearance and appearance as manifestation of the thing in itself (p. 20) before concentrating on the problem of empirical appearances.

80. The phrase is "Anzeige eines übersinnlichen Substrats." Immanuel Kant, *Kritik der Urteilskraft* (1790), vol. 10 of *Werkausgabe*, B LVII, A LV; Kant, *Critique of Judgment*, trans. Werner S. Pluhar (Indianapolis: Hackett, 1987), p. 37*.

81. "Die Denklichkeit (deren Schein daher kommt daß sich auch keine Unmöglichkeit davon darthun läßt) ist ein bloßes Blendwerk wie ich denn die

Träumereyen des Schwedenbergs selbst, wenn iemand ihre Möglichkeit angriffe, mir zu vertheidigen getraute." Kant, "To Moses Mendelssohn [April 8, 1766]," in *Briefe*, pp. 32–33/91–92*.

82. *D* 949/327*.

83. *D* 949/327*.

84. *D* 949/327*.

85. *CPuR* A 252/348*.

86. *Ibid.*, B 351–52/385*.

87. The phrase is "Logik des Scheins." *CPuR* B 86/198*. Michelle Grier's *Kant's Doctrine of Transcendental Illusion* (Cambridge: Cambridge University Press, 2001) is one of the very few texts that point to the role of optical figures in Kant's philosophy, referring to Kant's reliance on optical figures as "one of the most interesting aspects of Kant's account of transcendental illusion" (p. 129 n. 51. See also pp. 273 n. 20 and 278–79). Yet even Grier does not interpolate Kant's philosophical texts with late eighteenth-century medial practices and quotes only Newton's *Opticks* while ignoring the use of the magic lantern in phantasmagorical projections.

88. "Es gibt also eine natürliche und unvermeidliche Dialektik der reinen Vernunft, [die] ... selbst, nachdem wir ihr Blendwerk aufgedeckt haben, dennoch nicht aufhören wird, ihr [der Vernunft] vorzugaukeln und sie unablässig in augenblickliche Verirrungen zu stoßen, die jederzeit gehoben zu werden bedürfen." *CPuR* B 355, A 298/386–87*. See also *CPuR* B 450/467–68* on the "natural and unavoidable semblance [*Schein*], which even if one is no longer fooled [*hintergehen*] by it, still deceives [*täuschen*], though it does not defraud [*betrügen*], and which thus can be rendered harmless, but never be destroyed." See also: "The transcendental semblance, on the other hand, does not cease even after one has uncovered it and has clearly seen into its nullity by transcendental criticism." *CPuR* A 297, B 353/386*.

89. *CPuR* B 723/618

90. This is "an illusion that cannot be avoided at all, just as little as we can avoid it that the sea appears higher in the middle than at the shores, since we see the former through higher rays of light than the latter, or even better, just as little as the astronomer can prevent the rising moon from appearing larger to him, even when he is not deceived by this illusion." *CPuR* A 297, B 354/386.

91. Kant, *Anthropologie in pragmatischer Hinsicht*, A 40, B 40/29*. A similar notion of illusion is also to be found in Kant's posthumously published lectures on metaphysics, where Kant refers to "illusion" as an "overhasty judgment" that

"the following one immediately contests": "we are not deceived by an optical box, for we know that it is not so; but we are moved to a judgment which is immediately refuted by the understanding"; *Kants Vorlesungen über die Metaphysik*, pp. 147–48/53–54. In contrast to these lectures on metaphysics, Kant's *Anthropology from a Pragmatic Point of View* was published during his lifetime, in 1798, but the text draws on earlier lectures. On the relation between Kant's critical turn and his lectures on anthropology see Zammito, *Kant, Herder, and the Birth of Anthropology*, pp. 255–307.

92. *CPuR* A 366/424. In the original German, the verb used here is *vorspiegeln*.

93. *CPuR* A 384/433. This problem, already addressed in the *Dreams of a Spirit Seer*, is resolved (or perhaps merely circumvented) in the *Critique of Pure Reason*, first by ascribing to both the soul and the organic body the same status as *Erscheinung* or "appearance," and second, by asserting that the things in themselves underlying these appearances may not be of "such altogether different...substances." *Ibid.*, A 385/434. See also: "But if one considers that the two kinds of objects are different not inwardly but only insofar as one of them appears outwardly to the other, hence that what grounds the appearance of matter as thing in itself might perhaps not be so different in kind, then this difficulty vanishes." *CPuR* B 427/456.

94. *CPuR* A 384/434*.

95. Karl Marx, *Das Kapital: Kritik der politischen Ökonomie. Band I: Der Produktionsprozeß des Kapitals* (1867/1872; Berlin: Ullstein, 1979), p. 21; Marx, *Capital: A Critique of Political Economy, Volume 1*, trans. Ben Fowkes (London: Penguin, 1976), p. 103.

96. "In der ganzen Ideologie [erscheinen] die Menschen und ihre Verhältnisse wie in einer Camera obscura auf den Kopf gestellt." Karl Marx and Friedrich Engels, "Die deutsche Ideologie," in Rolf Hecker and Richard Sperl (eds.), *Werke*, 43 vols. (Berlin: Dietz, 1958), vol. 3, p. 26; "The German Ideology," in *Marx and Engels: Collected Works*, trans. William Lough, 50 vols. (New York, 1976), vol. 5, p. 36.

97. *CPuR* A 384/434*.

98. "Gegenständlicher Schein der gesellschaftlichen Arbeitsbestimmungen" (61/176*), "gespenstige Gegenständlichkeit" (20/128*), "Es ist nur das bestimmte gesellschaftliche Verhältnis der Menschen, welches hier für sie die phantasmagorische Form eines Verhältnisses von Dingen annimmt" (52/165*). Marx, *Das*

Capital.

99. Kant, *Prolegomena*, A 159/102.

100. *CPuR* A 424, B 452/468*.

101. *D* 955/332.

102. Guyot, *Neue physikalische Belustigungen*, p. 159.

103. "Überhaupt liegt aller Syncretisterey gemeiniglich Mangel an Aufrichtigkeit zum Grunde, Eine Gemüthseigenschaft die diesem großen Künstler von Blendwerken (die, wie durch eine Zauberlaterne, Wunderdinge eine Augenblicke lang vorstellig machen, bald darauf aber auf immer verschwinden, indessen daß sie doch bey Unwissenden eine Bewunderung hinterlassen, daß etwas Außerordentliches darhinter stecken müsse, welches sie nur nicht haschen können) besonders eigen ist." Immanuel Kant, "To Friedrich Heinrich Jacobi. August 30, 1789," in *Briefe*, p. 157/319*.

104. Kant, *Anthropologie in pragmatischer Hinsicht*, A 40, B 40/29.

105. *CPuR* A 384/434*.

106. The phrase is "spekulative Einschränkung." Kant, *Kritik der praktischen Vernunft*, vol. 7 of *Werkausgabe*, A 255; *Critique of Practical Reason*, trans. Mary Gregor (Cambridge: Cambridge University Press, 1997), p. 117*. Hereafter cited as *CprR*.

107. "Mit Theorien des Übersinnlichen, wovon man kein Ende absieht … die Theologie zur Zauberlaterne von Hirngespenstern zu machen." *CPrR*, A 254/117*. Kant also describes the dialectic of practical reason as "the ground of an error of subreption (*vitium subreptionis*) and, as it were, of an optical illusion in the self-consciousness of what one does, as distinguished from what one feels." *Ibid.*, A 210/97.

108. The phrases are "augenblickliche Verirrungen," *CPuR* B 355, A 298/386–87*, and "Macht ihrer Illusion, " *CPuR* B 622/565.

109. *CPuR* B 355, A 298/386–87.

110. Kant, *Anthropologie in pragmatischer Hinsicht*, A 40, B 40/29*.

111. *CPrR*, A 255/117*.

CHAPTER TWO: GHOSTS AND PHANTASMAGORIA
IN HEGEL AND SCHOPENHAUER

1. Arthur Schopenhauer, "Versuch über das Geistersehn und was damit zusammenhängt" (1851), in *Parerga und Paralipomena: Kleine philosophische Schriften I*, vol. 4 of *Sämtliche Werke*, ed. Wolfgang Freiherr von Löhneysen, 5 vols. (Frankfurt

am Main: Suhrkamp, 1986), p. 275; Schopenhauer, "Essay on Spirit Seeing and Everything Connected Therewith," in *Parerga and Paralipomena: Short Philosophical Essays*, trans. E. F. J. Payne, 2 vols. (Oxford: Clarendon Press, 2000), vol. 1, p. 227. Hereafter cited as "E."

2. "E" 275/227*. See also "E" 351/292*: "an immediate actual presence, like that of a body acting on the senses, is by no means a necessary condition" of spirit apparitions.

3. "E" 277/228–29*.

4. See also "E" 360/299.

5. "E" 360/299*.

6. "E" 363/302*.

7. "E" 350/291*. See also "E" 289/239.

8. "E" 358/297.

9. "E" 281/232.

10. "E" 330/274.

11. "E" 319/264.

12. The merging of philosophy and physiology in Schopenhauer's work thus corresponds to the early nineteenth-century embodiment of the observer as analyzed by Jonathan Crary. See Jonathan Crary, *Techniques of the Observer: On Vision and Modernity in the Nineteenth Century* (Cambridge, MA: The MIT Press, 1990), esp. pp. 76–77 on Schopenhauer.

13. "Ein sehr komplizierter physiologischer Vorgang im Gehirne eines Tieres, dessen Resultat das Bewußtsein eines Bildes ebendaselbst ist." Arthur Schopenhauer, *Die Welt als Wille und Vorstellung II*, vol. 2 of *Sämtliche Werke*, ed. Wolfgang Freiherr von Löhneysen (Frankfurt am Main: Suhrkamp, 1986), p. 248; *The World as Will and Representation*, trans. E. F. J. Payne, 2 vols. (New York: Dover, 1958), vol. 2, p. 191. Hereafter cited as *WWP*.

14. The phrase is "Vorstellungsmaschine im menschlichen Gehirnkasten." Arthur Schopenhauer, "Vereinzelte, jedoch systematisch geordnete Gedanken über vielerlei Gegenstände" (1851), in *Parerga und Paralipomena: Kleine philosophische Schriften II*, vol. 5 of *Sämtliche Werke*, ed. Wolfgang Freiherr von Löhneysen (Frankfurt am Main: Suhrkamp, 1986), p. 54; "Stray yet Systematically Arranged Thoughts on a Variety of Subjects," in *Parerga and Paralipomena*, trans E. F. J. Payne, 2 vols. (Oxford: Clarendon Press, 2000), vol. 2, p. 42*. Whereas Payne translates the German *Vorstellung* as "representation," I will render this term in the following

as "presentation" in order to maintain the difference between *Vorstellung* and *Darstellung*. A similar comparison of our intellectual faculties with the optical instrument of the magic lantern is to be found in the second volume of *The World as Will and Presentation* (1819/1844). There, Schopenhauer compares our necessarily fragmented consciousness with "a magic lantern in the focus of which only one picture can appear at a time." *WWP II* 178/2:138. On this passage, see also Jonathan Crary, *Suspensions of Perception: Attention, Spectacle, and Modern Culture* (Cambridge, MA: The MIT Press, 1999), p. 55.

15. The phrase is "Im Entwerfen von Bildern im Raum [und]...in der Zeit." "E" 286/237*. See also: "But now the sense impression that provides the starting point for this process and unquestionably the whole material for empirical intuitive perception [*Anschauung*], is something entirely subjective. All the forms of knowledge by means of which the objective representation of intuitive perception arises from that material and is projected [*projiziert*] outwards, according to Kant's absolute correct demonstration, are also of subjective origin." Arthur Schopenhauer, "Fragmente zur Geschichte der Philosophie," in *Parerga und Paralipomena I*, p. 117; "Fragments for the History of Philosophy," in *Parerga and Paralipomena*, vol. 1, pp. 92–93*. See also "The understanding projects the sensation, by means of its form, as something external and different from its own person." *WWP I* 357/2:276.

16. The phrase is "ein hervorgerufener Zauber, ein bestandloser, an sich wesenloser Schein, der optischen Illusion und dem Traume vergleichbar." *WWP I* 567/1:419–20*.

17. *WWP I* 567/1:420*.

18. Arthur Schopenhauer, "Fragmente zur Geschichte der Philosophie," in *Parerga und Paralipomena I*, p. 106; "Fragments for the History of Philosophy," in *Parerga and Paralipomena*, vol. 1, pp. 82–83.

19. "I think the transcendental ideality, i.e. the cerebral phantasmagoria, of the whole thing here becomes uncommonly clear." Schopenhauer, "Vereinzelte, jedoch systematisch geordnete Gedanken," 51/2:40*.

20. Immanuel Kant, *Kritik der praktischen Vernunft*, vol. 7 of *Werkausgabe*, ed. Wilhelm Weischedel, 12 vols. (Frankfurt am Main: Suhrkamp, 1974), A 255; Kant, *Critique of Practical Reason*, trans. Mary Gregor (Cambridge: Cambridge University Press, 1997), p. 117*. Hereafter cited as *CPrR*

21. *WWP I* 564/1:417.

22. *WWP I* 567/1:419. In its rhetoric of veiling and unveiling, as well as in its

invocation of the term "phantasmagoria," Schopenhauer's philosophy resembles that of Marx, who describes the commodity's "phantasmagorical form" as "spreading a veil of objectivity" over social relations (*sachlich verschleiert*). Karl Marx, *Das Kapital: Kritik der politischen Ökonomie. Band I: Der Produktionsprozeß des Kapitals* (1867/1872; Berlin: Ullstein, 1979), pp. 61 and 55; *Capital: A Critique of Political Economy, Volume 1*, trans. Ben Fowkes (London: Penguin, 1976), pp. 165* and 169*.

23. The phrase is "eine unvermeidliche, obzwar nicht unauflösliche Illusion." *CPuR* A 341, B 399/411*.

24. "E" 358–59/298*.

25. "E" 363/302*.

26. In his treatise *On the Will in Nature* (1836/1854) Schopenhauer contrasts the "nexus physicus" (physical connection) with a "nexus metaphysicus" (metaphysical connection) and postulates that "the dividing walls of individuation and separation, however solid they may be, do occasionally permit a [metaphysical] communication to take place behind the curtain, as it were, or, like a secret game under the table; and that just as with somnambulist clairvoyance there is a lifting of the individual isolation of knowledge, likewise there may also be a lifting of the individual isolation of the will" (daß die Scheidewände der Individuation und Sonderung, so fest sie auch seien, doch gelegentlich eine [metaphysische] Kommunikation, gleichsam hinter den Kulissen, oder wie ein heimliches Spielen unterm Tisch, zulassen könnten; und daß, wie es, im somnambulen Hellsehn, eine Aufhebung der individuellen Isolation der Erkenntnis gibt, es auch eine Aufhebung der individuellen Isolation des Willens geben könne). Arthur Schopenhauer, *Über den Willen in der Natur* (1836/1854), in *Sämtliche Werke*, ed. Wolfgang Freiherr von Löhneysen, 5 vols. (Frankfurt am Main: Suhrkamp, 1986), vol. 3, p. 437; Schopenhauer, *On the Will in Nature: A Discussion of the Corroborations from the Empirical Sciences That the Author's Philosophy Has Received Since Its First Appearance*, trans. E. F. J. Payne (New York: Berg, 1992), pp. 112–13*.

27. "E" 363/302.

28. "E" 364/302*.

29. The phrase is "eine unmittelbare, im Wesen an sich der Dinge gegründete Kommunikation"; "E" 364–65/303*.

30. See also "E" 349/290. The reference to the *Spiritual Telegraph* does not appear in the first edition of the text in 1851 and goes back to an addition made by Schopenhauer in his personal copy of the text. For a comparison of language

with the telegraph see *WWP I*, 78/39. On the interrelation of nineteenth-century physiological research into the human nervous system and the emerging technology of the telegraph, see also Laura Otis, *Networking: Communicating with Bodies and Machines in the Nineteenth Century* (Ann Arbor: University of Michigan Press, 2001).

31. On Johann Christian Reil's dynamic brain physiology see Michael Hagner, *Homo Cerebralis—Der Wandel vom Seelenorgan zum Gehirn* (Frankfurt am Main: Insel, 2000), pp. 157–70.

32. The phrases are "schwierige, schwache und mittelbare Kommunikation" and "nur auf Umwegen." "E" 294/243*.

33. The term is "Apparat der Halbleitung." Johann Christian Reil, "Ueber die Eigenschaften des Ganglien-Systems und sein Verhältnis zum Cerebralsystem" [On the qualities of the ganglion system and its relation to the cerebral system], in *Archiv für die Physiologie* [Archive for Physiology] 7 (1807): p. 210. See also Hagner, *Homo Cerebralis*, p. 162. For an influential summary and adaptation of Reil's theory see Carl Alexander Ferdinand Kluge, *Versuch einer Darstellung des animalischen Magnetismus als Heilmittel* [Attempt at presenting animal magnetism as a curative force] (Berlin: C. Salfeld, 1811), pp. 156–81.

34. Immanuel Kant, *Kritik der reinen Vernunft*, in vols. 3 and 4 of *Werkausgabe*, B 44; Kant, *Critique of Pure Reason*, trans. and ed. Paul Guyer and Allen W. Wood (Cambridge: Cambridge University Press, 1999), p. 177. Hereafter cited as *CPuR*.

35. Joseph Philippe François Deleuze, *Histoire critique du magnétisme animal*, 2 vols. (Paris: Mame, 1813), vol. 1, p. 281: "Si comme Kant l'a prétendu, le temps et l'espace n'existent que dans notre manière d'envisager les objets, s'ils ne sont que les conditions nécessaires de notre pensée, les formes originaires et virtuelles de notre sensibilité, les produits de notre sensorium, comme les couleurs sont le produit le notre oeil, alors les intelligences pures, qui connoissent les choses indépendamment de ces formes, doivent voir l'avenir comme le présent et le passé." See also Deleuze, *Mémoire sur la faculté de prévision* (Paris: Crochard, 1836), p. 31.

36. The term is "Fernsehen." "E" 318/264*. On the constitutive role of late nineteenth-century spiritualist theories of psychic "television in time and space" for the concurrent emergence of the technical medium see Chapter 5, "Psychic Television."

37. "E" 318/263–64*. See also "E" 362–63/301: "A consequence of this is that

clairvoyance is a confirmation of the Kantian doctrine of the ideality of space, time and causality." Friedrich Korn also claims that "soul sympathy" can overcome the "limits of time and space." Korn, *Die Existenz der Geister und ihre Einwirkung auf die Sinnenwelt; psychologisch erklärt und historisch begründet* [The existence of spirits and their workings on the sensory world, psychologically explained and historically justified] (Weimar: B. F. Voigt, 1841), p. 40. See also Dietrich Georg Kieser, *System des Tellurismus oder thierischen Magnetismus: Ein Handbuch fuer Naturforscher und Aerzte* [System of tellurism or of animal magnetism: A handbook for natural scientists and physicians], 2 vols. (Leipzig: F. L. Herbig, 1822), vol. 2, p. 66.

38. "E" 321/266*.

39. "E" 278/229.

40. "E" 323/268; "E" 319/265*.

41. Justinus Kerner, *Die Seherin von Prevorst: Eröffnungen über das innere Leben des Menschen und über das Hereinragen einer Geisterwelt in die unsere* (Stuttgart: Cotta, 1829); *The Seeress of Prevorst: Being Revelations Concerning the Inner-Life of Man, and the Inter-Diffusion of a World of Spirits in the One We Inhabit*, trans. C. Crowe (New York: Harper, 1845). The phrase is "gewissermaßen faktisch." "E" 318/264*.

42. The phrase is "ein sinnlich übersinnliches Ding." Marx, *Capital*, 50/165*.

43. For "facts of animal magnetism," see "E" 278/229; for "indication" (*Anzeige*), see "E" 319/265*.

44. "E" 364/303*; "E" 364/302*.

45. The terms are "mystische Bildersprache" and "transzendentes Thema." *WWP II* 421/2:326*.

46. Immanuel Kant, *Träume eines Geistersehers, erläutert durch Träume der Metaphysik*, in *Vorkritische Schriften bis 1768*, vol. 2 of *Werkausgabe*, ed. Wilhelm Weischedel (Frankfurt am Main: Suhrkamp, 1977), p. 945; Kant, *Dreams of a Spirit Seer, Elucidated by Dreams of Metaphysics*, in *Theoretical Philosophy 1755–1770*, trans. and ed. David Walford (Cambridge: Cambridge University Press, 1992), p. 325 n. Hereafter cited as *D*.

47. *WWP II* 422/ 2:326*.

48. *D* 945/325*.

49. Charles Bonnet's account of polyps, which are able to regenerate themselves after the loss of individual members, served already in Schiller's *Letters on Aesthetic Education* (1795) as a model for an organic connection between the

individual and the social aggregate: "That polypoid character of the Greek States, in which every individual enjoyed an independent existence but could, when need arose, grow into the whole organism, now made way for an ingenious clock-work" (Jene Polypennatur der griechischen Staaten, wo jedes Individuum eines unabhängigen Lebens genoß, und wenn es Not tat, zum Ganzen werden konnte, machte jetzt einem kunstreichen Uhrwerke Platz). Friedrich Schiller, *Über die ästhetische Erziehung des Menschen in einer Reihe von Briefen* (1795), vol. 8 of *Werke und Briefe in zwölf Bänden*, ed. Otto Dann, 12 vols. (Frankfurt am Main: Deutscher Klassiker Verlag, 1992), p. 572; Schiller, *On the Aesthetic Education of Man in a Series of Letters*, trans. Elizabeth M. Wilkinson and L. A. Willoughby (Oxford: Clarendon Press, 1982), p. 35.

50. The concept of communication also appears in Korn's *The Existence of Spirits*: "Communication of this kind is the actual penetration of one soul by another, by means of the nerve spirit." Korn, *Die Existenz der Geister*, p. 41.

51. Johann Gottlieb Fichte, *Einleitungsvorlesungen in die Wissenschaftslehre* (1813), in J. H. Fichte (ed.), *Sämmtliche und Nachgelassene Werke*, 11 vols., reprint (Berlin: de Gruyter, 1971), vol. 9, p. 4.

52. *D* 949/327.

53. The phrase is "als Anlage ... vorhanden." Fichte, *Einleitungsvorlesungen in die Wissenschaftslehre*, p. 6.

54. *Ibid.*, p. 20.

55. The phrase is "Windbeutelei intellektualer Anschauung." *WWP I* 566/1:419*.

56. *WWP II* 241/2:186.

57. *Ibid.* A polemical comparison of Fichte's intellectual intuition with spirit seeing can also be found in Friedrich Nicolai's essay "On Superstition in Philosophy" (1808): "Like the hypochondriac, the superstitious person creates the notion of the appearing ghost from his intuition and within its limits.... Both are thus as impossible to refute as Mr. Fichte, who insists on the irrefutability of his Doctrine of Science: we are supposed to credit everything which he assures us he intuits [anzuschauen]. He then cleverly adds that 'if we deny his intuition [*Anschauung*], we have only denied it, not disproved it.'" Nicolai, "Ueber Aberglauben in der Philosophie. Drey Vorlesungen" [On superstition in philosophy: Three lectures], in *Philosophische Abhandlungen: Zweyter Band* (Berlin: F. Nicolai, 1808), pp. 48–49.

58. See, for instance: "At this point, it is quite clear that the doctrine of

science, as a condition of its being understood, demands absolutely of the reader that he himself first do something on his own." Fichte, *Einleitungsvorlesungen in die Wissenschaftslehre*, in *Sämmtliche und Nachgelassene Werke*, vol. 9, p. 14.

59. G. W. F. Hegel, *Phänomenologie des Geistes* (Frankfurt am Main: Suhrkamp, 1986); Hegel, *Phenomenology of Spirit*, trans. A. V. Miller (Oxford: Oxford University Press, 1977). Hereafter cited as *Ph*. For "Anstrengung des Begriffs," see *Ph* 56/35*; for "Schrein des inneren, göttlichen Anschauens," see *Ph* 55/35.

60. G. W. F. Hegel, "Differenz des Fichteschen und Schellingschen Systems der Philosophie" (1801), in *Jenaer Schriften*, vol. 2 of *Werke*, ed. Eva Moldenhauer and Karl Markus Michel, 20 vols. (Frankfurt am Main: Suhrkamp, 1970), pp. 42–43.

61. The phrase is "Identität der Identität und Nichtidentität." Hegel, "Differenz," p. 96.

62. *Ph* 48/29*.

63. The phrase is "Arbeit des Begriffs." *Ph* 65/43*. See also *Ph* 19–20/7–8 on the opposition between esoteric and exoteric knowledge, esp. 20/8*: "The comprehensible form of science is the way open and equally accessible to all."

64. *Ph* 68/46*.

65. *Ph* 68/46*.

66. *Ph* 70/47.

67. *Ph* 69/47.

68. "Schon daß wir von einer Schranke wissen, ist Beweis unseres Hinausseins über dieselbe.... Nur das Ungewußte wäre eine Schranke des Wissens; die gewußte Schranke dagegen ist keine Schranke desselben; von seiner Schranke wissen heißt daher von seiner Unbeschränktheit wissen." G. W. F. Hegel, *Enzyklopädie der philosophischen Wissenschaften: Die Philosophie des Geistes* (Frankfurt am Main: Suhrkamp, 1986); Hegel, *Hegel's Philosophy of Mind* [sic]: *Being Part Three of the Encyclopaedia of the Philosophical Sciences*, ed. J. N. Findlay, trans. William Wallace (Oxford: Clarendon, 1971), pp. 36/23–24. Hereafter cited as *En*.

69. The phrase is "unüberschreitbare Grenze." *CPuR* B 421/452. See also "The great gulf that separates the supersensory from appearances" (die große Kluft, welche das Übersinnliche von den Erscheinungen trennt). Immanuel Kant, *Kritik der Urteilskraft*, vol. 10 of *Werkausgabe*, ed. Wilhelm Weischedel, 12 vols. (Frankfurt am Main: Suhrkamp, 1996), B LIV, A LII: Kant, *Critique of Judgment*, trans. Werner S. Pluhar (Indianapolis: Hackett, 1987), p. 35*.

70. The phrase is "Logik des Scheins," *CPuR* B 86/198*.

71. *Ibid.*, B 88/200*.

72. *Ph* 80/56*.

73. See Johann Heinrich Lambert, *Phänomenologie oder die Lehre vom Schein: Neues Organon*, ed. Günter Schenk, 2 vols. (1764; Berlin: Akademie-Verlag, 1990), vol. 2, p. 665. A possible connection between Hegel's and Lambert's *Phenomenology* is also indicated by Friedrich Kittler's *Optische Medien: Berliner Vorlesung 1999* (Berlin: Merve, 2002), p. 123; Kittler, *Optical Media: Berlin Lectures 1999*, trans. Anthony Enns (Malden, MA: Polity, 2010), p. 96.

74. *Ph* 76/53*.

75. *CPuR* A 45, B 63/186.

76. *Ph* 118/89*. In his essay "On Truth and Lie in an Extra-Moral Sense," Nietzsche attacked the assumption that the supersensory manifests itself in the world of empirical appearances. Nietzsche wrote: "Appearance is a word that contains many temptations, and for this reason I avoid using it as far as possible. For it is not true that the essence of things appears in the empirical world" (Das Wort Erscheinung enthält viele Verführungen, weshalb ich es möglichst vermeide: denn es ist nicht wahr, dass das Wesen der Dinge in der empirischen Welt erscheint). Friedrich Nietzsche, "Ueber Wahrheit und Lüge im aussermoralischen Sinne," in *Sämtliche Werke: Kritische Studienausgabe*, ed. Giorgio Colli and Mazzino Montinari, 15 vols. (Munich: Deutscher Taschenbuch Verlag, 1999), vol. 1, p. 884; Friedrich Nietzsche, "On Truth and Lying in a Non-Moral Sense," in *The Birth of Tragedy and Other Writings*, ed. Raymond Geuss and Ronald Speirs, trans. Ronald Speirs (Cambridge: Cambridge University Press), p. 148.

77. *Ph* 118/89.

78. *Ph* 118/89, emphasis in the original.

79. *Ph* 119/89*.

80. See G. W. F. Hegel, *Wissenschaft der Logik* (Frankfurt am Main: Suhrkamp, 1986), p. 177; Jacob Friedrich Abel, *Philosophische Untersuchungen über die Verbindung der Menschen mit höhern Geistern* (Stuttgart: Metzler, 1791), p. 129.

81. G. W. F. Hegel, *Vorlesungen über die Ästhetik I*, vol. 13 of *Werke*, ed. Eva Moldenhauer and Karl Markus Michel, 20 vols. (Frankfurt am Main: Suhrkamp, 1986), p. 300.

82. *Ibid.* An explicit comparison between absolute spirit and the ghost of Hamlet's father can be found in the *Lectures on the History of Philosophy*: "It goes ever on and on, because spirit is progress alone. Spirit often seems to have forgotten and

lost itself, but inwardly opposed to itself, it is inwardly working ever forward (as when Hamlet says of the ghost of his father, 'Well said, old mole! cans't work i' the ground so fast?'), until grown strong in itself it bursts asunder the crust of earth which divided it from the sun, its Notion, so that the earth crumbles away.... This work of the spirit to know itself, this activity to find itself, is the life of the spirit, and the spirit itself." G. W. F. Hegel, *Vorlesungen über die Geschichte der Philosophie III*, vol. 20 of *Werke*, 20 vols., ed. Eva Moldenhauer and Karl Markus Michel (Frankfurt am Main: Suhrkamp, 1986), p. 456; Hegel, *Lectures on the History of Philosophy, Volume 3: Medieval and Modern Philosophy*, trans. E. S. Haldane and Frances Simson (Lincoln: University of Nebraska Press, 1995), pp. 546–47. See *Hamlet*, the mole scene (1.4.24 and 1.5.170).

83. The terms are "wunderbar," *En* 143/109, and "unmittelbare Einwirkung des Geistes auf einen anderen," *En* 128/97*. On this part of the *Encyclopedia of the Sciences*, see also John H. Smith, "Sighting the Spirit: The Rhetorical Visions of Geist in Hegel's Encyclopedia," in David Michael Levin (ed.), *Sites of Vision: The Discursive Construction of Sight in the History of Philosophy* (Cambridge, MA: The MIT Press, 1997), pp. 240–65.

84. *En* 143/109*.

85. For "schauende Seele," see *En* 145/111*; for "Fernsehen," *En* 142/109*.

86. For "Hellsehen," see *En* 135/103*; for "ohne die Vermittlung des Lichtes," see *En* 140/107. The fantasy of an "unmediated" vision also surfaces in Schelling's *Ueber den Zusammenhang der Natur mit der Geisterwelt* (1810), where Schelling describes ghostly visions and clairvoyance as a "kind of seeing without pictures" (eine Art bilderlosen Anschauens). F. W. J. Schelling, *Ueber den Zusammenhang der Natur mit der Geisterwelt* (1810), in Manfred Schröter (ed.), *Werke: Vierter Ergänzungsband* (Munich: Beck, 1959), p. 167 (original pagination 9:65); Schelling, *Clara, or, On Nature's Connection to the Spirit World*, trans. Fiona Steinkamp (Albany: State University of New York Press, 2002), p. 47*.

87. The phrase is "schauendes Wissen," *En* 144/110*. See also 150/114*; "genius," *En* 135/103*.

88. *En* 135/103*.

89. The surprising proximity of magnetic clairvoyance to this mode of speculative knowledge is inadvertently highlighted by William Wallace's English translation of Hegel's *Encyclopedia*, which renders the "schauendes Wissen" of the feeling soul as "intuitive knowledge" and as "clairvoyant's knowledge." *Hegel's*

Philosophy of Mind, pp. 110 and 114.

90. *En* 16/7*.

91. *En* 136/103–104*.

92. *En* 144/110*.

93. *En* 16/7*.

94. *En* 133/101*.

95. *En* 133/101*.

96. "E" 323/268–69.

97. "E" 323/269*.

98. *En* 16/7.

99. Karl Rosenkranz, *Georg Friedrich Wilhelm Hegels Leben* (Berlin: Dunker & Humblot, 1844), pp. 12–13.

100. On Hegel's mode of excerpting books and its relation to his transformation of scientific data into a philosophical "subject," see also Friedrich Kittler, *Die Nacht der Substanz* (The night of substance) (Bern: Benteli, 1989). An abridged version of this argument is to be found in a later essay where Kittler states succinctly that "Hegel's absolute spirit is a concealed index card box" (Hegels absoluter Geist ist ein versteckter Zettelkasten). Friedrich Kittler, "Memories Are Made of You," in Peter Koch and Sybille Krämer (eds.), *Schrift, Medien, Kognition: Über die Exteriorität des Geistes* (Tübingen: Stauffenburg, 1997), p. 197.

101. *Ph* 453/374.

102. These texts are cited in "E" 353/293; "E" 334/278, and "E" 294/243.

103. See "E" 345/286; "E" 349/290; "E" 357/296.

104. G. W. F. Hegel, *Vorlesungen über die Ästhetik II*, vol. 14 of *Werke*, ed. Eva Moldenhauer and Karl Markus Michel, 20 vols. (Frankfurt am Main: Suhrkamp, 1986), p. 205.

105. "Der Mensch ist diese Nacht, dies leere Nichts, das alles in ihrer Einfachheit enthält, ein Reichtum unendlich vieler Vorstellungen.... Dies [ist] die Nacht, das Innere der Natur, das hier existiert—reines Selbst. In phantasmagorischen Vorstellungen ist es ringsum Nacht; hier schießt dann ein blutig[er] Kopf, dort ein[e] andere weiße Gestalt plötzlich hervor und verschwinden ebenso. Diese Nacht erblickt man, wenn man dem Menschen ins Auge blickt—in eine Nacht hinein, die furchtbar wird; es hängt die Nacht der Welt hier einem entgegen." G. W. F. Hegel, *Jenaer Realphilosophie: Vorlesungsmanuskripte zur Philosophie der Natur und des Geistes von 1805–1806*, ed. Johannes Hoffmeister (Hamburg: Felix

Meiner, 1967), pp. 180–81.

106. Many of the arguments developed in Slavoj Žižek's reading of this passage were previously formulated by Georges Bataille and Alexandre Kojève. See Alexandre Kojève, *Introduction à la lecture de Hegel* (Paris: Gallimard, 1947), p. 575; Georges Bataille, "Hegel, Death and Sacrifice" (1955), *Yale French Studies* 78 (1990), pp. 9–28, Slavoj Žižek, *The Ticklish Subject: The Absent Centre of Political Ontology* (London: Verso, 1999), pp. 29–41. None of these readings links Hegel's description of "phantasmagorical presentations" to Robertson's phantasmagoria.

107. "Geschichte," "eine träge Bewegung und Aufeinanderfolge von Geistern, eine Galerie von Bildern, deren jedes mit dem vollständigen Reichtume des Geistes ausgestattet [ist]." *Ph* 590/492*.

108. A relationship between Hegel's description of a "gallery of images" and the magic lantern is also suggested by Kittler's *Optical Media*. See Kittler, *Optische Medien*, p. 146/112.

109. *Ph* 590/492*.

110. "Ich habe versucht, diesen Zug der geistigen Gestaltungen der Philosophie in ihrem Fortgehen mit Andeutung ihres Zusammenhangs zu entwickeln, vor Ihren Gedanken vorüberzuführen. Diese Reihe ist das wahrhafte Geisterreich, das einzige Geisterreich, das es gibt—eine Reihe, die nicht eine Vielheit, noch auch eine Reihe bleibt als Aufeinanderfolge, sondern eben im Sichselbsterkennen sich zu Momenten des einen Geistes, zu dem einen und denselben gegenwärtigen Geiste macht. Und dieser lange Zug von Geistern sind die einzelnen Pulse, die er in seinem Leben verwendet." Hegel, *Vorlesungen über die Geschichte der Philosophie III*, pp. 461–62/553*.

111. A philosophical text that also features this narrative trope is Schelling's *On Nature's Relationship with the Spirit World: A Conversation* (1810), which emphasizes the resemblance of its heroine Clara with a picture from an ancestral gallery; Schelling, *Ueber den Zusammenhang der Natur mit der Geisterwelt: Ein Gespräch* [On the relationship between nature and the spiritual world: A dialogue]. The text emphasizes the resemblance of its protagonist, Clara, with a picture from an ancestral gallery. See Schelling, *Ueber den Zusammenhang*, pp. 115, 117 (original pagination 9: 13, 15), and Schelling, *Clare, or, Nature's Connection to the Spirit World*, pp. 10, 11. In Christoph Martin Wieland's *Euthanasia* (1805), the picture gallery is also described as a ghostly medium of memory that renders it possible that a deceased soul "see its previous life . . . like in a picture gallery" (ihr ehemaliges Leben . . . wie

in einer Bildergallerie zu beschauen). Wieland, *Euthanasia: Drey Gespräche über das Leben nach dem Tode* [Euthanasia: Three conversations on life after death] (Leipzig: Göschen, 1805), p. 191. But this assumption is proposed by the enthusiast Selmar, whereas the enlightened Willibald claims that after its death, a soul loses not just its body, but also its memory of its previous life.

112. When seeing Theodore for the first time, Princess Matilda seems to take Theodore himself for a ghost: "Do I dream? or is not that youth the exact resemblance of Alfonso's picture in the gallery?" Horace Walpole, *The Castle of Otranto: A Gothic Story*, ed. W. S. Lewis and E. J. Clery (Oxford: Oxford University Press, 1998), p. 54. See also p. 88: "He is the very image of that picture." Also see "his resemblance to Alfonso" (84) and "Still more was he troubled with the resemblance of Theodore to Alfonso's portrait" (99).

113. *Ibid.*, pp. 112–13.

114. *Ph* 591/492*.

115. See Joachim Ritter, *Hegel und die französische Revolution* (Frankfurt am Main: Suhrkamp, 1965).

116. Friedrich Nietzsche, "Hegel's gothische Himmelstürmerei," in *Sämtliche Werke*, vol. 11, p. 253.

117. The phrase is "die Erinnerung und Schädelstätte des absoluten Geistes, die Wirklichkeit, Wahrheit und Gewißheit seines Throns." *Ph* 591/493*.

118. Edmund Burke, "First Letter on a Regicide Peace," in *The Writings and Speeches of Edmund Burke, Volume 9: The Revolutionary War, 1794–1797, Ireland*, ed. R. B. McDowell (Oxford: Clarendon Press, 1991), pp. 190–91.

119. Thomas Carlyle, *The French Revolution: A History*, ed. Ruth Scurr (1837; London: Continuum, 2010), p. 183. These comparisons of the French Revolution with a specter and the phantasmagoria form the opposite to Karl Marx's opening of his *Communist Manifesto* and his frequent invocation of the phantasmagoria in his *Eighteenth Brumaire*.

120. *Ph* 590/492.

121. *WWP I* 567/1:420*.

CHAPTER THREE: GHOST NARRATIVES AND THE GOTHIC NOVEL

1. Immanuel Kant, "An Fräulein Charlotte von Knobloch 10. Aug [1763]," in *Briefe*, ed. Jürgen Zehbe (Göttingen: Vandenhoeck & Ruprecht, 1970), p. 21; Kant,

Correspondence, trans. and ed. Arnulf Zweig (Cambridge: Cambridge University Press, 1999), pp. 70–71*.

2. *Ibid.*, 24/73 and 25/74*.

3. Immanuel Kant, *Träume eines Geistersehers, erläutert durch Träume der Metaphysik*, in *Vorkritische Schriften bis 1768*, vol. 2 of *Werkausgabe*, ed. Wilhelm Weischedel, 12 vols. ed. Wilhelm Weischedel (Frankfurt am Main: Suhrkamp, 1977), p. 923; Kant, "Dreams of a Spirit Seer, Elucidated by Dreams of Metaphysics," in Immanuel Kant, *Theoretical Philosophy 1755–1770*, trans. and ed. by David Walford (Cambridge: Cambridge University Press, 1992), p. 305. Hereafter cited as *D*.

4. *Ibid.*

5. Jakob Friedrich Abel, *Philosophische Untersuchungen über die Verbindung der Menschen mit höheren Geistern* (Stuttgart: Mezler, 1791). While the text was published in 1791, two years after the first book version of Schiller's novel *The Ghost Seer* came out, Abel's 1786 book, *The Sources of Our Mental Presentations*, already contained a two-page introductory note that announced a later treatise dedicated to showing "that impressions by spirits cannot be considered as a special source of our mental presentations." Jacob Friedrich Abel, *Ueber die Quellen der menschlichen Vorstellungen* (Stuttgart: Bey Johann Benedict Mezler, 1786), no pagination.

6. Abel, *Philosophische Untersuchungen über die Verbindung der Menschen mit höheren Geistern*, p. 105.

7. *Ibid.* See also p. III: "obwohl auf der andern Seite die Unmöglichkeit einer Geisterverbindung...aus philosophischen Gründen nicht dargethan werden kann, so daß zulezt alles davon abhängt, ob irgend ein Faktum vorhanden sey, das uns hievon überzeuge."

8. The text was submitted in 1779 as Schiller's first dissertation at the Hohe Karlsschule. Two of the three readers' reports took offense with Schiller's fervent embrace of experience, condemning his writing as "obscure" and "exuberant." The thesis therefore did not receive its imprimatur, and the prospective military doctor had to spend another year at the boarding school, submitting a second dissertation, which was also rejected, until Schiller's third dissertation was finally accepted in 1780. Reports by Dr. Reuß and Surgeon-Major Klein, quoted in *Philosophische Schriften I*, ed. Lieselotte Blumenthal and Benno von Wiese, vol. 21 of *Schillers Werke: Nationalausgabe*, ed. Julius Petersen, Gerhard Fricke, et. al. (Weimar: Böhlaus Nachfolger, 1963), pp. 114–15; *Friedrich Schiller: Medicine, Psychology,*

and Literature, ed. Kenneth Dewhurst and Nigel Reeves (Berkeley: University of California Press, 1978), p. 167.

9. Friedrich Schiller, "Die Philosophie der Physiologie" (1779), in *Theoretische Schriften*, ed. Rolf-Peter Janz, vol. 8 of *Werke und Briefe in zwölf Banden*, ed. Klaus Harro Hilzinger et. al. (Frankfurt am Main: Deutscher Klassiker Verlag, 1992), p. 41; "Philosophy of Physiology," in *Friedrich Schiller: Medicine, Psychology, and Literature*, p. 152*.

10. "Ein Wesen, das eines teils durchdringlich, andern teils undurchdringlich wäre, und läßt sich ein solches denken?—Gewiß nicht." *Ibid.*, 41/152*.

11. "Die Erfahrung beweist sie. Wie kann die Theorie sie verwerfen?." *Ibid.*, 42/153*.

12. Abel, *Philosophische Untersuchungen über die Verbindung der Menschen mit höheren Geistern*, p. 107.

13. The phrase is "Vernunftgründe einerseits und wirkliche Erfahrung oder Erzählung andererseits" *D* 971/345*. On the distinction between "stories" or "histories" (*Geschichte*) and "philosophy," see Abel, *Philosophische Untersuchungen über die Verbindung der Menschen mit höheren Geistern*, p. 192

14. *D* 962–63/338*. "Eben dieselbe Unwissenheit macht auch, daß ich mich nicht unterstehe, so gänzlich alle Wahrheit an den mancherlei Geistererzählungen abzuleugnen, doch mit dem gewöhnlichen obgleich wunderlichen Vorbehalt, eine jede einzelne derselben in Zweifel zu ziehen, allen zusammen genommen aber einigen Glauben beizumessen. Dem Leser bleibt das Urteil frei; was mich aber anlangt, so ist zum wenigsten der Ausschlag auf die Seite der Gründe des zweiten Hauptstücks bei mir groß genug, mich bei Anhörung der mancherlei befremdlichen Erzählungen dieser Art ernsthaft und unentschieden zu halten."

15. See Peter Weber, "Die *Berlinische Monatsschrift* als Organ der Aufklärung," in Peter Weber (ed.), *Berlinische Monatsschrift (1783–1796)* (Leipzig: Reclam, 1986), pp. 412–34.

16. "Ich verstehe aber unter dem öffentlichen Gebrauche seiner eigenen Vernunft denjenigen, den jemand als Gelehrter von ihr vor dem ganzen Publikum der Leserwelt macht." Immanuel Kant, "Beantwortung der Frage: Was ist Aufklärung?" (1784), in *Schriften zur Anthropologie, Geschichtsphilosophie, Politik und Pädagogik 1*, vol. 11 of *Werkausgabe*, ed. Wilhelm Weischedel (Frankfurt am Main: Suhrkamp, 1977), p. 55; Immanuel Kant, "An Answer to the Question: What Is Enlightenment?," in *Practical Philosophy*, trans. and ed. Mary J. Gregor

(Cambridge: Cambridge University Press, 1996), p. 18*. On Kant's "What Is
Enlightenment?," see also Dorothea von Mücke, "Authority, Authorship, and Audience: Enlightenment Models for a Critical Public," *Representations* 111 (Summer
2010), pp. 60–87.

17. Josias Ludwig Gosch, *Fragmente über den Ideenumlauf*, ed. Georg Stanitzek
and Hartmut Winkler (1789: Berlin: Kadmos, 2006) "Vermöge der Mittheilung der
Begriffe wird das menschliche Geschlecht einer fortschreitenden Vervolkomm-
nung fähig" (p. 121) and "Aeusserst viel verdanken wir wahrlich der Erfindung der
Buchdruckerkunst" (p. 158). The book contains a whole chapter on "the mechanism of the circulation of ideas" (pp. 107–16).

18. Kant, "An Fräulein Charlotte von Knobloch 10. Aug [1763]," in *Briefe*,
22/71*, emphasis in the original.

19. *Ibid.*, 23/72*.

20. On the rise of mesmerism and its relation to print as a medium that allows
for the proliferation of esoteric theories, see Robert Darnton, *Mesmerism and the
End of Enlightenment in France* (New York: Schocken, 1970). On occultism and
print in the late eighteenth century see also Sabine Doering-Manteuffel, *Das
Okkulte: Eine Erfolgsgeschichte im Schatten der Aufklärung. Von Gutenberg bis zum
World Wide Web* [The occult: A success story in the shadow of enlightenment from
Gutenberg to the World Wide Web] (Munich: Siedler Verlag, 2008).

21. *D* 923/305.

22. The phrase is "herumgehende Geistergeschichten." *D* 965/340*.

23. "Nun trat die *Buchdruckerei* hinzu und gab beschriebenen Lumpen Flü-
gel. In alle Welt fliegen sie; mit jedem Jahr, mit jeder Tagesstunde vom ersten
erwachenden Morgenstrahl an wachsen dieser literarischen Fama die Schwingen,
bis an den Rand der Erde... worüber Menschenstimmen schweigen, darüber sprechen und schreien gegossene Buchstaben, merkantilische Hefte." Johann Gottfried
Herder, *Briefe zu Beförderung der Humanität*, ed. Heinz Stolpe, 2 vols. (Berlin:
Aufbau, 1971), vol. 2, pp. 92–93.

24. The phrase is "mit der Buchdruckerei nämlich kam *alles* an den Tag." *Ibid.*,
p. 93.

25. "Ein Anderes aber ist es in unsern Tagen, da durch einfache Druck-
werkzeuge das schlechteste, wie das beste Werk mit wunderbarer Schnelligkeit
vertausendfacht und in die Welt ausgestreut werden kann. *Jetzt erhält und verbreitet
sich das Schlechtere länger und mehr als ehemals*, und nimmt an Zahl an gleicher

Menge zu, wie es der mittelmäßigen Köpfe, der Halbgelehrten, der Leute mit
unedeln Nebenabsichten überhaupt mehr gibt, als der ausgezeichneten, zum Lehr-
amt wahrhaft geweihten Geister, denen es um nichts als das Gute zu thun ist.
Daher rührt die zahllose Fluth schriftstellerischer Werke, welche das Gepräge der
Elendigkeit offen tragen, und die Jrrthümer und Geistes- und Herzensschwächen
ihrer Verfasser Andern mitzutheilen bestimmt sind." Heinrich Zschokke, "Eine
Warnung vor den Gefahren der Lesesucht," [Warning of the dangers of reading
addiction] in *Stunden der Andacht zur Beförderung wahren Christenthums und häusli-
cher Gottesverehrung* [Hours of devotion for the promotion of true Christianity and
domestic worship of God], vol. 5, *Andachtsbuch für die Jugend, Sechste verbesserte
Original-Ausgabe* [Book of devotions for the youth, sixth improved edition] (Aarau:
Heinrich Remigius Sauerländer, 1821), p. 131. Paradoxically, Zschokke himself
wrote ghost and knight novels in his youth. See also Johann Georg Heinzmann,
Appell an meine Nation: Über die Pest der deutschen Literatur [Call to my nation: On
the plague of German literature] (Bern: Auf Kosten des Verfassers, 1795), p. 125:
"Keine Nation hat in den letzten Jahren so viel gedruckt, als die Deutsche...so hat
man eine Meeresfluth von Büchern."

26. *D* 967/342.

27. *D* 969/343.

28. *D* 969/343. See also: "Women are particularly prone to lend credence to
stories of prophecy, interpretation of dreams, and all kinds of other marvelous
things." *D* 967/342.

29. *D* 968/342–43*.

30. *D* 981/352–53*. See also *D* 972/346 on Kant's "philosophical brain child"
(*philosophische Hirngeburt*) and its resemblance to Swedenborg's "monstrous"
(*mißgeschaffen*) theory. On theories of maternal imagination and its role in giving
birth to monsters see Marie-Hélène Huet, *Monstrous Imagination* (Cambridge, MA:
Harvard University Press, 1993). See also Philip K. Wilson, "Eighteenth-Century
'Monsters' and Nineteenth-Century 'Freaks': Reading the Maternally Marked
Child," *Literature and Medicine* 21.1 (Spring 2002), pp. 1–25.

31. Kant, "An Ludwig Ernst Borowski [March 1790]," in *Briefe*, p. 162/338. It
is striking that Borowski, to whom the letter was addressed, undermines Kant's
intention by actually publishing the letter as an appendix to a treatise of his
that criticizes Cagliostro and mystical enthusiasm. See Ludwig Ernst Borowski,
"Über den Hang zur Schwärmerei und die Mittel dagegen," in *Cagliostro, einer der*

merkwürdigsten Abentheurer unsres Jahrhunderts: Seine Geschichte, nebst Raisonnement über ihn und den schwärmerischen Unfug unsrer Zeit überhaupt (Königsberg: Gottlieb Lebrecht Hartung, 1790), pp. 160–62. In the first edition of the book, both Kant's letter and Borowski's treatise were published without revealing the respective authors.

32. Friedrich Schiller, *Der Geisterseher: Aus den Papieren des Grafen von O*, in *Historische Schriften und Erzählungen II*, ed. Otto Dann, vol. 7 of *Werke und Briefe* (Frankfurt am Main: Deutscher Klassiker Verlag, 2002); Schiller, *The Ghost-Seer, or Apparitionist*, ed. Jeffrey L. Sammons, trans. Henry G. Bohn (Columbia, SC: Camden House, 1992). Hereafter cited as *G*.

33. *G* 589/2*.

34. *G* 590/2.

35. *G* 591/4.

36. *G* 597/8. See also: "I have a hidden guardian" (*verborgenen Aufseher*). *G* 594/6*.

37. The phrases are "schwärmerische Melancholie," *G* 588/1*; "[Mit der Geisterwelt in Verbindung zu stehen] war jederzeit seine Lieblingsschwärmerei gewesen," *G* 599/10; and "geheime Künste," *G* 597/8*.

38. "Wenige, worunter der Prinz war, hielten dafür, daß man sein Urteil in diesen Dingen zurückhalten müsse," *G* 598/8*; *D* 963/338*. In the conclusion of his *Essay on the Connection between the Animal and the Spiritual Nature of Man* (1780), Schiller himself had also invoked the possibility that even after death, the soul may be able to intervene into the material world—by reincarnation or by appearing as a spirit. Describing the human soul after the dissolution of the human body as "observing the universe from new perspectives," Schiller wrote: "But can one be sure that this sphere is lost to it? We now lay many a book aside that we do not understand, but we may understand it better some years hence." Friedrich Schiller, "Versuch über den Zusammenhang der tierischen Natur des Menschen mit seiner geistigen" (1780), in *Theoretische Schriften*, pp. 162–63; Schiller, "Essay on the Connection between the Animal and Spiritual Nature of Man," in *Friedrich Schiller: Medicine, Psychology, and Literature*, p. 285. On Schiller's openness to the possibility of genuine spiritual occurrences, see his letter to Christian Gottfried Körner in which Schiller reports on a conversation with Herder: "I talked about the Ghost Seer and how this essay [Aufsatz] had attained a certain celebrity. The matter pleased him, and we further embarked upon it. He has his own fertile ideas

in this, too, and leans toward the assumption of a mutual interaction of spirits [wechselseitigen Ineinanderwirkens der Geister] according to unknown laws.... A vivid thought of mine could awaken a similar one in somebody close to me, etc." Schiller to Christian Gottfried Körner, August 8, 1787, in *Briefwechsel: Schillers Briefe 17.4.1785–31.12.1787*, ed. Karl Jürgen Skrodzki, vol. 24 of *Schillers Werke: Nationalausgabe*, ed. Julius Petersen, Gerhard Fricke, et. al (Weimar: Böhlaus Nachfolger, 1989), pp. 124–25.

39. *G* 600/10.

40. *G* 604/14*.

41. *G* 605/14.

42. *Ibid.*

43. *G* 606/15*.

44. *G* 606/15. The fact that the Prince is able to recognize the "features" of the Armenian, even though the Armenian was wearing a mask in St. Mark's Square, is probably a mistake arising from the speed with which Schiller wrote this novel. At the same time, the dubious recognitions in this text correspond to the Gothic effacement of individuality analyzed by Eve Kosofsky Sedgwick in "The Character in the Veil: Imagery of the Surface in the Gothic Novel," *PMLA* 96 (1981), pp. 255–70.

45. *G* 615/22.

46. *G* 617/24.

47. For a list of these treatises, see Chapter 1, "The Magic Lantern of Philosophy: Specters of Kant," notes 54 and 62. Already in 1926, Ernst Weizmann had pointed to Funk's *Natural Magic* as one of the sources consulted by Schiller. See Weizmann, "Die Geisterbeschwörung in Schillers Geisterseher," *Jahrbuch der Goethe-Gesellschaft* 26 (1926), pp. 174–93.

48. On Philidor, see Deac Rossell, "Die Laterna magica," in Bodo von Dewitz and Werner Nekes (eds.), *Ich sehe was, was Du nicht siehst!: Sehmaschinen und Bilderwelten. Die Sammlung Werner Nekes* (Göttingen: Steidl, 2002), p. 142, and Mervyn Heard, *Phantasmagoria: The Secret Life of the Magic Lantern* (Hastings, UK: Projection Box, 2006), pp. 63–79.

49. Johann Samuel Halle, *Magie, oder die Zauberkräfte der Natur, so auf den Nutzen und die Belustigung angewandt worden*, 4 vols. (Berlin: Bey Joachim Pauli, 1784), vol. 1, p. 232.

50. Similar to Schiller's novel, Abel's *Philosophical Investigations* also explains

Schröpfer's conjuring of spirits as made possible by the secret use of a magic lantern: "so ließ z.E. Schröpfer ein Bild aus der Zauberlaterne in einen durch die Kunst gemachten Rauch fallen, und stellte dadurch dasselbe schwebend in der Luft vor" (p. 152).

51. Cajetan Tschink, *Geschichte eines Geistersehers: Aus den Papieren des Mannes mit der eisernen Larve*, 3 vols. (Vienna: F. J. Kaiserer, 1790–93); Tschink, *The Victim of Magical Delusion* (London: Robinson, 1795); Lorenz Flammenberg [Karl Friedrich Kahlert], *Der Geisterbanner: Eine Wundergeschichte aus mündlichen und schriftlichen Traditionen* (Vienna: Johann Baptist, 1792); Flammenberg, *The Necromancer* (1792; London: Skoob, 1989). The quotes are from Tschink, *The Victim of Magical Delusion*, vol. 1, p. 81, and vol. 2, pp. 197–200; Kahlert actually mentions a "camera obscura" (207) in a passage that can only refer to a magic lantern. In the translator's preface to *The Victim of Magical Delusion*, Peter Will also emphasizes that "many extraordinary phenomena which, to the uninformed, appear to originate from supernatural causes, either may be contrived by means of natural magic, or arise from the wild irregular flights of a heated and disordered imagination" (p. v).

52. Walter Scott, "Introduction," in Horace Walpole, *The Castle of Otranto: A Gothic Story* (Edinburgh: James Ballantyne and Co., 1811), p. xxvi. Scott's text was originally published without the author's name.

53. The phrase is "ein Beitrag zur Geschichte des Betrugs und der Verirrungen des menschlichen Geistes." *G* 1000/1*.

54. Johann Christoph Adelung, *Geschichte der menschlichen Narrheit; oder, Lebensbeschreibungen brühmter Schwarzkünstler, Goldmacher, Teufelsbanner, Zeichen- und Liniendeuter, Schwärmer, Wahrsager, und anderer philosophischer Unholden*, 5 vols. (Leipzig: Weygand, 1785–89).

55. The phrases are "eine bigotte knechtische Erziehung...hatte seinem zarten Hirne Schreckbilder eingedrückt," *G* 648/46; and "ein bezauertes Schloß, in das man nicht ohne Grauen seinen Fuß setzte," *G* 647/46*.

56. The phrase is "Geister ausgespien aus Gräbern." Friedrich Schiller, *Die Räuber*, ed. Herbert Stubenrauch, vol. 3 of *Schillers Werke: Nationalausgabe*, ed. Julius Petersen, Gerhard Fricke, et.al. (Weimar: Böhlaus Nachfolger, 1953), p. 117; for "images," see Schiller, "Die Philosophie der Physiologie," p. 144/272.

57. The phrase is "fanatische Begeisterung," *G* 630/33*.

58. *G* 638/39 and *G* 642/41.

59. *G* 655/51. On the Armenian as embodiment or personification of a secret

society, see Stefan Andriopoulos, "Occult Conspiracies: Spirits and Secret Societies in Schiller's *Ghost Seer*," *New German Critique* 103 (Winter 2008), pp. 65–81; on the "invisible hand" in political economy and the Gothic novel, see Stefan Andriopoulos, "The Invisible Hand: Supernatural Agency in Political Economy and the Gothic Novel," *English Literary History* 66 (1999), pp. 739–58.

60. G. W. F. Hegel, *Jenaer Realphilosophie: Vorlesungsmanuskripte zur Philosophie der Natur und des Geistes von 1805–1806*, ed. Johannes Hoffmeister (Hamburg: Felix Meiner, 1967), pp. 180–81.

61. The unreliability of the Sicilian's story also speaks to the question of how credible allegedly authentic ghost narratives truly are. In terms that echo the preamble to Kant's *Dreams of a Spirit Seer*, the Prince dismisses the evidence of the Sicilian because it contradicts the established theoretical assumptions of science: "The testimony of a villain...can have no weight against truth and sound reason. Does a man who has already deceived me several times...deserve credit when he appears against human reason and the eternal laws of nature?" G 637/38*.

62. G 627/31*.

63. G 629/32.

64. G 630/33. See Charlotta Elisabeth Konstantia von der Recke, *Nachricht von des berüchtigten Cagliostro Aufenthalte in Mittau, im Jahre 1779, und von dessen dortigen magischen Operationen* [On the notorious Cagliostro's stay in Mittau, in the Year of 1779, and on his magical operations there] (1787); reprinted in: *Cagliostro: Dokumente zu Okkultismus und Aufklärung* [Cagliostro: Documents on occultism and enlightenment], ed. Klaus H. Kiefer (Munich: Beck, 1991), pp. 20–143.

65. G 635/37. Immediately prior to this, the Armenian has entered the scene, standing motionless amid the celebration: "His appearance struck every one with terror." G 633/35*.

66. Ann Radcliffe, *The Mysteries of Udolpho: A Romance*, ed. Bonamy Dobrée (1794; Oxford: Oxford University Press, 1980), p. 248.

67. *Ibid.*, pp. 248–49.

68. Edmund Burke, *A Philosophical Enquiry into the Origin of our Ideas of the Sublime and Beautiful*, ed. Adam Phillips (1759; Oxford: Oxford University Press, 1990), p. 54.

69. Radcliffe, *The Mysteries of Udolpho*, p. 249.

70. Charles Maturin's *Melmoth, The Wanderer* describes the "monotony" (pp. 76, 110, 115, 357) and "repetition" (p. 112) that characterize monastic life as

creating a kind of void that makes any kind of change desirable: "I am a clock that has struck the same minutes and hours for sixty years. The monotony of my existence would make a transition, even to pain, desirable" (p. 110). Similar to Radcliffe's *Udolpho*, the disruption of this monotony comes in the form of terror, one that is described as intensely embodied: "All this detail, that takes many words to tell, rushed... on my body. I was all physical feeling,—all intense corporeal agony" (p. 192). Charles Maturin, *Melmoth, The Wanderer*, ed. Douglas Grant (1820; Oxford: Oxford University Press, 1989).

71. Horace Walpole, *The Castle of Otranto: A Gothic Story*, ed. W. S. Lewis and E. J. Clery (Oxford: Oxford University Press, 1998), p. 19.

72. Walpole, "Preface to the First Edition," in *ibid.*, p. 6.

73. *G* 702 and 703/70.

74. The term is "Schrecken," *G* 700/68*. On terror and the sublime see Burke, *A Philosophical Enquiry into our Ideas of the Beautiful and the Sublime*, p. 36: "Whatever... is in any sort terrible, or is conversant about terrible objects, or operates in a manner analogous to terror, is a source of the sublime."

75. *G* 700/68*.

76. Schiller's representation of the enchanting power of images is appropriated and radicalized in a scene from Matthew Lewis's *The Monk*, which describes Ambrosio's falling in love with Matilda as founded upon his previous idolatrous adoration of a painted Madonna. See Matthew Lewis, *The Monk: A Romance*, ed. Howard Anderson (Oxford: Oxford University Press, 1980), pp. 81–84. Within the German literary tradition, this trope was then reappropriated in E. T. A. Hoffmann's novel *The Devil's Elixirs* (1815), which explicitly quotes Lewis's *The Monk*.

77. See Schiller's letter to his publisher Göschen from March 1789: "Wenn Sie eine Vignette oder Titelkupfer dazu wollen, so würde ich entweder die Entrevue des Prinzen mit der schönen Unbekannten in der Kirche, welche auf dem neulich überschickten Mscrpte. vorkommt, oder die Erscheinung des 2ten Marquis von Lanoy, die den ersten Abschnitt des Geistersehers im 4ten Hefte beschließt, dazu vorgeschlagen haben." Schiller to Göschen, March 8, 1789, quoted in *Historische Schriften und Erzählungen II*, p. 1035.

78. The phrase is "ein überirdisches Wesen," *G* 720/78. The equivalence between the spirit apparition in the first part and the apparition of the Greek woman in the second part is also emphasized by Friedrich Kittler, "Die Laterna magica der Literatur: Schillers und Hoffmanns Medienstrategien," *Athenäum:*

Jahrbuch für Romantik 4 (1994), p. 228, and by Liliane Weissberg, *Geistersprache: Philosophischer und literarischer Diskurs im späten achtzehnten Jahrhundert* [Spirit language: Philosophical and literary discourse in the late eighteenth century] (Würzburg: Königshausen & Neumann, 1990), p. 127.

79. G 720/78*.

80. G 721/78.

81. The terms are "Erscheinung," G 702 and 703/70, and "metaphysische Träumereien," G 707/73.

82. G 1007/92. On Schiller's literary anti-Catholicism, see Ritchie Robertson, "Schiller and the Jesuits," in Nicholas Martin (ed.), *Schiller: National Poet—Poet of Nations* (Amsterdam: Rodopi, 2006), pp. 179–200.

83. On *The Ghost Seer* in relation to the "secret society novel" see Andriopoulos, "Occult Conspiracies."

84. G 650/48*. Here, Schiller's novel seems to cite from his earlier text, "Über die Krankheit des Eleven Grammont" [On the illness affecting the pupil Grammont] (1780), which described "pietistic fanaticism" as the source of Grammont's melancholy and pathological skepticism: "Pietistic fanaticism seems to have laid the foundations of the whole subsequent ailment. This sharpened his conscience, rendered him extremely sensitive towards all moral and religious matters, and confused his powers of reasoning. The study of metaphysics finally made him suspicious of all truth and forced him to the other extreme, where skeptical reflection frequently brought him, who had previously exaggerated religion, to the point of doubting its very cornerstone." Friedrich Schiller, "Über die Krankheit des Eleven Grammont," in *Theoretische Schriften*, p. 59; Schiller, "On the Illness Affecting the Pupil Grammont," in *Friedrich Schiller: Medicine, Psychology and Literature*, p. 181*.

85. G 676/63*.

86. In an often-quoted letter to his later wife, Caroline von Beulwitz, and her sister, Charlotte Lengfeld, from January 1789, Schiller claimed that developing these skeptical arguments made him doubt his own faith: "My Ghost Seer...had...nearly shaken my Christianity.... The incident provided me an occasion to bring about out a philosophical discussion, which I already found necessary, in order to present before the reader's eyes the freethinking phase through which I let the prince wander. On this occasion, I developed some of my own ideas, which you may discern in this (for God save me, that I should think completely like the prince in the darkening of his mind)." Schiller to Caroline von Beulwitz and

Charlotte Lengfeld, January 1789, in *Briefwechsel: Schillers Briefe 1.1.1788–28.2.1790*, ed. Eberhard Haufe, vol. 25 of *Schillers Werke: Nationalausgabe*, ed. Julius Petersen, Gerhard Fricke, et.al. (Weimar: Böhlaus Nachfolger, 1979), p. 190. According to Wolfgang Riedel's *Die Anthropologie des jungen Schiller* (Würzburg: Königshausen & Neumann, 1985), Schiller did not read Kant's critical philosophy before 1791, but in the spring of 1788, Schiller's friend Körner sent him a text that stressed the "limits of human cognition" (die Gränzen des menschlichen Wissens) in terms clearly borrowed from the *Critique of Pure Reason*. See Schiller, *Philosophische Schriften I*, pp. 157–58, and Riedel, *Die Anthropologie des jungen Schiller*, pp. 240–41 and 246.

87. On the veil in Schiller's work, see also his poem "Das verschleierte Bild zu Sais." The trope of removing a veil also surfaces earlier in *The Ghost Seer* in the Prince's response to the Sicilian's offer to demonstrate his ability of raising a spirit: "Ich würde denjenigen als meinen Wohltäter...umarmen, der hier meine Zweifel zerstreute und die Decke von meinen Augen zöge.... Lassen Sie mich eine Erscheinung sehen." *G* 600/10. On the veil in general, see Uwe C. Steiner, *Verhüllungsgeschichten: Die Dichtung des Schleiers* (Munich: Fink, 2006).

88. *G* 695 note. This editorial note was included only in the first version of the text, printed in six installments in Schiller's journal *Thalia*.

89. For bibliographical references see note 51 above.

90. Anonymous, *Enthüllte Geistergeschichten: Zur Belehrung und Unterhaltung für Jedermann; ein Pendant zu Schillers Geisterseher* (Leipzig: Supprian, 1797). Jakob Brückner, *Angelika, Tochter des grossen Banditen Odoardo, Prinzen von Peschia aus dem Hauße Zanelti: Ein Seitenstück zu Schillers Geisterseher* (Leipzig: Hinrichs, 1801). A similar wave of spin-offs and sequels was engendered by the most popular robber novel of the period, Christian August Vulpius's *Rinaldo Rinalidini der Räuberhauptmann: Eine romantische Geschichte unseres Jahrhunderts*, 4 vols. (Leipzig: Wienbrack, 1798); the sixth edition was published in 1824. Two years after publishing the novel, which ended with Rinaldini's death, Vulpius declared his protagonist only seemingly dead and gave in to public demand for continuing the story by publishing two further volumes. See Christian August Vulpius, *Rinaldo Rinaldini: Forsetzung des Räuberhauptmanns Rinaldini* (Leipzig: Gräff, 1800). In addition, other authors also published "sequels" and "counterparts" to the popular text, such as J. J. Brückner, *Gräfin Dionora Mortagno, Rinaldo Rinaldinis Geliebte; ein Romantisches Gemälde in 8 Büchern, als Anhang zu Rinaldo Rinaldini* (Leipzig:

Joachim, 1801) or J. F. E. Albrecht, *Dolko, der Bandit, Zeitgenosse Rinaldo Rinaldinis* (Heidelberg: Herold 1801). See also Marion Beaujean, *Der Trivialroman in der zweiten Hälfte des 18. Jahrhunderts* (Bonn: Bouvier, 1964), pp. 147–48.

91. H. Krappe, *Geistererscheinungen im Grabe der Scipionen: Aus Papieren, die...auf dem Esquilin gefunden worden* (Leipzig: Taubert, 1816); Karl August Gottlieb Seidel, *Die Geisterseherin*, 3 vols. (Leipzig: Reinicke, 1794–98); Christian Heinrich Spiess, *Der Alte Ueberall und Nirgends: Eine Geistergeschichte* (Leipzig: Kleefeld, 1803); Leonhard Wächter, *Die Teufelsbeschwörung* (Berlin: Maurer, 1791), translated into English as *The Sorcerer: A Tale* (London: Johnson 1795); Johann Heinrich Zschokke, *Geister und Geisterseher oder Leben und frühes Ende eines Nekromantisten: Eine warnende Anekdote unserer Zeit* (Kuestrin: Oehmigke, 1789). See furthermore Sophie Albrecht, *Graumännchen, oder die Burg Rabenbühl, eine Geistergeschichte altdeutschen Ursprungs* (Hamburg: Buchhandlung der Verlagsgesellschaft, 1799); Ignatz Ferdinand Arnold, *Das Bildniss mit dem Blutflecken, eine Geistergeschichte nach einer wahren Anekdote* (Zerbst: Füchsel, 1800); Benedikte Naubert, *Velleda: Ein Zauberroman* [Velleda: A magic novel] (Leipzig: Schäfer, 1795); and Francisco Quevedo y Villegas, *Reisen in die andere Welt. Oder: Ueber-und unterirdische Visionen und Phantasien verschiedener Geisterseher* [Journeys into the other world; or, Celestial and subterranean visions and phantasies of various ghost seers] (Leipzig: Weygang, 1787).

92. See Ernst Friedrich Follenius, *Friedrich Schillers Geisterseher: Aus den Memoires des Grafen von O*** (Strassburg: bey Grünefeld, 1796), first English translation published as *The Armenian; or the Ghost Seer: A History Founded on Fact* (London: Symonds, 1800).

93. Carl A. Grosse, *Der Genius: Aus den Papieren des Marquis C* von G***, 4 vols. (Halle: Hendel, 1791–95).

94. Carl August Grosse, *The Genius: or, The Mysterious Adventures of Don Carlos de Grandez*, 2 vols., trans. Joseph Trapp (London: Allen and West, 1796); Grosse, *Horrid Mysteries: A Story*, 3 vols., trans. Peter Will (London: William Lane, 1796).

95. Jane Austen, *Northanger Abbey*, ed. John Davie (1798/1817; Oxford: Oxford University Press, 1990), pp. 35, 34, 23–24.

96. Ludwig Tieck, "An Heinrich Wackenroder" (June 12, 1792), in *William Lovell*, ed. Walter Münz (Stuttgart: Reclam, 1986), pp. 691–92.

97. *Ibid.*, p. 692.

98. See Johann Gottfried Hoche, *Vertraute Briefe über die jetzige abentheuerliche*

Lesesucht und über den Einfluß derselben auf die Verminderung des häuslichen und öffentlichen Glücks [Intimate letters on the current frivolous reading addiction and on its influence on the diminution of domestic and public happiness] (Hannover: Ritscher, 1794); Johann Rudolph Gottlieb Beyer, *Ueber das Bücherlesen in so fern es zum Luxus unserer Zeit gehört* [On the reading of books in so far as it is part of the luxuriousness of our time] (Erfurt: Keyer, 1796); Johann Andreas Keyn, *Ueber die Lesesucht der Jugend, nebst einigen Vorschlägen, wie Eltern und Lehrer dieselbe zu mäßigen und zu leiten trachten sollen* [On the reading addiction of our youth, together wirth several proposals how parents and teachers should seek to alleviate and guide it] (Regensburg: Zeidler, 1803). See also Albrecht Koschorke, "Lesesucht—Zeichendiät: Die Weimarer Klassik als Antwort auf die Medienrevolution des 18. Jahrhunderts," [Weimar classicism as a response to the media revolution of the eighteenth century] in Claus Pias (ed.), *Neue Vorträge zur Medienkultur* (Weimar: Verlag und Datenbank für Geisteswissenschaften, 2000), pp. 115–36; John A. McCarthy, "The Art of Reading and the Goals of the German Enlightenment," *Lessing Yearbook* 16 (1984), pp. 79–94; and Martha Woodmansee, "Toward a Genealogy of the Aesthetic: The German Reading Debate of the 1790s," *Cultural Critique* 11 (Winter 1988–89), pp. 203–21.

99. Hoche, *Vertraute Briefe*, p. 68.

100. See Reinhard Wittmann, "Was There a Reading Revolution at the End of the Eighteenth Century?," in Guglielmo Cavallo and Roger Chartier (eds.), *A History of Reading in the West*, trans. Lydia Cochrane (Amherst: University of Massachusetts Press, 1999), pp. 284–312. Wittmann alleges that the market share of novels grew from 2.6 percent in 1740 to 11.7 percent in 1800 (p. 302). On the lending library and the Gothic novel, see Jörg Schönert and Georg Jäger (eds.), *Die Leihbibliothek als Institution des literarischen Lebens im 18. und 19. Jahrhundert: Organisationsformen, Bestände und Publikum* [The lending library as an institution of literary life in the eighteenth and nineteenth century] (Hamburg: Hauswedell, 1980), pp. 7–60.

101. On the interrelation between the "circulation" of pernicious reading material and "reading societies," see also Hoche, *Vertraute Briefe*, p. 98: "Die Lesegesellschaften...stiften bis jetzt im allgemeinen mehr Schaden als Nutzen, und bedürfen wol eines Censors. Durch sie kommt so manches in Umlauf was den Sitten...höchst nachtheilig ist."

102. See Christian Gottlob Kayser (ed.), *Vollständiges Bücherlexikon enthaltend*

alle von 1750 bis zu Ende des Jahres 1832 in Deutschland und in den angrenzenden Ländern gedrückten Bücher [Complete dictionary of books, containing all volumes printed between 1750 and 1832 in Germany and its neighboring countries] (Leipzig 1836), supplement of vol. 6. See also Beaujean, *Der Trivialroman*, p. 178.

103. On women and the young generation as subject to "reading addiction," see Dominik von König, "Lesesucht und Lesewut," [Reading addiction and reading rage] in Herbert G. Göpfert (ed.), *Buch und Leser* [Book and reader] (Hamburg: Hauswedell, 1977), pp. 89–112, esp. p. 97.

104. "An Ludwig Ernst Borowski [March 1790]," Kant, *Briefe*, p. 160/337*.

105. *Ibid.*

106. *Ibid.*, p. 161/338*.

107. Heinzmann, *Appell an meine Nation*, pp. 396–97.

108. The phrase is "Meeresfluth von Büchern." Heinzmann, *Appell an meine Nation*, p. 125.

109. "Das *Romanlesen* hat, außer manchen anderen Verstimmungen des Gemüts, auch dieses zur Folge, daß es die Zerstreuung habituell macht." Immanuel Kant, *Anthropologie in pragmatischer Hinsicht*, in *Schriften zur Anthropologie, Geschichtsphilosophie, Politik und Pädagogik II*, vol. 12 of *Werkausgabe*, p. 521; Immanuel Kant, *Anthropology from a Pragmatic Point of View*, trans. Robert B. Louden (Cambridge: Cambridge University Press, 2006), p. 102.

110. J. A. Bergk, *Die Kunst, Bücher zu lesen* (Jena: In der Hempelschen Buchhandlung, 1799), pp. 250–51. In similar terms, Hoche described the authors of ghost novels as "veritable enemies of human reason" (wirkliche Feinde des menschlichen Verstandes). Hoche, *Vertraute Briefe*, p. 24.

111. The phrase is "wenn alle Augenblicke neue ungewöhnliche Erscheinungen, wie in einem Guckkasten, vor ihm vorbeigehen." Bergk, *Die Kunst, Bücher zu lesen*, p. 250.

112. *Ibid.*, p. 252.

113. Hoche, *Vertraute Briefe*, p. 21.

114. "Neben diesem erwecken alle Romane die Neigung für das Wunderbare und Ausserordentliche, und einen Eckel gegen den natürlichen Lauf der Dinge. Die gewohnten Arbeiten, bey denen sich die Mädchen zu Hausmüttern bilden sollten, werden unerträglich und erzeugen Langeweile, die nur durch *neue Erschütterungen der Einbildungskraft überwunden wird*." Friedrich Burchard Benken (ed.), *Weltklugheit und Lebensgenuß; oder praktische Beyträge zur Philosophie des Lebens*

[Practical cleverness and the enjoyment of life, or practical contributions to the philosophy of life], 3 vols., 3rd ed. (Hannover, 1806), vol. 1, p. 243.

115. Tieck, *William Lovell*, pp. 162–63.

116. Five hundred pages later, the text gives a different explanation for Balder's ostensible hallucination as Andrea Cosimo, the novel's conspirator, recalls in his diary how he amused himself with walking as a specter through Balder's room. *Ibid.*, p. 636.

117. *Ibid.*, pp. 162–63.

CHAPTER FOUR: ROMANTICISM AND THE MARVELOUS FACTS OF ANIMAL MAGNETISM AND CLAIRVOYANCE

1. Ludwig Tieck, "Über Shakespeare's Behandlung des Wunderbaren" (1793), in Ludwig Tieck, *Schriften 1789–1794*, ed. Achim Hölter, vol. 1 of *Schriften in zwölf Bänden*, ed. Manfred Frank et al., 12 vols. (Frankfurt am Main: Deutscher Klassiker Verlag, 1991).

2. On ghosts in *Hamlet* and sixteenth-century and seventeenth-century theological debates, see Stephen Greenblatt, *Hamlet in Purgatory* (Princeton, NJ: Princeton University Press, 2001).

3. Tieck, "Über Shakespeares Behandlung," p. 685.

4. See also "The Enlightenment and the Anti-Marvelous," in Lorraine Daston and Katharine Park, *Wonders and the Order of Nature, 1150–1750* (New York: Zone Books, 1998).

5. Tieck, "Über Shakespeares Behandlung," p. 719, emphasis in the original. On this passage, see also Dorothea von Mücke, *The Seduction of the Occult and the Rise of the Fantastic Tale* (Stanford: Stanford University Press, 2003), p. 5.

6. Tieck, "Über Shakespeares Behandlung," p. 697.

7. *Ibid.*, p. 687. On the transformation of the ghostly into a simulacrum that stands in for the power of Romantic poetry, see also David Wellbery, "Verzauberung: Das Simulakrum in der romantischen Lyrik" [Enchantment: The simulacrum in Romantic poetry], in Andreas Kablitz and Gerhard Neumann (eds.), *Mimesis und Simulation* (Freiburg im Breisgau: Rombach, 1998), pp. 452–77.

8. Tieck, "Über Shakespeares Behandlung," p. 687.

9. *Ibid.*, p. 692. Tieck gives an extensive comparison of dreams and theatrical illusion (see pp. 691 and 692), and he returns this analogy repeatedly. See, for instance, p. 702, where he states: "The illusion of a dream and of a marvelous play

end according to the same laws." See also pp. 703 and 705.

10. *Ibid.*, p. 710. Analyzing the opening of Macbeth, Tieck similarly states: "it is the terror…that fills us with dread and deceives us in the most lively manner" (der Schreck ist es hier…was uns mit Grausen erfüllt, und uns auf die lebendigste Art täuscht). *Ibid.*, p. 712. On suddenness, see also Karl-Heinz Bohrer, *Suddenness*, trans. Ruth Crowley (New York: Columbia University Press, 1994).

11. Thirty years later, in 1826, Tieck similarly praised Kleist for his art of "producing terror" (*Schrecken [zu] erregen*). Ludwig Tieck, "Heinrich von Kleist" (1826), in Ludwig Tieck, *Kritische Schriften*, 4 vols. (Leipzig: Brockhaus, 1848), vol. 2, p. 54.

12. Tieck, "Über Shakespeare's Behandlung," pp. 707–708. The same phrase is employed by Tieck when contrasting Shakespeare's genius with imitators who "lack the art of putting to sleep reason and its judgments" (weil sie nicht die Kunst besitzen, den richtenden Verstand einzuschläfern). *Ibid.*, p. 686.

13. J. A. Bergk, *Die Kunst, Bücher zu lesen* (Jena: In der Hempelschen Buchhandlung, 1799), p. 249.

14. *Ibid.*, p. 250.

15. Tieck, "Über Shakespeares Behandlung," pp. 689–90. Another explicit comparison of the representation of the marvelous in drama and in narrative fiction is to be found on p. 707. The importance of narrative fiction for his essay also comes to the fore in the description of "reading"—rather than seeing—*Othello* and *Macbeth* (p. 609) and in Tieck's invocation of Jacques Cazotte's fantastic tale *Le diable amoureux* as a parallel to the mixture of comical and terrifying elements in Shakespeare's work (p. 704). For a compelling reading of Tieck's essay that has its focus on this reference to Cazotte, see Mücke, *The Seduction of the Occult*, pp. 4–9.

16. Ludwig Tieck, "An Heinrich Wackenroder" (June 12, 1792), in *William Lovell*, ed. Walter Münz (Stuttgart: Reclam, 1986), p. 692. See Chapter 3 at note 96 for a longer quotation from this letter.

17. Tieck, "Über Shakespeare's Behandlung," p. 697.

18. Johann Peter Eckermann, "Gespräche mit Goethe," in J. P. Eckermann, *Gespräche mit Goethe*, ed. Christoph Michel, vol. 39 of Johann Wolfgang von Goethe, *Sämtliche Werke: Briefe, Tagebücher und Gespräche*, ed. Dieter Borchmeyer et al. (Frankfurt am Main: Deutscher Klassiker Verlag, 1999), p. 221.

19. "Die Novelle…[stellt] einen großen oder kleinen Vorfall in's hellste Licht…der, so leicht er sich ereignen kann, doch wunderbar, vielleicht einzig ist."

Ludwig Tieck, "Vorbericht zur dritten Lieferung" (1829), in *Schriften: Elfter Band Schauspiele* (Berlin: G. Reimer, 1829), p. lxxxvi.

20. *Ibid.*, p. lxxxvii.

21. Tieck, "Über Shakespeares Behandlung," pp. 697 and 693.

22. Johann Wolfgang von Goethe, "Unterhaltungen deutscher Ausgewanderten," in *Romane und Novellen I*, vol. 6 of *Werke: Hamburger Ausgabe in 14 Bänden*, ed. Erich Trunz 14 vols., 14th ed. (Munich: Beck, 1996), pp. 159–61.

23. On the serial production of novelties in news reporting, see Niklas Luhmann, *The Reality of the Mass Media*, trans. Kathleen Gross (Stanford: Stanford University Press, 2000), p. 28.

24. Ludwig Tieck to Georg Joachim Goeschen, June 16, 1800, quoted in Manfred Frank, "Kommentar" in Ludwig Tieck, *Phantasus*, ed. Manfred Frank, vol. 6 of *Schriften in zwölf Bänden*, pp. 1147–48.

25. Ludwig Tieck, *Phantasus: Eine Sammlung von Mährchen, Schauspielen und Novellen*, 3 vols. (Berlin: In der Realschulbuchhandlung, 1812–1816).

26. E. T. A. Hoffmann, *Fantasiestücke in Callot's Manier: Blätter aus dem Tagebuch eines reisenden Enthusiasten. Mit einer Vorrede von Jean Paul*, 4 vols. (Bamberg: C. F. Kunz, 1814/1815).

27. E. T. A. Hoffmann, *Die Elixiere des Teufels: Nachgelassene Papiere des Bruders Medardus, eines Capuziners. Herausgegeben von dem Verfasser der Fantasiestücke in Callot's Manier*, 2 vols. (Berlin: Dunker & Humblot, 1815).

28. E. T. A. Hoffmann, *Nachtstücke* (1816–17), in *Nachtstücke / Klein Zaches / Prinzessin Brambilla*, vol 3. of *Werke 1816–1820*, ed. Hartmut Steinecke, with Gerhard Allroggen (Frankfurt am Main: Deutscher Klassiker Verlag, 2009). Hoffmann, "The Sandman," in *The Tales*, vol. 1 of *Selected Writings*, ed. and trans. Leonard J. Kant and Elizabeth C. Knight (Chicago: University of Chicago Press, 1969), pp. 137–67.

29. On Hoffmann's private staging of a phantasmagoria, which took place in the winter of 1800 in the Berlin home of his uncle, Johann Ludwig Doerffer, see Rupert Gaderer, *Poetik der Technik: Elektrizität und Optik bei E. T. A. Hoffmann* [The poetics of technology: Electricity and optics in E. T. A. Hoffmann] (Freiburg im Breisgau: Rombach, 2009), pp. 11–13 and 16–17.

30. "But it seemed to you that you had to gather together all that had occurred—the marvelous, the magnificent, the dreadful, the joyous, the ghastly—and convey it in the very first word so that it strike everybody, like an

electrical shock" (Aber es war dir, als müßtest du nun gleich im ersten Wort alles Wunderbare, Herrliche, Entsetzliche, Lustige, Grauenhafte, das sich zugetragen, recht zusammengreifen, so daß es, wie ein elektrischer Schlag, alle treffe). Hoffmann, *Werke*, p. 26, *Selected Writings*, p. 148*. For a close reading of this passage see Michael Gamper, *Elektropoetologie: Fiktionen der Elektrizität 1740–1870* [Electropoetics: Fictions of electricty, 1740–1870] (Göttingen: Wallstein, 2009), p. 245.

31. Tieck also employs the term *Schlag*/"jolt" repeatedly. See Tieck, "Über Shakespeares Behandlung," pp. 686, 696, 703, 710.

32. "Der elektrische Schlag, der durch alle Deine Fibern und Nerven zitterte." E. T. A. Hoffmann, *Fantasiestücke in Callot's Manier*, ed. Harmut Steinecke (Franfurt am Main: Deutscher Klassiker Verlag, 1993), p. 280. For a more detailed analysis of E. T. A. Hoffmann's poetics in its interrelation to early nineteenth-century optical and electrical technologies, see Gaderer, *Poetik der Technik* and Gamper, *Elektropoetologie*. For a different interpretation of shock in the early nineteenth-century literature of the fantastic as related to the discourses of normality and perversion, see Mücke, *The Seduction of the Occult*, esp. pp. 80–97, where she develops a reading of Tieck's novella *Love Charm* (*Liebeszauber*), which became part of his collection *Phantasus*.

33. Hoffmann, Letter from July 20 1813, see also letter from July 13, 1813, quoted in Hoffmann, *Fantasiestücke in Callot's Manier*, pp. 724 and 725.

34. Gotthilf Heinrich Schubert, "Von dem thierischen Magnetismus und einigen ihm verwandten Erscheinungen," in *Ansichten von der Nachtseite der Naturwissenschaft* (Dresden: In der Arnoldischen Buchhandlung, 1808), pp. 326–84. There is no English translation of Schubert's treatise, but Catherine Crowe, who translated a book by Justinus Kerner that we will discuss below, published in 1848 a highly successful book entitled *The Night Side of Nature, or, Ghosts and Ghost Seers* (London: T. C. Newby, 1848). A good overview of German Romanticism and its appropriation of animal magnetism is to be found in Jürgen Barkhoff, *Magnetische Fiktionen: Literarisierung des Mesmerismus in der Romantik* (Stuttgart: J. B. Metzler, 1995). But Barkhoff chooses to ignore the link between spiritualism and mesmerism, disregarding authors such as Jung-Stilling, Kerner, and others—see p. 86 n.4.

35. E. T. A. Hoffmann, "Der Magnetiseur: Eine Familienbegebenheit," in *Fantasiestücke in Callot's Manier,* p. 180; Hoffmann, "The Mesmerist" in *Fantasy Pieces in Callot's Manner*, trans. Joseph M. Hayse (Schenectady, NY: Union College Press, 1996), p. 123. Hereafter cited as "M."

36. "M" 178/121 and 193/133.

37. "M" 181/124*.

38. "M" 183–85/126–27*.

39. "M" 186/128*.

40. "M" 187/129.

41. "M" 179/123*.

42. Similar arguments are also formulated in Jean Paul's essays "Glimpses into the Dream World" and "Speculations on Some Marvels of Organic Magnetism," which were published in 1814, as well. See Jean Paul, "Mutmassungen über einige Wunder des organischen Magnetismus" and "Blicke in die Traumwelt," in *Museum*, in *Vermischte Schriften I*, ed. Norbert Miller, vol. 3 of *Sämtliche Werke*, ed. Norbert Miller, with Wilhelm Schmidt-Biggemann, 4 vols. (Munich: Carl Hanser, 1976), pp. 884–920 and 1017–48.

43. "M" 179/123*. The phrase is "mich dünkt...ich höre deinen Freund Alban sprechen."

44. "M" 193/133*.

45. "M" 195/134–35*. On the Chevalier de Barbarin (sometimes also spelled Barberin) and the spiritualist magnetizers of Lyon, see Alan Gauld, *A History of Hypnotism* (Cambridge: Cambridge University Press, 1992), pp. 64–67.

46. "M" 196/135. Hoffmann's text likens this stance, not quite accurately, to that of the Marquis de Puységur, who had coined the terms "magnetic sleep" and "magnetic somnambulism" and who had formulated a spiritualist theory of animal magnetism. See Armand M. J. de Chastenet, Marquis de Puységur, *Mémoires pour servir à l'histoire et à l'établissement du magnétisme animal* (Paris: Dentu, 1784); Gauld, *A History of Hypnotism*, pp. 39–52.

47. Carl Alexander Ferdinand Kluge, *Versuch einer Darstellung des animalischen Magnetismus als Heilmittel* (Berlin: C. Salfeld, 1811); Ernst Daniel August Bartels, *Grundzüge einer Physiologie und Physik des animalischen Magnetismus* (Frankfurt am Main: Varrentrapp, 1812).

48. On sympathy and animal magnetism, see Friedrich Hufeland, *Über Sympathie* (Weimar: Landes-Industrie-Comptoirs, 1811).

49. The episode related by Ottmar may draw in this on a case history from Kluge's *Animal Magnetism*. See Kluge, *Versuch einer Darstellung des animalischen Magnetismus als Heilmittel*, pp. 325–26.

50. "M" 201/139*.

51. "M" 202/141.

52. The phrase is "schneidendes Werkzeug." "M" 204/143 and 203/142*.

53. "M" 210/147.

54. "M" 208/145. The phrase is "so war es mir gleich...ich müßte alles unbedingt tun, was er gebieten würde."

55. "M" 209/146*. "Nur in diesem *mit Ihm* und *in Ihm* sein kann ich wahrhaftig leben...ja, indem ich dieses schreibe, fühle ich nur zu sehr, daß nur *Er* es ist, der mir den Ausdruck gibt, mein Sein in ihm wenigstens anzudeuten" (emphasis in the original).

56."M" 205/143.

57. "M" 209/246. Hoffmann's text thereby anticipates late nineteenth-century and early twentieth-century anxieties about the unlimited power of hypnotism and Cold War fantasies of absolute mind control. See Stefan Andriopoulos, *Possessed: Hypnotic Crimes, Corporate Fiction, and the Invention of Cinema* (Chicago: University of Chicago Press, 2008) and "On Brainwashing: Mind Control, Media, and Warfare," special issue of *Grey Room* 45 (Fall 2011).

58. "M" 216/151.

59. "M" 214/149.

60. "M" 213/149.

61. "M" 186/127–28.

62. See also Maria's statement on Alban's stories, which describes the impact of his narratives in magnetic terms: "for Alban's narratives are usually, if not horrible and terrifying, then suspenseful in such a strange manner that their effect may be beneficial in a certain way but one feels nonetheless exhausted" (denn Alban's Erzählungen sind gemeinhim, wenn auch nicht schrecklich und schauderhaft, doch auf eine solche seltsame Weise spannend, daß der Eindruck zwar in gewisser Art wohltätig ist, aber man sich doch erschöpft fühlt" "M" 194/133.

63. Kluge, *Versuch einer Darstellung des animalischen Magnetismus als Heilmittel*, pp. 3–4. See, similarly, Bartels, *Grundzüge einer Physiologie und Physik des animalischen Magnetismus*, p. VI.

64. Justinus Kerner, *Die Seherin von Prevorst: Eröffnungen über das innere Leben des Menschen und über das Hereinragen einer Geisterwelt in die unsere* (Stuttgart: Cotta, 1829).

65. Justinus Kerner, *Geschichte zweyer Somnambülen: Nebst einigen andern Denkwürdigkeiten aus dem Gebiete der magischen Heilkunde und der Psychologie* [History

of two somnambulants: Together with to some other notabilia from the realm of magic medicine and psychology] (Karlsruhe: Braun, 1824); Kerner, *Geschichten Besessener neuerer Zeit: Beobachtungen aus dem Gebiete kakodämonisch-magnetischer Erscheinungen* [Histories of possession in more recent times: Observations in the tealm of cacodemonic-magnetic phenomena] (Karlsruhe: Braun, 1834); Kerner, *Die somnambülen Tische: Zur Geschichte und Erklärung dieser Erscheinung* (Stuttgart: Ebner, 1853).

66. I quote in the following from the first edition from 1829 and from a reprint of the latest, most comprehensive edition in volume 4 and 5 of an anthology of Kerner's works from 1914: *Kerners Werke: Auswahl in sechs Teilen*, 6 vols., ed. Raimund Pissin (Berlin: Deutsches Verlagshaus Bong, 1914).

67. "Will man sie mit einem Menschen vergleichen, so kann man sagen: sie war ein im Augenblicke des Sterbens, durch irgend eine Fixierung, zwischen Sterben und Leben zurückgehaltener Mensch, der schon mehr in die Welt, die nun vor ihm, als in die, die hinter ihm liegt, zu sehen fähig ist"; *Kerners Werke* vol. 4, p. 58. Margaret Fuller, *Summer on the Lakes, in 1843* (Boston: Charles Little, 1844), p. 147, contains the following translation of this passage: "Should we compare her with anything human, we would say she was as one detained in the moment of dissolution, betwixt life and death; and who is better able to discern the affairs of the world that lies before than that behind him."

68. Immanuel Kant, *Träume eines Geistersehers, erläutert durch Träume der Metaphysik*, in *Vorkritische Schriften bis 1768*, vol. 2 of *Werkausgabe*, ed. Wilhelm Weischedel (Frankfurt am Main: Suhrkamp, 1977), p. 940; Kant, *Dreams of a Spirit Seer, Elucidated by Dreams of Metaphysics*, in *Theoretical Philosophy 1755–1770*, trans. and ed. David Walford (Cambridge: Cambridge University Press, 1992), p. 319. Hereafter cited as *D*.

69. *D* 940/319.

70. "But when the soul separates itself from the body, then it will not have the same sensory intuition [*Anschauung*] of this world; it will not intuit [*anschauen*] the world as it appears, but rather as it is. Accordingly the separation of the soul from the body consists in the change of sensory intuition to spiritual intuition." Immanuel Kant, *Immanuel Kants Vorlesungen über die Metaphysik: Zum Drucke befördert von dem Herausgeber der Kantischen Vorlesungen über die philosophische Religionslehre* (1821; Darmstadt: Wissenschaftliche Buchgesellschaft, 1988), p. 255; Kant, *Lectures on Metaphysics*, trans. and ed. Karl Ameriks and Steve Naragon (Cambridge:

Cambridge University Press, 1997), p. 104*. Kant's lectures go so far as to applaud Swedenborg for his description of the "other world": "The thought of Swedenborg is in this quite sublime." *Ibid.*, p. 257/105.

71. *Ibid.*, p. 259/105–106*.

72. Kluge, *Versuch einer Darstellung des animalischen Magnetismus als Heilmittel*, p. 109

73. Schubert, *Ansichten von der Nachtseite der Naturwissenschaft*, p. 357. See also *ibid.*, p. 359 n.: "Da auf diese Weise der Tod dem Zustand des Somnambulismus so nahe verwandt ist."

74. *Ibid.*, p. 357.

75. Jean Paul, "Mutmassungen über einige Wunder des organischen Magnetismus," p. 916. See also *ibid.*, p. 914, on "the similarity between the conditions of clairvoyance and dying."

76. *Kerners Werke*, vol. 4, p. 43.

77. Kerner, *Die Seherin von Prevorst*, p. 18. For a more detailed analysis of Kerner's orientalism in *The Seeress of Prevorst* and his reliance on ethnographic modes of writing, see Stefan Andriopoulos, "Ethnographie des Jenseits: Justinus Kerners *Die Seherin von Prevorst* und Edgar Allan Poes *Facts in the Case of M. Valdemar*," in David Wellbery (ed.), *Kultur-Schreiben als romantisches Projekt: Romantische Ethnographie im Spannungfeld zwischen Imagination und Wissenschaft* (Würzburg: Königshausen & Neumann, 2012), pp. 245–56.

78. "Dies ist nicht nur ein poetischer Ausdruck, sondern wirklich wahr. Wir sehen, daß Menschen in Momenten des Todes oft schon in eine andere Welt hinüberschauen und von dieser Kunde geben; wir sehen wir ihr Geist da oft, schon wie aus dem Körper getreten, sich in Entfernungen hin zu offenbaren vermag, während er die Hülle doch noch nicht völlig verlassen hat. Kann man sich diesen Menschen in diesen Momenten (die bei Sterbenden oft nur wie Blitze sind) jahrelang hingehalten denken, so haben wir das Bild dieser Seherin, und hierin sehe ich nur *buchstäbliche* Wahrheit, keine Dichtung." *Ibid.*, pp. 58–59, emphasis in the original.

79. *Kerners Werke*, vol. 4, p. 56, emphasis in the original.

80. See the passage from the editor's final note, which is addressed to the unnamed narrator of "The Lonely Castle" and not included in the published English translation: "Da ich...am Ende auch nicht einmal recht weiß, ob Sie wirklich existieren." "M" 225.

81. *Kerners Werke*, vol. 4, p. 54.

82. "Ohne alle Theorie, nur als Tatsache getreu." *Kerners Werke*, vol. 5, p. 9.

83. *Ibid.*, p. 68.

84. *Ibid.*, p. 235.

85. *Kerners Werke*, vol. 5, p. 40.

86. *Ibid.*

87. *Ibid.*, p. 57.

88. Emmerich's visions were not only documented, but also shaped by Brentano, who read regularly from apocryphal writings and mystical literature to the nun. But in the preface to his transcription of her visions, the poet describes his own role as that of a "writer" (*Schreiber*, p. 13), who recorded those "spiritual travels," in a "four-year long, daily, intense observation" (durch vierjährige, tägliche, angestrengte Beobachtung, p. 24) that the stigmatized Anna Katharina Emmerich undertook to the Holy Land. All quotes are from Clemens Brentano, *Das Bittere Leiden unsers Herrn Jesu Christi nach den Betrachtungen der Gottseligen Anna Katharina Emmerich I*, ed. Bernhard Gajek, vol. 26 of *Sämtliche Werke und Briefe*, ed. Jürgen Behrens, Wolfgang Frühwald, and Detlev Lüders (Stuttgart: Kohlhammer, 1980). On Brentano's project, see also Gabriele Brandstetter, "Reliquienberg und Stigmata: Clemens Brentano und Anna Katharina Emmerick—der Blut-Kreislauf der Schrift," in Bettine Menke and Barbara Vinken (eds.), *Stigmata Poetiken der Körperinschrift* (Munich: Fink, 2004), pp. 243–68; Wolfgang Frühwald, *Das Spätwerk Clemens Brentanos (1815–1842): Romantik im Zeitaler der Metternich schen Restauration* (Tübingen: Niemeyer, 1977). On Brentano s reading of mystical literature and apocryphal writings to the nun, see Bernhard Gajek, "Der romantische Dichter und das Christentum: Clemens Brentanos religiöse Schriften," in Hartwig Schulz (ed.), *Clemens Brentano: 1778–1842. Kolloquium zum 150. Todestag* (Bern: Peter Lang, 1993), pp. 109–31, esp. pp. 115 and 120.

89. Joachim Bodamer, "Vorwort," in Justinus Kerner: *Die Seherin von Prevorst*, 9th ed. (1958; Stuttgart: Steinkopf, 2007), p. 18.

90. Chauncy Hare Townshend, *Facts in Mesmerism, with Reasons for a Dispassionate Inquiry into It* (London: Longman, 1840). See also Charles Caldwell, *Facts in Mesmerism, and Thoughts on Its Causes and Uses* (Louisville, KY: Prentice and Weissinger, 1842). Johann Gottlieb Fichte, "Tagebuch über den animalischen Magnetismus," in *Vermischte Schriften aus dem Nachlaß*, vol. 11 of *Fichtes Werke*, ed. Immanuel Hermann Fichte (Berlin: de Gruyter, 1962), pp. 295–344. On Fichte's

appropriation of mesmerism, see also Sean Franzel, "'Welches Gesetz ist der Mensch in seiner Wirksamkeit': Pedagogy and Media in Fichte's Encounter with Mesmerism," *The Germanic Review* 84.1 (Winter 2009), pp. 3–25.

91. Arthur Schopenhauer, *Über den Willen in der Natur* (1836/1854), in *Sämtliche Werke*, ed. Wolfgang Freiherr von Löhneysen, 5 vols. (Frankfurt am Main: Suhrkamp, 1986), vol. 3, pp. 423–58; Schopenhauer, *On the Will in Nature: A Discussion of the Corroborations from the Empirical Sciences That the Author's Philosophy Has Received Since Its First Appearance*, trans. E. F. J. Payne (New York: Berg, 1992), pp. 102–28.

92. Arthur Schopenhauer, "Versuch über das Geistersehn und was damit zusammenhängt" (1851), in *Parerga und Paralipomena: Kleine philosophische Schriften I*, vol. 4 of *Sämtliche Werke*, ed. Wolfgang Freiherr von Löhneysen, 5 vols. (Frankfurt am Main: Suhrkamp, 1986), p. 275; Schopenhauer, "Essay on Spirit Seeing and Everything Connected Therewith," in *Parerga and Paralipomena: Short Philosophical Essays*, trans. E. F. J. Payne, 2 vols. (Oxford: Clarendon Press, 2000), vol. 1, p. 227. Hereafter cited as "E."

93. "E" 348/289.

94. The phrase is "die vollkommene Ähnlichkeit in dem ganz eigentümlichen Hergang und Beschaffenheit der angeblichen Erscheinungen." "E" 355/295.

95. "E" 334/277.

96. "E" 324/270.

97. "E" 323/268*. Schopenhauer introduces the notion of experimental metaphysics for the first time in *On the Will in Nature*, p. 429/107.

98. "Der animalische Magnetismus... ist gewissermaßen eine Experimentalmetaphysik.... Wenn nun aber schon in der bloßen Physik die Experimente und Thatsachen uns noch lange nicht die richtige Einsicht eröffnen, sondern hiezu die oft sehr schwer zu findende Auslegung derselben erfordert ist; wie viel mehr wird dies der Fall sein bei den mysteriösen Tatsachen jener empirisch hervortretenden Metaphysik! Die rationale, oder theoretische Metaphysik wird also mit derselben gleichen Schritt halten müssen, damit die hier aufgefundenen Schätze gehoben werden. Dann aber wird eine Zeit kommen, wo Philosophie, animalischer Magnetismus und die in allen ihren Zweigen beispiellos vorgeschrittene Naturwissenschaft gegenseitig ein so helles Licht auf einander werfen, daß Wahrheiten zu Tage kommen werden, welche zu erreichen man außerdem nicht hoffen durfte. Nur denke man hiebei nicht an die metaphysischen Aussagen und

Lehren der Somnambulen: diese sind meistens armselige Ansichten, entsprungen aus den von der Somnambule erlernten Dogmen, und deren Mischung mit dem, was sie im Kopf ihres Magnetiseurs vorfindet; daher keiner Beachtung wert." "E" 322–23/268–69.

99. See, for instance, *E* 331/275: "This is confirmed by the easy and artless way in which the clairvoyante of Prevorst cultivates her spiritual acquaintances, for example, vol. ii, p. 120 (1st edn.), where she quite calmly lets a spirit stand and waits until she has had her soup. J. Kerner himself also says in several places (for example, vol. I, p. 209) that she seemed to be awake, but never yet entirely. At all events it might be possible to reconcile this with her own statement (vol, ii, p. 11, 3rd edn., p. 256) that, whenever she sees spirits she is wide awake." See also *E* 311/258: "Further, *a confirmation of this is given* by the impression, described in the Seherin von Prevorst (1st edn., vol. ii, p. 73; 3rd edn., p. 325), which certain verses, relating to somnambulistic events, made during wakefulness on the clairvoyante who knew nothing of them."

100. The phrase is "Leichtgläubigkeit unsers sonst sehr achtungswerthen und verdienstvollen Justinus Kerner." *E* 323/269.

101. Alphonse Cahagnet, *The Celestial Telegraph; or, The Secrets of the Life to Come, Revealed Through Magnetism* (New York: J. S. Redfield, 1851); the original French edition was published under a different title: *Magnétisme: arcanes de la vie future dévoilés: ou, L'existence, la forme, les occupations de l'ame après sa séparation du corps* (Paris: Cahagnet, 1848).

102. Margaret Fuller to Ralph Waldo Emerson, May 29, 1843, in *The Letters of Margaret Fuller*, ed. Robert N. Hudspeth, 6 vols. (Ithaca: Cornell University Press, 1984), vol. 3, p. 124.

103. See Margaret Fuller, *Summer on the Lakes, in 1843* (Boston: Charles Little, 1844), pp. 133–65. A few years after the publication of "Facts in the Case of M. Valdemar," Poe reviewed Fuller's *Summer on the Lakes* as "a remarkable assemblage of sketches." Edgar Allan Poe, "Sarah Margaret Fuller," in *Edgar Allan Poe: Essays and Reviews*, ed. G. R. Thompson (New York: Library of America, 1984), p. 1172.

104. Justinus Kerner, *The Seeress of Prevorst; Being Revelations Concerning the Inner-Life of Man, and the Inter-Diffusion of a World of Spirits in the One We Inhabit.* From the German, by Mrs. Crowe (New York: Harper's, 1845). Crowe also published *The Night Side of Nature, Or Ghosts and Ghost Seers* (1848; New York: E. P. Dutton, 1904).

105. [Anonymous], *Rambles and Reveries of an Art-Student in Europe* (Philadelphia, 1855), pp. 36–38.

106. On the parallels between Mrs. H.'s and Valdemar's final moments, see *Rambles and Reveries*, p. 37; Sidney E. Lind, "Poe and Mesmerism," *PMLA* 62.4 (December 1947), pp. 1092–93; and Thomas Ollive Mabbott (ed.), *Collected Works of Edgar Allan Poe*, vol. 3, *Tales and Sketches 1843–1849* (Cambridge, MA: Harvard University Press, 1978), p. 1229: "A third source, pointed out as long ago as 1855, is the conclusion of *The Seeress of Prevorst*." Bruce Mills mentions in a footnote that both Kerner's and Poe's texts conceive of somnambulism as a state hovering between life and death, but he does not refer to Kerner in his analysis of Poe's literary texts. See Bruce Mills, *Poe, Fuller, and the Mesmeric Arts: Transition States in the American Renaissance* (Columbia: University of Missouri Press, 2006), p. 123 n. 7.

107. Edgar Allan Poe, "The Facts in the Case of M. Valdemar," in *The Short Fiction of Edgar Allan Poe*, ed. Stuart Levine and Susan Levine (Urbana: University of Illinois Press, 1990), p. 134.

108. Kerner/Crowe, *The Seeress*, p. 24.

109. *Ibid.*, p. 55.

110. Fuller, *Summer on the Lakes*, p. 152. See also *ibid.*, p. 147: "she was as one detained in the moment of dissolution."

111. Poe, "Facts in the Case of M. Valdemar," p. 134.

112. *Ibid.*, p. 137.

113. *Ibid.*, p. 137.

114. In 1839, Latimer Clark described William Cooke's needle telegraph as "a trembling tongue of steel." Quoted in Laura Otis: "The Other End of the Wire: Uncertainties of Organic and Telegraphic Communication," *Configurations* 9.2 (2001), p. 183. On the role of telegraphy for Poe's narrative, see also Adam Frank, "Valdemar's Tongue, Poe's Telegraphy," *ELH* 72.3 (Fall 2005), pp. 635–62.

115. Edgar Allen Poe, "The Mesmeric Revelation," in: *The Short Fiction of Edgar Allan Poe*, p. 141.

116. Poe, "Facts in the Case of M. Valdemar," p. 138, emphasis in the original. A poststructuralist interpretation of this sentence as a figuration of the condition of possibility of language, one in which the speaker is always already absent, is to be found in Jacques Derrida, "Discussion of Roland Barthes' 'To Write: Intransitive Verb,'" in Richard Macksey and Eugenio Donato (eds.), *The Languages of Criticism and the Sciences of Man: The Structuralist Controversy* (Baltimore: Johns Hopkins

University Press, 1970), pp. 155–56. See also Roland Barthes, "Textual Analysis of a Tale of Poe," in Marshall Blonsky (ed.), *On Signs* (Baltimore: Johns Hopkins University Press, 1985), pp. 84–97, as well as Jacques Derrida, *Speech and Phenomena and Other Essays on Husserl's Theory of Signs*, trans. David B. Allison and Newton Garver (Evanston, IL: Northwestern University Press, 1973), pp. 1 and 96–97.

117. Poe, "Facts in the Case of M. Valdemar," p. 138.

118. *Ibid.*, p. 139. It is this passage that is compared in *Rambles and Reveries* with the description of Mrs. H.'s death in the American edition of Kerner's *The Seeress of Prevorst*: "After a short interval, her soul also departed; leaving behind a totally unrecognizable husk—not a single trace of her former features remaining" (p. 38). These two passages are also juxtaposed by Lind and Mabbott. But both the author of *Rambles and Reveries*, as well as Lind and Mabbott, ignore the crucial similarity between Kerner's and Poe's representations of Mrs. H. and Valdemar being "arrested in the moment of dying." In addition, they also do not take note of how Poe's literary text transforms Kerner's thought experiment into an ostensibly real one.

119. Poe, "Facts in the Case of M. Valdemar," p. 137.

120. Edgar A. Poe, "The Facts of M. Valdemar's Case," in *The American Review: A Whig Journal of Politics, Literature, Art, and Science* 2.12 (December 1845), pp. 561–65.

121. *Broadway Journal*, December 20, 1845, p. 365.

122. *Broadway Journal*, December 27, 1845, p. 390.

123. *Spirit of the Times*, December 23, pp. 24 and 25; *Baltimore Saturday Visiter*, January 1848.

124. "Mesmerism in America: Astounding and Horrifying Narrative," London *Sunday Times*, January 4, 1896; "Mesmerism in America," London *Morning Post*, January 5, 1846; "Mesmerism in America. Death of M. Valdemar of New York," London *Popular Record of Modern Science*, January 10, 1846.

125. Edgar A. Poe, Esq., *Mesmerism "in articulo mortis": An Astounding & Horrifying Narrative, Shewing the Extraordinary Power of Mesmerism in Arresting the Progress of Death* (London: Short & Co., 1846).

126. Archibald Ramsay to Edgar Allan Poe, November 30, 1846, in *Poe and His Friends: Letters Relating to Poe*, vol. 17 of *The Complete Works of Edgar Allan Poe*, ed. James A. Harrison (1902: New York 1965), pp. 268–69, emphasis in the original.

127. Edgar Allan Poe to Archibald Ramsay, December 30, 1846, in *The Letters*

of Edgar Allan Poe, ed. John Ward Ostrom, 2 vols. (New York 1966), vol. 2, p. 337, emphasis in the original.

128. See on this also *Rambles and Reveries*, p. 34: "To hoax seemed one of the chief pleasures of his [Poe's] life.... 'The Facts in the Case of M. Valdemar' and other stories have such a wonderful appearance of truth, are so plausible, that from the very earnestness with which they are written, they deceive."

129. Quoted in Arthur Hobson Quinn, *Edgar Allan Poe: A Critical Biography* (Baltimore: Johns Hopkins University Press, 1998), p. 485.

CHAPTER FIVE: PSYCHIC TELEVISION

An early version of this chapter was published under the same title in *Critical Inquiry* 31.3 (Spring 2005), pp. 618–37.

1. Walter Reisser, "Bildfunk, Fernsehen und Tonfilm" [Image radio, television, and sound film], *Rundfunkjahrbuch* [Radio yearbook] (1930), p. 299. For a similar point of view, see Hans Bredow, "Vor einer wichtigen Entwicklungsstufe" [On the verge of an important development], *Kameraden des Films: Funk und Schallplatte, 12. Beiblatt zum Film-Kurier* [Comrades of film: Radio and phonography, 12th supplement to the *Film Messenger*] (June 1929), p. 1.

2. *Wochenende*, 1929. On this point, see also Birgit Schneider, "Die kunstseidenen Mädchen. Test- und Leitbilder des frühen Fernsehens" [The rayon girls: Early television prototypes and models], in Stefan Andriopoulos and Bernhard Dotzler (eds.), *1929: Beiträge zur Archäologie der Medien* [1929: Contributions to the archaelogy of the media] (Frankfurt am Main: Suhrkamp, 2002), pp. 54–79.

3. "Horch, was kommt von draußen rein."

4. Ernst Steffen, "Das Fernkino im Haus" [Telecinema in your home]," *Daheim: Ein deutsches Familienblatt* [At home: A German family paper], 65.23 (1929), p. 3.

5. Eduard Rhein, "Wollen wir fernsehen?" [Do we want to see televisually?], *Die Sendung* [Broadcast] 6 (1929), p. 726.

6. Rhein, "Wollen wir fernsehen?," p. 726. Frank Warschauer, "Rundfunk heute und morgen" [Radio today and tomorrow] (1928), in Ernst Glaeser (ed.), *Fazit: Ein Querschnitt durch die deutsche Publizistik* [On balance: A cross section of German journalism] (Kronberg im Taunus: Scriptor 1977), pp. 307–308; see also Theodor Kappstein's comment: "The miracle is not just the 'dearest child of faith,' as was said in olden times. The miracle is now also the 'favorite child of technology.'" Theodor H. Kappstein, "Der Zauberer Rundfunk" [Radio the magician],

Die Sendung [Broadcast] 6 (1929), p. 22.

7. Ernst Bloch, "Die Angst des Ingenieurs" (1929), in *Gesamtausgabe*, 16 vols. (Frankfurt am Main: Suhrkamp, 1985), vol. 9, p. 354. Available in English as Ernst Bloch, "The Anxiety of the Engineer," in *Literary Essays*, trans. Andrew Joron et al. (Stanford: Stanford University Press, 1998), p. 310*; Eugen Diesel, "Das Unheimliche des technischen Zeitalters" [The uncanny of the technical age], *Zeitwende* 5 [Turning points] 5.6 (1929), p. 241.

8. Diesel, "Das Unheimliche des technischen Zeitalters," p. 239.

9. *Ibid.*, pp. 241 and 243.

10. Diesel's text can hence be read as an anticipation of Günther Anders's culturally conservative remarks on "the world as phantom and matrix" or of Jean Baudrillard's apocalyptically charged theories of simulation.

11. Amtsgerichtsrat i.R. Geheimrat Drießen, "Privathäusliche Phänomenik" [Domestic phenomena], *Zeitschrift für psychische Forschung* [Journal for psychic research] 5.6 (1929), pp. 178–82.

12. *Ibid.*, pp. 181, 179, 180.

13. Walter Benjamin, "Erfahrung und Armut" (1933), in *Aufsätze, Essays, Vorträge*, vol. 2 of *Gesammelte Schriften*, ed. Rolf Tiedemann and Hermann Schweppenhäuser (Frankfurt am Main: Suhrkamp, 1972), p. 214. Available in English as "Experience and Poverty," trans. Rodney Livingstone, in *Walter Benjamin: Selected Writings, Volume 2: 1927–1934*, ed. Michael Jennings, Howard Eiland, and Gary Smith (Cambridge, MA: Harvard University Press, 1999), p. 732*.

14. Friedrich Kittler, *Optische Medien: Berliner Vorlesung* (Berlin: Merve, 2002), p. 290; Kittler, *Optical Media: Berlin Lectures 1999*, trans. Anthony Enns (Malden, MA: Polity, 2010), p. 207*.

15. Wolfgang Hagen, whose work has highlighted the importance of occultism for the development of radio, has traced the development of the concept of "radio" to William Crookes's 1870s experiments into radiation as the "fourth state of matter." See Wolfgang Hagen, "Vom Ort des Radios: Vortrag zur Eröffnung von *Recycling The Future*" [On the place of radio: Keynote to the symposium *Recycling the Future*], Vienna, December 4, 1997. in Robert Adrian and Gerfried Stocker (eds.), *Recycling the Future*, http://www.whagen.de/vortraege/1997/OnthePlaceOfTheRadio%20Wien/OnthePlace/hagen.html?page=vortraege/radort/RADORT.HTM.

16. Raphael Eduard Liesegang, *Das Phototel: Beiträge zum Problem des electrischen*

Fernsehens [The phototel: Contributions on the problem of electrical television] (Düsseldorf: Liesegang, 1891). On the alleged 'first use' of the term *Fernsehen*, see Siegfried Zielinski, *Audiovisionen: Kino und Fernsehen als Zwischenspiele in der Geschichte* [Audiovisions: Cinema and television as historical interludes] (Reinbek: Rowohlt, 1989), p. 26, and Joseph Hoppe, "Chronologie," in *TV-Kultur*, p. 19.

17. Albert Freiherr von Schrenck-Notzing, "Translator's Introduction" (1890), in Charles Richet, *Experimentelle Studien auf dem Gebiete der Gedankenübertragung und des sogenannten Hellsehens: Autorisierte Deutsche Ausgabe von Schrenck-Notzing* [Experimental studies in the field of thought transmission and so-called clairvoyance. Authorized German edition by Schrenck-Notzing] (Stuttgart: Ferdinand Enke, 1891), pp. 2–3. See also Charles Richet, "Relation de diverses expériences sur la transmission mentale, la lucidité, et autres phénomènes non explicables par les données scientifiques actuelles" [Report on several experiments with mental transmission, clairvoyance, and other phenomena inexpicable to our existing sciences] *Proceedings of the Society for Psychical Research* 5 (1888–89), pp. 18–168, and Richet, "Further Experiments in Hypnotic Lucidity or Clairvoyance," *Proceedings of the Society for Psychical Research* 6 (1889–1890), pp. 66–83.

18. "Fernsehen" appears in Richet's *Experimentelle Studien*, p. 230. Earlier references are to be found in Hegel's and Schopenhauer's texts analyzed in Chapter 2. See, in addition, Carl Kiesewetter, "Fernsehen und Telepathie in der älteren okkultistischen Literatur" [Television and telepathy in older occultist literature], *Sphinx* 8 (1889), pp. 97–104; Heinrich Bruno Schindler, *Das magische Geistesleben: Ein Beitrag zur Psychologie* [Magical spirit life: A contribution to psychology] (Breslau: Korn, 1857), p. 139; Eduard Stern, " Fernsehen, Fernhören," [Television, telehearing], *Archiv für den Thierischen Magnetismus* [Archive for animal magnetism] 7.2 (1820), pp. 161–63.

19. Richet, *Experimentelle Studien*, p. 227.

20. Patent record 30105, January 6, 1884, cited in Josef Mühlbauer, *Fernsehen: Das Wunder und das Ungeheuer* [Television: The miracle and the monster] (Basel: Herder, 1959), p. 15.

21. See Albert Abramson, *The History of Television 1880 to 1941* (London: McFarland 1987), p. 6.

22. For a more detailed description of the Nipkow device, see Joseph Hoppe, "Wie das Fernsehen in die Apparate kam" [How television became an apparatus], in Wulf Herzogenrath, Thomas Gaethgens, Sven Thomas Hoenisch, and Peter

Hoenisch (eds.), *TV-Kultur: Das Fernsehen in der bildenden Kunst seit 1879* [TV cul-ture: Television in art since 1879] (Dresden: Verlag der Kunst, 1997), p. 28, and David E. Fisher and Marshall Jon Fisher, *Tube: The Invention of Television* (New York: Harvest, 1997) p. 16.

23. Christoph Ries, *Sehende Maschinen: Eine kurze Abhandlung über die geheim-nisvollen Eigenschaften der lichtempfindlichen Stoffe und die staunenswerten Leistun-gen der sehenden Maschinen* [Seeing machines: A short treatise on the mysterious properties of photosensitive elements and the astonishing achievements of seeing machines] (Diessen vor München: Jos. C. Huberts, 1916), p. 38. See also Ries, *Die elektrischen Eigenschaften und die Bedeutung des Selens für die Elektrotechnik* [Electrical qualities of selenium and its significance for electrical engineering] (Berlin-Nikolassee: Harrwitz, 1914). For a more detailed analysis of Ries's treatise on "seeing machines" see Bernhard Dotzler, "Die Schaltbarkeit der Welt," in *1929: Beiträge zur Archäologie der Medien*, p. 312.

24. Hans E. Hollmann, "Fernseher von einst und jetzt" [Television, then and now], *Helios: Fachzeitschrift für Elektrotechnik* [Helios: A professional journal of electrical engineering] 35 (1929), p. 54.

25. Liesegang, *Das Phototel*; Benedict Schöffler, *Die Phototelegraphie und das Elektrische Fernsehen* [Phototelegraphy and electrical television] (Vienna: Wilhelm Braumüller, 1898); Fritz Lux, *Der elektrische Fernseher* [The electrical televisor] (Ludwigshafen: n.p., 1903).

26. Walter Bormann, *Die Nornen: Forschungen über Fernsehen in Raum und Zeit* [The Norns: Inquiries into television in space and time] (Leipzig: Max Altmann, 1909), p. XIV.

27. Carl du Prel, *Fernsehen und Fernwirken* [Television and action at a distance], vol. 2 of *Die Entdeckung der Seele durch die Geheimwissenschaften* [The discovery of the soul by means of the secret sciences], 2 vols. (Leipzig: Ernst Günthers Verlag, 1895); Bormann, *Die Nornen*; J. Körmann-Alzech, *Telepathie, Gedankenübertragung, Gedankenlesen. Die Svengalis. Fernsehen. Fernwirken. Gespenster lebender Personen. Das zweite Gesicht* [Telepathy, thought transmission, thought reading, Svengalis, television, action at a distance, ghosts of living persons, second sight], vol. 4 of *Offenbarung der Wunder und Geheimnisse aller Zeiten: Auf Grund alter Ueberlieferun-gen und der neuesten Forschungen* [Marvels and secrets from throughout the ages revealed] (Leipzig: U. F. Schlöffel's Verlag, 1904).

28. Carl du Prel, "Das Fernsehen in Zeit und Raum" [Television in time and

space], *Sphinx* 14 (1892), p. 9.

29. Bormann, *Die Nornen*, p. 98.

30. Carl du Prel (ed.), *Immanuel Kants Vorlesungen über die Psychologie. Mit einer Einleitung "Kants mystische Weltanschauung"* [Immanuel Kant's lectures on psychology: With an introduction on "Kant's mystical worldview"] (Leipzig: Ernst Günthers Verlag, 1889); du Prel, "Fernsehen als Funktion des transzendentalen Subjekts," *Sphinx* 15 (1893), pp. 200–209 and 305–16. The reference to earlier philosophical theories is also common in 1920s studies on telepathy and clairvoyance—see, for instance, Rudolf Tischner, *Über Telepathie und Hellsehen. Experimentell-theoretische Untersuchungen* [On telepathy and clairvoyance: Experimental-theoretical studies] (Munich and Wiesbaden: J. F. Bergmann, 1921), p. 3: "Telepathy and clairvoyance were in earlier times considered completely established. Philosophers such as Hegel, Schelling, Schopenhauer, J. H. Fichte, Ed. v. Hartmann as well as numerous physicians speak of thought transference and clairvoyance as facts."

31. Du Prel, *Fernsehen und Fernwirken*, p. 1. The text is based on a longer article on "Television in Time and Space" in *Sphinx* 15 (1893).

32. "This close-range clairvoyance should be distinguished from 'spatial television' over distances of many miles and also from 'temporal television.' In other words, clairvoyance is based on a process unique to itself, whereas spatial and temporal television appear both to be based on a separate and entirely different process." Du Prel, *Die Entdeckung der Seele durch die Geheimwissenschaften* (Leipzig: Ernst Günthers Verlag 1894), vol. 1, p. 163.

33. Du Prel, *Fernsehen und Fernwirken*, pp. 5 and 79. In a similar vein, Bormann wrote: "Everything called up by the visionary medium presents itself directly to the eye, in motion and in full color." Bormann, *Die Nornen*, p. 130.

34. Du Prel, *Fernsehen und Fernwirken*, p. 1.

35. *Ibid.*

36. *Ibid.*, p. 2.

37. William Crookes, "Address by the President," *Proceedings of the Society for Psychical Research* 12 (1896–1897), p. 348. On this point, see also Wolfgang Hagen, "Der Okkultismus der Avantgarde um 1900" [The occultism of the avant-garde around 1900], in Sigrid Schade and Georg Christoph Tholen (eds.), *Konfigurationen: Zwischen Kunst und Medien um 1900* [Configurations: Between art and media around 1900], (Munich: Fink, 1999), p. 351.

38. See Bormann, *Die Nornen*, p. 97: "To explain this, Lombroso drew on the concept of radioactivity, just as Hellenbach had used the ether and du Prel the 'od.'" The "od" was considered by Karl von Reichenbach to be a force that pervades all nature, manifesting itself in persons of sensitive temperament. See, for instance, Karl von Reichenbach, *Letters on Od and Magnetism: Published for the First Time in English, with Extracts from his Other Works, so as to Make a Complete Presentation of the Odic Theory*, trans. and ed. F. D. O'Byrne (1852; London: Hutchinson, 1926).

39. Heinrich Hertz, *Ueber die Beziehungen zwischen Licht und Elektricität* [On the relations between light and electricity] (Bonn: Emil Strauß, 1889), p. 5.

40. *Ibid.*, p. 15. On Hertz's discovery see Oliver Lodge, *The Work of Hertz and Some of His Successors: Being the Substance of a Lecture Delivered at the Royal Institution on Friday Evening, 1 June 1894* (New York: Nostrand, 1894).

41. See Stanley Goldberg, "In Defense of Ether: The British Response to Einstein's Special Theory of Relativity, 1905–1911," *Historical Studies in the Physical Sciences* 2 (1970), pp. 89–125. For a 1924 account of electromagnetic waves that still took recourse to the "world-ether hypothesis," see Albert Neuburger, *Die Wunder der Fernmeldetechnik: Über Telegraphie und Telephonie zum Rundfunk* [The marvels of telecommunication: From telegraphy and telephony to radio] (Leipzig: Hachmeister & Thal, 1924), p. 123.

42. Bormann, *Die Nornen*, p. X.

43. *Ibid.*, p. XIV.

44. On this point, see Hoppe, "Wie das Fernsehen in die Apparate kam," p. 31.

45. Bormann, *Die Nornen*, p. XIV.

46. Körmann-Alzech, *Telepathie, Gedankenübertragung, Gedankenlesen. Die Svengalis. Fernsehen. Fernwirken. Gespenster lebender Personen. Das zweite Gesicht*, p. 3.

47. Bormann, *Die Nornen*, pp. XIII–XIV, see also p. 114. On the interrelation of telegraphy and occultism, see also Richard Noakes, "Telegraphy Is an Occult Art: Cromwell Fleetwood Varley and the Diffusion of Electricity to the Other World," *British Journal of the History of Science* 32 (1999), pp. 421–59.

48. Du Prel, *Fernsehen und Fernwirken*, p. 281.

49. William Crookes, "Some Possibilities of Electricity," *Fortnightly Review*, n.s. 51 (February 1892), p. 174. This essay by Crookes has frequently been remarked upon. See, for instance Hugh G. J. Aitken, *Syntony and Spark: The Origins of Radio*

(New York: Wiley, 1976), p. 111.

50. On Lodge's 1894 experiments see Hagen, "Vom Ort des Radios."

51. Oliver Lodge, "On the Difficulty of Making Crucial Experiments as to the Source of the Extra or Unusual Intelligence Manifested in Trance-Speech, Automatic Writing, and Other States of Apparent Mental Inactivity," *Proceedings of the Society for Psychical Research* 10 (1894), p. 18.

52. On Crookes's spiritualist experiments, see William Crookes, "Notes of Séances with D. D. Home," *Proceedings of the Society for Psychical Research* 6 (1889–1890), pp. 98–127, as well as Crookes, "Address by the President" in the same issue. See also Crookes, *Researches in the Phenomena of Spiritualism* (London, J. Burns, 1874) and *Psychic Force and Modern Spiritualism* (London: Longmans, Green, 1871). These texts have been republished as *Crookes and the Spirit World: A Collection of Writings by or concerning the Work of Sir William Crookes, O.M., F.R.S., in the Field of Psychical Research*, ed. M. R. Barrington (New York: Taplinger, 1972).

53. Crookes, "Some Possibilities of Electricity," p. 176.

54. See William Crookes, *On Radiant Matter: A Lecture Delivered to the British Association for the Advancement of Science, at Sheffield, Friday, August 22, 1879* (Philadelphia: James W. Queen & Co., 1879).

55. See Ferdinand Braun, "Über ein Verfahren zur Demonstration und zum Studium des zeitlichen Verlaufs variabler Ströme" [On a method for the recording and study of the temporal sequence of alternating currents], *Annalen der Physik und Chemie* [Annals of physics and chemistry] 60 (1897), pp. 552–59.

56. See, for example, Hollmann's statement: "Only with the improvement in amplification technology, however, was image telegraphy able to become a technology suitable for practical applications." Hollmann, "Fernseher von einst und jetzt," pp. 55–56.

57. See Crookes, "Address by the President," p. 338: "Is there any connexion between my old-standing interest in psychical problems and such original work as I may have been able to do in other branches of science? I think there is such a connexion."

58. Du Prel, *Die Entdeckung der Seele*, vol. 1, p. 172.

59. Kerstin Bergmann and Siegfried Zielinski, "'Sehende Maschinen': Einige Miniaturen zur Archäologie des Fernsehens" ['Seeing machines': Sketches in the archaelogy of television], in Stefan Münker and Alexander Roesler (eds.), *Televisionen* [Televisions] (Frankfurt am Main: Suhrkamp, 1999), p. 33.

60. See Albert Robida, *Le vingtième siècle* (Paris: Montgredien, 1883). On the role of literary "functional utopias," see Monika Elsner, Thomas Müller, and Peter Michael Spangenberg, "Der lange Weg eines schnellen Mediums: Zur Frühgeschichte des deutschen Fernsehens" [The long journey of a fast medium: On the early history of German television], in William Uricchio (ed.), *Die Anfänge des deutschen Fernsehens: Kritische Annäherungen an die Entwicklung bis 1945* [The beginnings of German television: Critical approaches to development before 1945] (Tübingen: Niemeyer, 1991), pp. 153–206, esp. p. 158.

61. Liesegang, *Das Phototel*, p. III. See also Ernst Kapp, *Grundlinien einer Philosophie der Technik* [Outlines of a philosophy of technology] (Braunschweig: Westermann, 1877). Already in 1853, Carl Gustav Carus had written: "The hammer is the extended arm and fist.... The achromatic lens is an imitation of the eye's lens.... Telegraph currents are analogous to nerve currents." Quoted in Liesegang, *Das Phototel*, p. III.

62. Liesegang, *Das Phototel*, pp. 1 and IV.

63. *Ibid.*, pp. 111 and 89.

64. Lux, *Der elektrische Fernseher*, pp. 6–7 and 3.

65. Du Prel, *Fernsehen und Fernwirken*, p. 206. See also the statement: "Such visions in mirrors and crystals cannot be objective, but must rather be simply projections from the organs of vision." *Ibid.*, p. 194. And see [Anonymous], "Recent Experiments in Crystal-Vision," *Proceedings of the Society for Psychical Research* (1889), pp. 486–521. For a theory of mirror magic in the explanation of psychic television, see Heinrich Jürgens, *Anleitung zum bewußten Hellsehen* [Instructions for conscious clairvoyance] (Freiburg im Breisgau: Hermann Bauer Verlag, 1932), p. 19. Here, Jürgens also turns to technological analogies for the purpose of elucidating telepathic occurrences: "In this way, we are all living magic mirrors. But to put it in terms of modern technology, we are all also walking radios. We have inside us a transmitter and we have inside us a receiver. Unbeknownst to ourselves, we are thus constantly receiving thought pictures created by our fellow human beings" (p. 43). On the use of radio as an explanation for mental telepathy, see the book by the novelist Upton Sinclair, *Mental Radio: Does it Work, and How? With an Introduction by Professor William McDougall* (London: T. Werner Laurie, 1930).

66. Carl du Prel, *Die Magie als Naturwissenschaft. Erster Theil: Die magische Physik* [Magic as natural science, pt. 1: Magical physics] (Jena: Hermann Costenoble, 1899), pp. 13–14.

67. *Ibid.*, p. 14.

68. *Ibid.*, pp. 15 and 16.

69. *Ibid.*, pp. 18–19.

70. *Ibid.*, p. 22.

71. *Ibid.*

72. *Ibid.*, p. 23.

73. "Wie können wir fernsehend werden?" Carl du Prel, *Die Magie als Natur-wissenschaft. Zweiter Theil. Die magische Psychologie* [Magic as natural science, pt. 2: Magical psychology] (Jena: Hermann Costenoble, 1899), p. 293.

74. *Ibid.*, p. 304. See also p. 295: "In external suggestion, we possess a lever for releasing magic forces."

75. Du Prel, *Die Magie als Naturwissenschaft. Erster Theil*, p. 15.

76. On early representations of cinema as a hypnotic medium, see Stefan Andriopoulos, *Possessed: Hypnotic Crimes, Corporate Fiction, and the Invention of Cinema* (Chicago: University of Chicago Press, 2008); on brainwashing and media, see "Brainwashing: Mind Control, Media, and Warfare," ed. Andreas Killen and Stefan Andriopoulos, special issue, *Grey Room* 45 (Fall 2011).

77. [Anonymous], "Neuer Fernsehstart in Deutschland" [A new launch of television in Germany], *Rundfunk und Fernsehen* [Radio and television] 7 (1950), p. 10; see also [Anonymous], "Fernsehen. Appell ans Unterbewußtsein" [Television: Appeal to the subconscious], *Der Spiegel*, April 2, 1958, pp. 61–63.

78. "Aside from these copy telegraphs...there were [in the 1890s] a great number of fantastical television projects based on the use of selenium, which had been discovered in the year 1873. In fact, only the English scientist Bidwell made serious experiments in broadcasting pictures using selenium compounds." Arthur Korn, "Die Bildtelegraphie und das Problem des elektrischen Fernsehens" [Image telegraphy and the problem of electrical television], in Peter Craemer and Adolf Franke (eds.), *Deutsche Beiträge zur Internationalen Tagung der Fernmeldetechniker Como 1927* [German contributions to the International Congress of Telecommunications Technologists, Como, 1927] (Berlin: Europäischer Fernsprechdienst, 1927), p. 51.

79. The opposite view is held by Friedrich Kittler. See his *Optische Medien*, p. 290, *Optical Media*, pp. 207–208*: "Television means...to subject all the complexities of the image to high tech.... Literatures or fantasies are therefore irrelevant. In contrast to film, television could not be dreamed of before its

development.... Television was no wish of so-called man, but a civilian byproduct of mostly military electronics."

80. Du Prel, *Die Magie als Naturwissenschaft. Erster Theil*, p. 23.

Index

Zone Books series design by Bruce Mau
Typesetting by Meighan Gale
Image placement and production by Julie Fry
Printed and bound by Maple Press